Advancing Evidence-Based Practice

Through Program Evaluation

Advancing Evidence-Based Practice Through Program Evaluation

A Practical Guide for School-Based Professionals

JULIE Q. MORRISON

AND

ANNA L. HARMS

OXFORD
UNIVERSITY PRESS

Oxford University Press is a department of the University of Oxford. It furthers
the University's objective of excellence in research, scholarship, and education
by publishing worldwide. Oxford is a registered trade mark of Oxford University
Press in the UK and certain other countries.

Published in the United States of America by Oxford University Press
198 Madison Avenue, New York, NY 10016, United States of America.

© Oxford University Press 2018

CIP data is on file at the Library of Congress
978-0-19-060910-8

To my parents, Gerald and Shirley Quatman, whose love and support I can always count on and to my husband and best friend, David, and our children, William, Andrew, and Henry.

—J.Q.M.

To my husband, Tim, and son, Lucas, for their constant support and laughs; and to my MIBLSI colleagues for their encouragement, collaboration, and relentless efforts to improve educational systems and outcomes for students.

—A.L.H.

CONTENTS

ACKNOWLEDGMENTS

This book is best viewed as a culmination of the collective wisdom of the evaluators in the U.S. Department of Education; The Office of Special Education Programs' SIGnetwork, under the leadership of Jennifer Coffey; and of the tireless champions in Michigan's Integrated Behavior and Learning Support Initiative (MIBLSI), under the leadership of Steve Goodman. We greatly appreciate both Jennifer and Steve's efforts to create adult learning organizations where we are all challenged to do better to achieve positive, measurable outcomes for students. Too many individuals have influenced our thinking and practices to identify by name, but we want to specifically acknowledge members of the SIGnetwork John Eagle, Amy Gaumer Erickson, Pat Mueller, and Pattie Noonan, as well as colleagues at MIBLSI Melissa Nantais, Jennifer Rollenhagen, and Christine Russell who served as reviewers. Their expertise and insights were extremely valuable in the development of this book. We would also like to thank our graduate student reviewers for their thoughtful feedback: Emma Clarke, Taylor Creek, Tiaunne Duffy, Devin Frazier, Brittany Hall, Jamie Jones, Natalie Justice, Aubrey Rogers, and Kylie Watzka. Finally, we would like to thank Sarah Harrington and Andrea Zekus at Oxford University Press, whose editorial support and guidance has made this venture a very positive experience.

Advancing Evidence-Based Practice
Through Program Evaluation

Introduction to Program Evaluation

The school bell signals the start of dismissal at Central Elementary. With buses lined up and students gathering their belongings, another day of instruction draws to a close. What was accomplished? Will the students be able to demonstrate mastery of the content in time to show gains by the end of the school year? The educators at Central Elementary, like the ones at many schools, recognize that the school has many interventions and supports in place, but more are required to address the needs of all of the students. Implementation of academic interventions and instructional supports is inconsistent among the educators. Behavior remains a concern in seventh and eighth grade students. A small number of students can be very disruptive to other students' learning. Educators are directed to gather data regarding their students' academic and behavioral performance in school, but the volume of data can be overwhelming! Despite these challenges, there is strong school and districtwide commitment to meeting all students' needs through the implementation of a multitier system of academic and behavioral supports (i.e., integrating Response to Intervention and a Positive Behavioral Interventions and Supports frameworks). The members of the school leadership team are highly regarded among their colleagues, and they are passionate about data-based decision making and shared leadership. So at the end of another school day the question remains: How do the educators at Central Elementary know what they are doing is having the desired impact on student learning and behavior?

This book is designed for educators (a) who seek answers to the question "how will we know what we are doing is having the desired impact on student learning and behavior?" and those (b) who are eager to learn from current efforts in order to increase the likelihood of future success. Practical skills in program evaluation are crucial to professionals' ability to critically examine student performance on value indicators and identify opportunities for improving outcomes in the face of scarce resources. School-based professionals (i.e., teachers, administrators, school psychologists, school counselors, school social workers, others) are in an ideal position to play a significant role in supporting school improvement efforts and improving outcomes for struggling students by applying the knowledge and skills characteristic of program evaluation.

WHAT IS PROGRAM EVALUATION?

It is not hard to find a definition of **program evaluation**. There are many. The assortment of definitions largely reflects a varying emphasis on the role of program evaluation in informing decisions or giving participants a voice. In the early years of program evaluation, Scriven (1967) defined evaluation as judging the worth or merit of something. Most subsequent definitions have incorporated elements of this initial definition. For this book, we adopt the definition used by Fitzpatrick, Sanders, and Worthen (2011) in their comprehensive textbook, which defines evaluation as "the identification, clarification, and application of defensible criteria to document an evaluation object's value (worth and merit) in relation to those criteria" (p. 7).

Program evaluations serve a variety of functions within the field of education. Evaluation findings are used to demonstrate accountability for implementing programs as planned, achieving intended outcomes, continuous program improvement, resource allocation, and the development of policies and procedures. A data-driven focus lends credibility and fairness to the evaluation process and counters any tendencies toward bias in decision making. Furthermore, program evaluation has gained prominence as schools and districts strive to build their capacity for evaluation and sustain organizational learning (Preskill & Boyle, 2008).

Throughout this book we use the term *evaluation* as short for *program evaluation*, consistent with the vernacular used within the field of evaluation. As educators, we recognize the importance of distinguishing between the evaluation of a program and the evaluation of personnel (i.e., teacher evaluation). Personnel evaluation is associated with human resources and the development, evaluation, and selective retention of teachers, administrators, and staff. In contrast, program evaluation uses systematic and precise methods of inquiry to arrive at a judgment of value, quality, utility, effectiveness, or significance that informs recommendations for continuous improvement of a program. The Joint Committee on Standards for Educational Evaluation (Yarbrough, Shulha, Hopson, & Caruthers, 2011) has defined a program as a set of planned systematic activities. This entails:

- Using managed resources
- Achieving specified goals related to specific needs
- Specific, identified, participating human individual or groups
- Specific contexts
- Having documentable outputs, outcomes, and impacts
- Following assumed (explicit or implicit) systems of beliefs (diagnostic, causal, intervention, and implementation theories about how the program works)
- Specific, investigable costs and benefits (p. 3)

This book focuses on school-based programs designed for further implementation of a multi-tier system of supports (MTSS) framework, described later in this chapter.

Effective schools and school systems recognize that program evaluation is critical to addressing key questions regarding whether a program is achieving its goals and what efforts can be taken to improve aspects of the program that are not working well. To the degree that school improvement efforts target changes in educators' practices, program evaluation can be used to recognize successes and boost professional supports. In short, "good evaluation is an essential part of good programs" (Fitzpatrick et al., 2011, p. 4).

THE DISTINCTION BETWEEN PROGRAM EVALUATION AND RESEARCH

Program evaluation shares many characteristics in common with research in terms of rigor and the systematic use of data collection methods and data analytic techniques to address an evaluation or research question. There are, however, important distinctions between research and evaluation in terms of their purpose, who is driving the agenda, generalizability of the results, and the criteria to judge adequacy (Yarbrough et al., 2011). The primary purpose of research is to contribute to a body of knowledge in a field of study. Hypotheses are selected by the researcher who drives the theory-building enterprise. The results of a research study are expected to generalize to other contexts and thus have implications for attaining similar outcomes in other settings on future occasions. The criteria involved in judging the adequacy of research include internal validity (i.e., whether changes in an independent variable/treatment brought about changes in a dependent variable/outcome) and external validity (whether the results are expected to generalize to other settings and participants over time).

The primary purpose of evaluation is to inform decision making. Program evaluations are driven by the client stakeholders (i.e., program coordinators, administrators, leadership team), often in collaboration with the evaluator. Evaluations are designed in light of the specific needs of the local context (e.g., identification of evaluation questions to be addressed, scope and sequence of the professional learning sessions, timeline for implementation, selection of assessment instruments). Although it is possible that the findings from an evaluation of one school district, for example, could be generalized to another school district, it is not an assumed inference given the unique characteristics of each district. Finally, criteria to judge adequacy for evaluation were established by the Joint Committee on Standards for Educational Evaluation and include accuracy, utility, feasibility, propriety, and evaluation accountability. These Program Evaluation Standards are outlined in Appendix A and described in full in *The Program Evaluation Standards: A Guide for Evaluators and Evaluation Users* (Yarbrough et al., 2011).

A LITTLE MORE CONTEXT: EVALUATIONS OF MULTI-TIER SYSTEM OF SUPPORTS

A little more context is warranted before continuing with an overview of program evaluation approaches and the role of the internal and external evaluator as a change agent. Program evaluation is pervasive in education. State departments of education, funding agencies, and taxpayers demand accountability for programs designed to support students in schools. Although there are countless applications of evaluation for programs serving students from preschool through high school, in this book we focus on the evaluation of programs that feature a **multi-tier system of supports**, or MTSS, framework, as highlighted in the Spotlight on Evaluation in Action describing the evaluation and research contributions of Amanda VanDerHeyden (see Box 1.1).

Box 1.1

Spotlight on Evaluation in Action: Connecting Program Evaluation and Research

Despite the distinction between program evaluation and research, information gathered as part of a program evaluation can lend itself to a future research study just as empirical research can advance evaluation tools and techniques. The work of Amanda VanDerHeyden and her collaborators exemplifies this seamless connection between evaluation and research in the context of a Response to Intervention (RTI) initiative. Her sustained role in evaluating district-level implementation and outcomes of the System to Enhance Educational Performance (STEEP) RTI model (VanDerHeyden, Witt, & Gilbertson, 2007; Witt & VanDerHeyden, 2007) has informed her research in RTI. Her research, in turn, has greatly contributed to how RTI initiatives are evaluated. Together with her collaborators, VanDerheyden has advanced research in the areas of universal screening (i.e., identifying technically adequate measures, and establishing decision rules [Griffiths, VanDerHeyden, Skokut, & Lilles, 2009; VanDerHeyden, 2010; VanDerHeyden, 2013; VanDerHeyden & Witt, 2005; VanDerHeyden, Witt, & Naquin, 2003]); the development of curriculum-based measures in early childhood, writing, and math [Burns, VanDerHeyden, & Jiban, 2006; Gansle, Noell, VanDerHeyden, Slider, Hoffpauir, Whitmarsh, & Naquin, 2004; Gansle, VanDerHeyden, Noell, Reseter, & Williams, 2006; VanDerHeyden, Broussard, & Cooley, 2006; VanDerHeyden, Broussard, Snyder, George, Lafleur, & Williams, 2011]; intervention evaluation [VanDerHeyden & Burns, 2005b], and systemwide risk reduction [Barnett, VanDerHeyden, & Witt, 2007; VanDerHeyden & Burns, 2005a; VanDerHeyden, Witt, & Barnett, 2005]. VanDerHeyden's efforts demonstrate how one can move fluidly between evaluation and research, capitalizing on what can be learned from each.

An MTSS framework is designed to meet the academic and behavioral needs of all students through the use of a continuum of instructional and behavioral supports and targeted, evidence-based interventions of increasing intensity matched to student need. An overview of what is meant by the term *evidence-based* is featured in this section (see Box 1.2). The MTSS framework is represented graphically as a pyramid (see Figure 1.1) with schoolwide, universal core research-based curriculum and instructional/behavioral supports

---

Box 1.2

WHAT IS "EVIDENCE-BASED" PRACTICE?

This book is dedicated to promoting program evaluation expertise to advance evidence-based practice in schools. Evidence-based practices are "practices and programs shown by high-quality research to have meaningful effects on student outcomes" (Cook & Odom, 2013, p. 135). The impetus behind identifying evidence-based practices stems from dissatisfaction with the widespread use of practices and programs that have no evidence base (i.e., the research-to-practice gap) and a commitment to the use of high-quality research to provide rigorous standards for determining effectiveness (Cook & Cook, 2011). To meet the standards for evidence-based practice, an intervention or program must meet prescribed guidelines with regard to research design (i.e., experimental or quasi-experimental, including single-case research), quality, and quantity demonstrating that the practice has a meaningful impact on student outcomes (Cook & Odom, 2013). Within education, there are several different approaches for categorizing evidence-based practices. What Works Clearinghouse (2011) used six classifications (i.e., practices with positive, potentially positive, mixed, indeterminate, potentially negative, and negative effects), whereas Gersten et al. (2005) recommended three classifications (i.e., evidence-based, promising, and not evidence-based), and Horner et al. (2005) supported the use of categorizing practices as either evidence-based or not evidence-based. In his book *Visible Learning*, John Hattie (2009) provided a synthesis of more than 800 metastudies using effect sizes to rank teaching and learning approaches and other factors in five other areas (i.e., teacher, curriculum, school, home, student) with regard to their impact on student achievement. His effect size graphic provides educators with an easy way of judging the effectiveness of common teaching and learning approaches. It is also important to recognize that many existing practices and programs have not yet been reviewed or do not yet have a compelling body of high-quality research to constitute an "evidence-based" classification (Cook & Smith, 2012). Practices and programs that have not been thoroughly researched might be implemented when evidence-based practices are not available or do not produce the desired outcome (Cook & Odom, 2013). Given these various classification approaches, it is important to consider the evidence for a practice or program within the context of the classification standards applied.

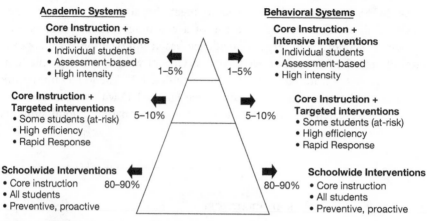

Figure 1.1. Multi-tier System of Supports Framework
Adapted from Graden, J. L., Stollar, S. A., & Poth, R. L. (2007). The Ohio Integrated Systems Model: Overview and lessons learned. In S. E. Jimerson, M. K. Burns, & A. M. VanDerHeyden (Eds.), *Handbook of response to intervention: The science and practice of assessment and intervention* (pp. 288–299). New York: Springer.

(tier 1) meeting the needs of the majority of the students (i.e., 80–90% of the students). Tier 2 is composed of core curriculum and instructional supports with the addition of evidence-based targeted interventions for those students whose needs are not met with tier 1 supports (i.e., 5–10% of the students). Finally, intensive, individualized evidence-based interventions are provided to the 1 to 5% of the students who demonstrate an inadequate response to targeted interventions implemented with fidelity. As MTSS frameworks, both **Response to Intervention (RTI)** and **Positive Behavioral Interventions and Supports (PBIS)** feature: (a) universal screening, (b) data-based decision making and problem solving, (c) continuous progress monitoring, (d) a continuum of evidence-based practices, and (e) a focus on fidelity of implementation (McIntosh & Goodman, 2016). Implementation of an MTSS initiative represents a fundamental shift in how educators gather, monitor, and respond to data to promote positive outcomes for students (Daly, Martens, Barnett, Witt, & Olson, 2007; Kratochwill, Volpiansky, Clements, & Ball, 2007).

At its core, MTSS is a "decision making framework that guides the selection, integration, and implementation of the best evidence-based academic and behavioral practices for improving important academic and behavioral outcomes for all students" (OSEP Center on Positive Behavioral Interventions and Supports, 2009, p. 1). The intended academic and behavioral outcomes of an MTSS initiative include increasing overall student achievement (Ervin, Schaughency, Goodman, McGlinchey, & Matthews, 2006); increasing appropriate behavior and decreasing office discipline referrals (McIntosh, Chard, Bolard, & Horner, 2006); providing early intervention for students at risk for academic failure (Al Otaiba & Torgensen, 2007); and improving the ways students are determined to be eligible for special education services, based on a lack of satisfactory response to intensive, research-based interventions implemented as intended (Fletcher, Coulter, Reschly, & Vaughn, 2004; Speece & Case, 2001).

Whereas many excellent resources exist to guide educators in the implementation of MTSS initiatives, the literature dedicated to the evaluation of an MTSS initiative is relatively sparse. Yet MTSS, with its emphasis on real-time, data-based decision making and systems change, provides an excellent context for advancing educators' knowledge and skills in program evaluation with content that is meaningful and relevant to supporting educators and meeting students' needs. This book builds on a foundation established by the *Evaluation Blueprint for School-wide Positive Behavior Support* (Algozzine et al., 2010) and Shapiro and Clemens's (2009) conceptual model for evaluating systems effects of RTI.

FORMATIVE AND SUMMATIVE EVALUATION

An understanding of the core components of MTSS is also useful for drawing a distinction between formative and summative evaluation. **Formative evaluation** focuses on the continuous improvement of the program. Formative evaluation questions include (Altschuld & Watkins, 2014; Fitzpatrick et al., 2011):

- To what degree is the program being implemented as planned?
- Which components are being implemented effectively?
- Which components need to be improved?
- How can the program be improved?
- Are the appropriate data being collected to inform decision making (i.e., problem solving and strategic planning)?

Summative evaluation occurs toward the end of a program cycle and focuses on whether the program met its objectives and should continue in its current form, continue with modifications, or terminate. Summative evaluation questions include (Altschuld & Watkins, 2014):

- Has the project attained its objectives?
- Under what conditions (e.g., schedule for implementation, resources used) were the results obtained?
- Were the outcomes obtained evident among all intended groups?

In illustrating the distinction between formative and summative evaluation, Robert Stake famously asserted, "When the cook tastes the soup, that's formative evaluation; when the guest tastes it, that's summative evaluation" (Scriven, 1991, p. 19). The popularity of this analogy has led Chen (2015) to point out its limitations, chiefly that: (a) formative evaluation is not limited to the early stages of the program and summative evaluation is not restricted to the program's final outcome stage; (b) formative evaluations do not always have a focus on continuous improvement and may be used early in a program's installation to determine whether the program should be discontinued; (c) that the final determination of the merit or worth of the program is not typically confided to the judgment of one "guest" stakeholder but often includes the judgment of multiple stakeholders, including those conducting the evaluation, and (d) the "guest" stakeholders' input should be elicited in the early stages of implementation rather than waiting until summative judgments are needed. Despite these points, the soup analogy is very useful in understanding the distinction between formative and summative evaluation.

Both formative and summative evaluation foci are essential to a comprehensive evaluation of an MTSS initiative. Formative evaluation efforts examine **implementation fidelity**, or the degree to which the core components of the initiative are implemented as planned, across the system as a whole and at each tier. Formative evaluation is also used to monitor student outcomes on academic and behavioral indicators across the school year. The formative evaluation of changes in adult practices and targeted student outcomes is used to inform ongoing adjustments, identify needed midcourse corrections, and recognize successful implementation. The summative evaluation of an MTSS initiative should focus on whether the objectives were met relative to the criterion for implementation in a given school. For a school district or project supporting numerous schools, the objective might be based on the percentage of schools attaining the criterion for implementation fidelity. The summative evaluation will also examine student outcomes to compare end-of-year academic and behavioral data relative to local or national norms and to analyze progress over the course of the school year for all students.

If the implementation of an effective MTSS initiative is a journey, the formative evaluation focus is represented by the dashboard that serves to monitor several key indicators continuously over time to gauge whether the project is on course to reach its intended destination given the intended route. The summative evaluation focus is reflected in the trip summary statistics (e.g., total miles, travel time), and judgments regard whether we arrived to our intended destination and whether it was worth the effort.

NEEDS ASSESSMENT, PROCESS EVALUATION, AND OUTCOME/IMPACT EVALUATION STUDIES

Three types of evaluation studies are conducted frequently in education: needs assessment, process evaluation, and outcome or impact evaluation. Although process evaluation is often equated with formative evaluation and outcome or impact evaluation is likened to summative evaluation, these terms are not synonymous. This section will describe these three types of evaluation studies and highlight how needs assessment, process evaluation, and outcome/impact evaluation studies can each serve a formative or summative purpose.

Needs Assessment

A **needs assessment** involves identifying and prioritizing needs for the purpose of determining the causes of the needs and developing solutions. A need is "a measureable gap between two conditions—what currently is and what should be" (Altschuld & Watkins, 2014, p. 6). Assessing needs requires a thorough under-standing of the current levels of performance with regard to implementation or outcome, a criterion or standard for the expected or desired level of performance, and a comparison of the two.

Contemporary thinking on needs assessment cautions against focusing solely on quantifiable, deficit-defined needs (i.e., indicators and outcomes), while (a) undervaluing needs expressed by key stakeholders and (b) failing to also consider current assets and capacity building opportunities to project a better future moving forward (Altschuld, Hung, & Lee, 2014; Altschuld & Watkins, 2014). Needs assessment questions pertinent to an MTSS initiative might include (Altschuld & Watkins, 2014):

- What is the expected level of performance at the system-level (i.e., district or school-level capacity for supporting implementation) and for tier 1 schoolwide supports; tier 2 targeted interventions; and tier 3 intensive, individual interventions?
- How do current levels of performance compare to these expected levels of performance?
- How should we prioritize diverse needs in terms of importance?
- Which strategies (or sets of solutions) can best reduce the data-driven or perceived gap between the actual and expected level of performance?
- What criteria can be used to evaluate the alternatives?

Many of the tools designed to measure MTSS implementation fidelity outlined in Chapter 2 are well suited to measure the current state of affairs with regard to MTSS structures and processes for the purposes of a needs assessment. Needs assessments are typically conducted prior to the adoption of a new program or at critical junctures in a program cycle, and thus they can serve both a formative and summative evaluative purpose. As such, needs assessments are often con-sidered a form of strategic or program planning rather than a type of evaluation (Wedman, 2014).

Process Evaluation

A **process evaluation** examines the delivery of a program. Process evaluations have three parts: (a) operationally defining or verifying what the program is (i.e., what is the program intended to be?), (b) assessing the degree to which the program was implemented as intended (i.e., what was actually delivered?), and (c) analyzing

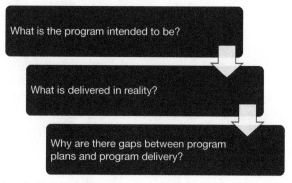

Figure 1.2. Parts of a Process Evaluation

the variability or gaps in the implementation (i.e., why are there gaps between the actual and intended program delivery?) (Scheirer, 1994). Each of these parts of a process evaluation (see Figure 1.2) will be described in this section.

WHAT IS THE PROGRAM INTENDED TO BE?

Process evaluation begins with an explicit, operational definition of the strategies, activities, and processes that constitute the intended program along with a clear understanding of the roles and responsibilities of the program administrators, facilitators, and consumers. Scheirer (1994) recommends identifying the program components based on the behaviors or practices the program is intended to affect, rather than focusing on goals and objectives. The core components of a school-based initiative might include professional learning opportunities for teachers, the implementation of evidence-based interventions, and systems for measuring adult implementation and student outcomes. Core components of an MTSS initiative might be identified from the *School-wide Tiered Fidelity Inventory* (reviewed in Chapter 2), whose subscales include teams, implementation/intervention, evaluation for tiers 1 and 2 and teams, resources, support plans, and evaluation for tier 3. After developing a complete listing of observable, measurable program components, the core components are prioritized for monitoring as part of the process evaluation. For each of the core components selected to be monitored, the program administrator and other team members need to determine which components can be adapted to the local setting and which components need to be delivered as designed (Scheirer, 1994). If the program component allows for local adaptions, the program manager and other members of the team will further outline a range of acceptable variations for each of the expected practices (Hall & Loucks, 1978). This process of developing a practice profile for specifying acceptable practices on a continuum from ideal to unacceptable will be described in greater detail in Chapter 2.

WHAT IS DELIVERED, IN REALITY?

The second part of a process evaluation involves measuring implementation fidelity or the degree to which the program components were implemented as planned. With the program components identified, the evaluator and leadership team need to select or develop tools to measure two key aspects of program delivery: (a) the degree of implementation in terms of the number and quality of program components actually delivered, and (b) the scope of implementation, in terms of the number of recipients (e.g., teachers and staff, students) reached and their characteristics (Scheirer, 1994).

Monitoring implementation is critical to identifying problems or barriers to successful implementation and in turn improve service delivery. Data regarding implementation practices can inform decision making and spur improvements in aspects of program implementation found to be off-track or lagging behind. Measuring implementation can also lead to the identification of variability in program delivery, which can be explored when analyzing outcomes (Scheirer, 1994). Only when measures of implementation are linked to the analysis of outcomes can valid conclusions be reached regarding the impact of the program. If the intended outcomes are not attained, process evaluation can provide decision makers with information regarding the pattern of implementation that yielded the less than desirable results to inform future program planning.

WHY ARE THERE GAPS BETWEEN PROGRAM PLANS AND PROGRAM DELIVERY?

In the third part of a process evaluation, implementation data are examined and variability in how the program was delivered are analyzed. Variability in implementation can be expected in most school-based programs. Variations can stem from differences among program deliverers (i.e., teachers and staff, program manager and other team members) and differences in recipients (i.e., students or teachers and staff). This third part of a process implementation is concerned with exploring why the variability exists, how it affects program effectiveness, and what actions can increase implementation fidelity. Variability could reflect participant-initiated modifications to implementation to meet the demands of a local context (e.g., school culture, student demographics, availability of resources). These variations might not compromise the core of the program that represents the "active ingredient" in affecting change and may contribute to positive outcomes and greater sustainability. Yet other variations may represent legitimate gaps between the intended program and the actual program being implemented. In these instances, the leadership team needs to engage in problem solving to address the mismatch between expected program delivery and the actual program delivery.

To the greatest extent possible, process evaluation data collection and analysis should be ongoing and timely. "Real-time" data is a descriptor used to reflect information that is gathered for use without delay for monitoring progress. Building a school's capacity for "real-time" data analysis for action planning and problem solving will require an infrastructure, such as that represented in the Implementation Drivers Framework, presented in Chapter 2.

Process evaluation serves a formative (program improvement) purpose with its emphasis on monitoring implementation practices and analyzing implementation variability. Box 1.3 further describes the relationship between process evaluation

Box 1.3

WORKING IN TANDEM: PROCESS EVALUATION AND PROGRAM DEVELOPMENT

Process evaluation can greatly enhance program development by providing a data-based decision-making lens to program development efforts. Scheirer (1994) identified four functions of process evaluation that support program development (p. 42):

1. Process measures provide feedback on the quality of ongoing intervention delivery—information that can stimulate greater efforts to make delivery congruent with an intended program.
2. Process data indicate who is receiving program services and to what extent, allowing program managers to assess whether the program is reaching its intended recipients.
3. Process evaluation increases knowledge of what program components contribute to outcomes achieved, enabling program managers to design more effective future programs.
4. Process evaluation aids in understanding how programs can be successfully implemented within complex human organizations and communities.

---

and program development. Process evaluation can also be summative (informing judgments of merit or worth) as implementation data can be treated as the outcome or dependent variable in an analysis of factors that facilitate or impede program implementation (Scheirer, 1994).

Outcome or Impact Evaluation

Outcome or **impact evaluation** focuses on the changes that occur as a result of a program's implementation. Outcomes can be intended or unintended and can range from immediate impacts to medium- and longer-term outcomes. The ability to draw valid inferences regarding the program's impact requires outcome data to be linked to the program implementation data garnered from ongoing process evaluation activities. Descriptive research methods are typically sufficient to summarize the program outcomes for school-based programs. This can include the time-series analysis (i.e., line graph with a goal line and aim line) of discipline data, percentage of students at or above benchmark for curriculum-based measures (e.g., DIBELS Next, aimsweb), or means and standard deviations to compare groups on a variety of other measures (e.g., attendance, norm-referenced state-mandated tests). Comparative designs can be used with inferential statistics to determine if there is a statistically significant difference between students participating in the program and those not participating. However, real-world constraints often preclude the use of experimental design requiring the random assignment of students to groups (i.e., intervention class/school vs. nonintervention class/school).

The challenges of ensuring students in the comparison or control group do not receive the intervention and an unwillingness to exclude students from participation in a program in which they would likely benefit render randomized control trials more appropriate for research than program evaluation. Quasi-experimental designs, which might involve comparing the outcomes of classrooms or schools that have demonstrated fidelity of implementation in contrast to the outcomes of classrooms or school with partial implementation, have appeal in addressing the impact of the initiative when implemented as intended.

PROGRAM EVALUATION APPROACHES

The field of evaluation is comprised of various approaches reflecting the varied backgrounds, disciplines, philosophical and theoretical orientations, and priorities of their developers. Evaluation approaches inform the manner in which the evaluation is planned and the types of evaluation methods that are used (Fitzpatrick et al., 2011). Fitzpatrick and colleagues classified the many different approaches into four broad categories. A selection of the program evaluation approaches represented by each category is presented in Table 1.1.

Evaluation approaches that are oriented to decisions to be made about the program are well suited for evaluating an MTSS initiative. Earlier in this chapter,

Table 1.1 THE FOUR CATEGORIES OF PROGRAM EVALUATION APPROACHES

APPROACHES ORIENTED TO DECISION TO BE MADE ABOUT THE PROGRAM
Context-input-process-product (CIPP) Utilization-focused evaluation
APPROACHES ORIENTED TO CHARACTERISTICS OF THE PROGRAM
Objectives-based evaluation Standards-based evaluation Theory-based evaluation
APPROACHES ORIENTED TO PARTICIPATION OF STAKEHOLDERS
Client-centered/Responsive evaluation Practical participatory evaluation Empowerment evaluation
APPROACHES ORIENTED TO COMPREHENSIVE JUDGMENTS ON THE QUALITY OF THE PROGRAM OR PRODUCT
Expertise-oriented evaluation Consumer-oriented evaluation

Compiled from Fitzpatrick, J. L., Sanders, J. R., & Worthen, B. R. (Eds.). (2011). *Program evaluation: Alternative approaches and practical guidelines* (4th ed.). Boston: Pearson Education, Inc.

Figure 1.3. Components of the Context, Input, Process, and Product Evaluation Model

MTSS was defined as a "decision making framework that guides the selection, integration, and implementation of the best evidence-based academic and behavioral practices for improving important academic and behavioral outcomes for all students" (OSEP, 2009, p. 1). Decision-oriented evaluation approaches focus on the role of evaluation in improving the quality of decisions made by program administrators. The *Evaluation Blueprint for School-wide Positive Behavior Support* (Algozzine et al., 2010) uses one such evaluation approach.

This **Context, Input, Process, and Product (CIPP)** approach, which was developed by Daniel Stufflebeam in the 1960s and revisited by Stufflebeam and Coryn (2014). See Figure 1.3. As a decision-oriented evaluation approach, evaluation is defined as the process of delineating, obtaining, reporting, and applying descriptive and judgmental information about a program's merit, worth, and significance to guide decisions, support accountability, disseminate effective practices, and increase understanding of the program (Stufflebeam, 2005). The CIPP approach is described here in relation to an evaluation of an MTSS initiative.

Context considerations seek to understand the unique setting and circumstances relevant to the program's implementation. Context evaluation decisions pertinent to the evaluation of an MTSS initiative might involve answers to these questions:

- What are the needs and problems of teachers and students?
- What strengths or capacity does the school or district have to address these needs?
- What should be the goals and intended outcomes for the MTSS implementation?

The *Evaluation Blueprint for School-wide Positive Behavior Support* also includes as context questions:

- Who provided support for implementation of this system?
- Who received support during implementation of this system?

Input considerations help program decision makers identify school or district organizational assets and opportunities for building capacity. The *Evaluation Blueprint for School-wide Positive Behavior Support* identified the following as input questions:

- What professional development was part of implementation support?
- Who participated in the professional development?
- What was the perceived value of the professional development?

Process (termed "Fidelity" in the *Evaluation Blueprint*) considerations focus on decisions concerning implementation and the possible need for modifications. Process evaluation questions might include:

- Is the program being implemented as planned?
- What planned or unplanned changes have been made?
- What barriers impede the fidelity of implementation?
- What modifications, adaptations, or refinements are needed?

Product (termed "Impact" in the *Evaluation Blueprint*) considerations focus on judging whether the program attained the desired outcomes given the context, inputs, and processes. Product questions might include:

- To what extent did the MTSS initiative contribute to positive changes in student outcomes?
- To what extent did the MTSS initiative contribute to a reduction in student needs?
- What are the next steps with regard to the initiative (i.e., should it be modified, continued as is, or scaled up?)

The *Evaluation Blueprint for School-wide Positive Behavior Support* featured "Replication, Sustainability, and Improvement" as a distinct consideration in addition to Context, Input, Fidelity, and Impact (Algozzine et al., 2010). Replication, Sustainability, and Improvement questions include:

- To what extent did implementation improve capacity for the state/region/district to replicate Behavior Support practices, sustain Behavior Support practices, and improve social and academic outcomes for students?
- To what extent did implementation change educational/behavioral policy?
- To what extent did implementation affect systemic educational practice?

Although the CIPP approach was initially developed to meet the needs of administrators focused on decision making, program improvement, and judging the merit or worth of the program, the CIPP approach has evolved over the years. In response to concerns that the CIPP was too narrowly focused on meeting the needs of decision makers while devaluing the input and information needs of others, the notion of context has been expanded to be more inclusive of the perspectives of a diverse range of stakeholders and program participants. We contend that educators (i.e., teachers, paraprofessionals, and related service professionals) all have a stake in using program evaluation to improve decisions, programs, systems, and outcomes in their schools.

Returning to the four categories of program evaluation approaches from Table 1.1, approaches oriented to the characteristics of the program focus primarily on a program's goals and objectives. A primary contribution of the objectives-based/standards-based/theory-based evaluation approaches is the emphasis on understanding the theory of change reflected in the causal links between program activities and the intended program outputs and outcomes. Determining the goals, objectives, and theory of change are critical initial steps in planning an evaluation of an MTSS initiative, as described later in Chapter 4. A recognized limitation of objectives-based/standards-based/theory-based evaluation approaches is a relative lack of consideration of the context in which the initiative operates (Fitzpatrick et al., 2011). Understanding the school and/or district context in which an MTSS initiative is to be implemented is critical to its success.

Program evaluation approaches oriented to stakeholders emphasize giving voice to the wants, needs, and aspirations of the program participants (e.g., educators and students). Qualitative research methods (i.e., interviews with teachers, students, or parents; focus groups) can yield valuable information to inform a needs assessment, process evaluation, or impact evaluation. Whereas a comprehensive evaluation of an MTSS initiative could include aspects of a client-centered, responsive evaluation or practical participatory evaluation, the expectations for an MTSS evaluation typically include quantitative measures of impact on student outcomes.

The final evaluation approach is oriented to expert, comprehensive judgments on the quality of a program or product. University program accreditation and consumer product reviews are examples of this category. Expertise- and consumer-oriented approaches have not typically been used to evaluate MTSS initiatives.

THE ROLE OF INTERNAL AND EXTERNAL EVALUATORS

The evaluation literature makes a distinction between **internal** and **external evaluators**. School-based professionals who collaborate on program evaluation activities within their school are internal evaluators, whereas professionals who engage in program evaluation through consultation with school-based professionals are external evaluators. Internal and external evaluator roles both have advantages and disadvantages. As an internal evaluator, a school-based practitioner can capitalize on his or her understanding of the school culture and history of improvement efforts, anticipate the school's governance and decision-making processes, maintain visibility to provide frequent prompts and feedback, and be available to communicate technical results on a timely basis (Volkov, 2011b). For example, an internal evaluator is in the best position to champion the implementation and evaluation efforts on a daily basis and address obstacles as they emerge. An internal evaluation will require a team effort. A school-based internal evaluator will need to build the capacity of the school team to an acceptable level where evaluation is perceived as an indispensable component in the daily and weekly operations of the school (Sonnichsen, 2000). The primary disadvantage of internal evaluation is the issue of perceived credibility (Volkov, 2011a). The *Program*

Evaluation Standards emphasizes the need for evaluator credibility, stating that "Evaluations should be conducted by qualified people who establish and maintain credibility in the evaluation context" (Yarbrough et al., 2011). A school-based team of professionals engaged in evaluating their MTSS implementation might be discounted as less objective and less credible than an external evaluator who is somewhat detached from the inner workings of the school. Internal evaluators can counter the perception of limited credibility by demonstrating their knowledge and skills in the evaluation process described in this book, applying the *Program Evaluation Standards* established by the Joint Committee on Standards for Educational Evaluation (Yarbrough et al., 2011) outlined in Appendix A and the *Guiding Principles for Evaluators* put forth by the American Evaluation Association (2004) provided in Appendix B, and building on collaborative relationships characterized by effective communication, respect, and trust.

External evaluators have the advantage of being perceived as more objective, more credible, and more knowledgeable in the technical aspects of evaluation. Through their variety of consulting experiences, external evaluators may have valuable insights regarding effective programs and practices in similar schools and school districts. Professional evaluators may also have additional technical expertise with evaluation tools and technologies. Many external evaluators working in education started their careers as school-based professionals with a passion for systems change, collaboration, and data-based decision making. External evaluators also recognize the primary limitation of their role, the perception that they are outsiders who do not truly understand "how we do things here" in the school or district. Contemporary thinking about the roles of internal and external evaluators focus on promoting a complementary and mutually beneficial partnership between the two roles, such that internal evaluators gain expertise and credibility and external evaluators gain a deeper understanding of the unique climate and culture of the school (Christie, Ross, & Klein, 2004; Dahler-Larsen, 2009; Nevo, 2001; VanHoof & Van Petegem, 2007; Watling & Arlow, 2002). For example, initiatives funded by grants often require that an external evaluator be in place to fulfill the grant reporting requirements. That individual, however, will have to work closely and collaboratively with individuals internal to the school who can facilitate access to data and entry to the social norms and culture of the school.

ORGANIZATIONAL LEARNING AND EVALUATION CAPACITY BUILDING

Organizational learning and **evaluation capacity building** are two related terms that have garnered a great deal of attention in recent years. Organizational learning refers to building an organization's capacity to learn and manage over time (Cousins, Goh, Elliott, & Bourgeois, 2014). The contributions of evaluation in promoting organizational learning is well-established in the evaluation literature (e.g., Cousins & Earl, 1995; Cousins, Goh, Elliot, & Bourgeois, 2014; Leviton,

2001; Owen & Lambert, 1995; Preskill & Torres, 1999). Cousins, Goh, and Clark (2005) contended that the effective use of evaluation data in schools can increase positive perceptions regarding the value of data-based decisions among teachers and other school-based professionals, thus advancing organizational change and program implementation. Evaluation capacity building is the ability to conduct an effective evaluation that meets acceptable standards of the discipline (Cousins et al., 2014). It involves establishing evaluation frameworks, processes, and procedures, a shared commitment to evaluation processes and the use of evaluation findings, dedicating resources to evaluation activities, integrating evaluation and decision-making processes, strategic planning for building and sustaining evaluation capacity, and fostering continuous learning about evaluation (Preskill & Boyle, 2008).

PROGRAM EVALUATORS AS CHANGE AGENTS IN SCHOOLS AND DISTRICTS

This book rests on our strong conviction that program evaluation enables individuals to support and lead the transformation in their school and district by determining the issues to be addressed, the goals to be prioritized, the benchmarks or indicators for assessing short-term progress toward the goals, and the decision-making process for changing course if the desired progress is not evident. This is not to minimize the challenge of systems change in educational systems. Consider the realities:

> Educational systems have multiple layers of infrastructure that have accumulated over time and that must be engaged directly if they are to support, rather than obstruct, transformation. As Engeström (2011) reminds us, interventions take place in complex and multilayered activity systems rife with reoccurring problems that are conceptualized as contradictions inherent in the structuring of the system. Interventions themselves are contested spaces, filled with tensions and resistance from a range of stakeholders (Gutierrez & Penuel, 2014, p. 20).

Strengthening a school's capacity for evaluation is an effective (and rewarding) way to increase the use of evidence-based practices, enhance organizational learning, and embrace results-driven accountability as a means of ensuring positive outcomes for all students. This book is designed for individuals and teams poised to lead the charge. Understanding the local context, the collective culture, and the priorities is essential to conduct a successful evaluation in a complex, potentially political system. An effective evaluator skilled in collaboration, problem-solving, and systems change has a valuable role to play in navigating the often choppy waters of school improvement. Throughout this book we will strive to provide you with the knowledge and skills required to conduct an effective program evaluation, with particular emphasis on evaluating MTSS initiatives.

SUMMARY POINTS

- Program evaluation is defined as "the identification, clarification, and application of defensible criteria to document an evaluation object's value (worth and merit) in relation to those criteria" (Fitzpatrick et al., 2011, p. 7).
- An MTSS framework is designed to meet the academic and behavioral needs of all students through the use of a continuum of instructional supports and targeted, evidence-based interventions of increasing intensity matched to student need.
- As MTSS frameworks, both RTI and PBIS feature: (a) universal screening, (b) data-based decision making and problem solving, (c) continuous progress monitoring, (d) a continuum of evidence-based practices, and (e) a focus on fidelity of implementation.
- MTSS is complex, multifaceted, and requires systemic change to build the capacity for sustainable, durable implementation with fidelity.
- Early in the adoption of a program and through all of the stages of implementation, a formative evaluation focuses on the continuous improvement of the program.
- Summative evaluation occurs toward the end of a program cycle or at key junctures and focuses on whether the program met its objectives and should continue in its current form, continue with modifications, or terminate.
- A needs assessment involves identifying and prioritizing needs for the purpose of determining the causes of the needs and developing solutions.
- Process evaluations involve three parts: (a) operationally defining or verifying what the program is (i.e., what is the program intended to be?), (b) assessing the degree to which the program was implemented as intended (i.e., what was actually delivered?), and (c) analyzing the variability or gaps in the implementation (i.e., why are there gaps between the actual and intended program delivery?).
- Outcome or impact evaluation focuses on the changes that occur as a result of a program's implementation. Outcomes can be intended or unintended and can range from immediate impacts to medium- and longer-term outcomes.
- Evaluation approaches inform the manner in which the evaluation is planned and the types of evaluation methods that are used.
- School-based professionals who collaborate on program evaluation activities within their school are internal evaluators, whereas professionals who engage in program evaluation through consultation with school-based professionals are external evaluators.
- Organizational learning refers to building an organization's capacity to learn and manage in difficult times.
- Evaluation capacity building is the ability to conduct an effective evaluation that meets acceptable standards of the discipline.

QUESTIONS TO FURTHER YOUR UNDERSTANDING

1. In what ways can an outcome or impact evaluation be formative and summative?
2. In what ways can a process evaluation be formative and summative?
3. Why is MTSS considered a framework rather than a prescriptive one-size-fits-all model? How might a needs assessment be used to facilitate the installation and implementation of an MTSS framework in a school or district?
4. What are some ways that an individual engaged in program evaluation can operate as a change agent in a school or district?

2

Evaluating Implementation

The school leadership team at Central Elementary meets after school on Tuesdays. Early in the school year, the team members were very busy ensuring teachers had the information and materials they needed to teach the expected behaviors schoolwide. New teachers and staff were provided an overview of Central Elementary's multi-tier system of supports (MTSS) framework and universal screening in reading was completed for the beginning (fall) benchmark period. Now with the school year well underway, some of the initial momentum has been lost. There remains a sense among a small but vocal group of teachers that MTSS is just another set of hoops that has come down the pike and if they wait it out, this too shall pass. Nobody is really sure how the implementation efforts are going. The school leadership team members recognize they need to be able to show evidence of success soon to keep the initiative moving forward.

A comprehensive program evaluation of MTSS includes an analysis of student performance and implementation fidelity. These data are important for crafting a complete picture of how well MTSS is working, ascertaining where implementation has lagged or failed to produce positive student outcomes, and designing a continuous improvement plan. In this chapter we explore the dimensions, methods, and tools for assessing implementation fidelity. We emphasize implementation fidelity based on the widely recognized, yet often overlooked premise that evidence-based programs require evidence-based implementation in order to achieve the desired impact.

Implementation is defined in the evaluation field as "all of the activities focused on the actual operation of a program once it moves from the drawing board and into action" (Love, 2003, p. 1). **Implementation fidelity** is the degree to which an intervention is implemented as intended (Moncher & Prinz, 1991; Yeaton & Sechrest, 1981), or more specifically, the degree to which a specified set of activities designed to put into practice a program of known dimensions is completed as intended (Fixsen, Naoom, Blase, Friedman, & Wallace, 2005). Conceptually, implementation fidelity parallels intervention fidelity (also known as treatment integrity), or the degree to which an intervention is implemented as planned

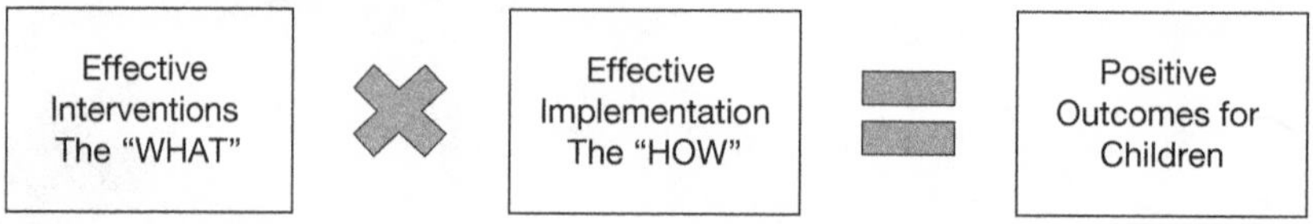

Figure 2.1. Why Fidelity of Implementation is Important for School-Based Initiatives
SOURCE: Fixsen, D., Blase, K., Metz, A., & Van Dyke, M. (2013). Statewide implementation of evidence-based programs. *Exceptional Children, 79*, 213–230. Reprinted with permission from Dean L. Fixsen and the National Implementation Research Network.

(Perepletchikova & Kazdin, 2005; Peterson, Homer, & Wonderlich, 1982; Sanetti & Kratochwill, 2014). At a systems level, implementation fidelity typically refers to the use of high-fidelity practitioner behaviors assessed on multiple occasions over time as defined by a framework, such as MTSS.

The National Implementation Research Network (NIRN) offers a simple formula (see Figure 2.1) to illustrate the critical importance of implementation for school-based initiatives (Fixsen, Blase, Metz & Van Dyke, 2013; Metz, 2012). The implication of this formula is that in the absence of effective implementation (implementation = zero), even the most effective intervention will fail to achieve the desired outcomes. Research has shown that the quality of implementation begins to decline within 10 days after teachers begin implementation of evidence-based practices, as busy teachers are inclined to omit components, implement them inaccurately, or abandon the practice altogether (Oliver, Wehby, & Nelson, 2015). Indeed, a poorly implemented effective intervention is no better than an ineffective intervention (intervention = zero) implemented with fidelity. Research has shown that a well-implemented but inherently less effective intervention can outperform a more effective intervention that is poorly implemented (Lipsey, 2009). As such, Cook and Odom (2013) contended, "implementation is the next, and arguably most critical, stage of evidence-based reforms" (p. 142).

DIMENSIONS OF FIDELITY

Fidelity is comprised of two dimensions: structural and process (Harn, Parisi, & Stoolmiller, 2013). The structural dimensions of fidelity pertain to the degree to which the core components of the program were implemented as intended (i.e., intervention adherence or program adherence; Dane & Schneider, 1998). Structural dimensions also involve consideration of exposure to the intervention (i.e., number, length, frequency, and duration of the sessions [Dane & Schneider, 1998; Durlak & DuPre, 2008; Gersten et al., 2005; Power et al., 2005]). Process dimensions encompass the quality of intervention delivery as evidenced through the practitioner's competence, decisions, language, timing, choice making, and judgment in implementing an intervention (Dane & Schneider, 1998; Durlak, 2010; Justice, Mashburn, Hamre, & Pianta, 2008; Kaderavek & Justice, 2010; O'Donnell, 2008).

THE NEED FOR FIDELITY MEASURES

Poor implementation has been identified as the most common reason programs fail to achieve their intended outcomes (Mills & Ragan, 2000; Yeaton & Sechrest, 1981). Neglecting to measure the degree to which a program was implemented with fidelity may lead to an erroneous conclusion that the program was ineffective when in fact it was effective. Conversely, a program could be perceived as effective when it was not.

The need to measure intervention and implementation fidelity has its roots in research. In order to establish the **internal validity** in a study, both the independent variable (the intervention) and the dependent variable (the outcome) needed to be measured with precision (Gresham, MacMillan, Beebe-Frankenberger, & Bocian, 2000; Hohmann & Shear, 2002). Without a systematic measure of the degree to which the intervention was implemented, the researcher is unable to verify that any changes observed in the outcome were due to the intervention and not to other extraneous variables (i.e., unplanned factors or outside influences). Therefore, intervention effects can only be attributed to the degree the intervention was implemented as planned (Cordray & Pion, 2006). Assessing fidelity helps the researcher account for negative or ambiguous findings (Hohmann & Shear, 2002). If the desired outcome was not attained, the researcher needs to determine whether the disappointing results were due to poor implementation or whether the intervention was simply ineffective.

Both intervention fidelity and implementation fidelity are critical in the evaluation an MTSS initiative (see Box 2.1). School-based professionals must assess the

---

Box 2.1

Spotlight on Why Implementation Fidelity Matters

On its release, the Institute for Education Sciences report, an *Evaluation of Response to Intervention Practices for Elementary School Reading* (Balu, Zhu, Doolittle, Schiller, Jenkins, & Gersten, 2015) drew considerable the attention among practitioners and researchers alike. EdCentral reported on the study in the article titled "New Study Raises Questions about RTI Implementation" (Loewenberg, 2015). Likewise, *Education Week* reported on the study in the article titled, "RTI Practice Falls Short of Promise: First Graders Who Were Identified for More Help Fell Further Behind" (Sparks, 2015) and published a response by an assembly of researchers lead by Amanda VanDerHeyden (i.e., "Four Steps to Implement RTI Correctly" [VanDerHeyden et al., 2016]). Clearly, this Institute for Education Sciences report was unsettling to educators committed to meet students' needs through the implementation of Response to Intervention and an integrated MTSS framework.

The study and the buzz it created highlights just how important implementation fidelity is to measure and communicate. A careful read of the Institute for Education Sciences report clarifies that the researchers did not (a) adequately

(continued)

Box 2.1 (Continued)

distinguish students who received intervention from those who did not when reporting outcomes, and (b) did not use any type of validated measure of implementation fidelity, both of which relate to structural dimensions of fidelity. In their response, VanDerHeyden et al. (2016) concluded, "Research has shown that RTI [response to intervention] practices can work to improve student outcomes. Yet, the most pernicious threat to RTI—and the Achilles' heel of all promising practices in education—is poor implementation" (p. 25). This conclusion echoes the most basic premise of implementation science, that even the most effective innovation, if implemented poorly, will fail to achieve the desired outcomes. The four essential steps to improve the impact of RTI/MTSS implementation, involves four steps. The first step is selecting efficient screening measures and administering them well. The second step involves strengthening core instruction. According to VanDerHeyden et al. (2016), "When there is a systemwide problem, it is foolish to try to provide interventions to all of those children as a first step in RTI . . . The process of trying to provide intervention to more than 20 percent of students rapidly overwhelms the system's resources." (p. 25). The third step to successful implementation is establishing effective intervention systems that match to what each student specifically needs. Decades of intervention research demonstrates that students with various reading challenges will not benefit equally from the same generic reading intervention protocol. The fourth step to increase the positive impact of an MTSS initiative involves varying intervention intensity through the use of research-based instructional actions (i.e., increasing the number of learning trials within an intervention strategy, providing more frequent and precise feedback to students, monitoring student growth and adjusting intervention tactics in response to student performance; VanDerHeyden et al., 2016). In sum, a one-size-fits-all intervention (or series of interventions) stretched over an extended period of time with little regard for how students are progressing individually and collectively should not be confused with a true MTSS framework implemented with fidelity. Implementation of the core MTSS components is essential for the initiative to have a measurable, meaningful impact on student outcomes. A compromised initiative will likely produce compromised results!

degree to which evidence-based academic and behavioral instruction and interventions are implemented as planned in order to evaluate individual, small group, and classwide responses to those interventions. Certainly high-stakes decisions regarding an individual student's response to intervention require documentation that the evidence-based intervention was implemented as intended (Gresham et al., 2000). An MTSS framework, however, is much more than just a continuum of increasingly intensive interventions. As a decision-making framework, MTSS initiatives require systemic change at the classroom, school, and district level. Fidelity of implementation must also consider the system's capacity to implement and sustain MTSS.

For a systemic initiative such as MTSS, measuring fidelity of implementation serves multiple purposes that include both accountability and continuous improvement. First, measuring fidelity is critical for attributing changes in outcomes (e.g., gains in reading fluency, decreases in disruptive behavior) to the planned program components, other contextual features, or the interaction between the two (Dane & Schneider, 1998; Perepletchikova & Kazdin, 2005). Assessing fidelity also makes it possible to detect variations in implementation (e.g., across classrooms or over time) and to determine the degree to which these variations contribute to the program outcomes (Durlak, 1998; Dusenbury, Brannigan, Falco, & Hansen, 2003; Zvoch, Letourneau, & Parker, 2007). A careful study of implementation fidelity can provide valuable information regarding how the active ingredients of the program function in the local school context and in turn inform the continuous improvement of the program. Conclusions drawn from assessing fidelity may guide the plan for training and coaching of teachers new to the school. Furthermore, MTSS initiatives are designed to be sustainable over time and scaled up to other school buildings within the district. Fidelity measures are critical to monitoring program drift over time and assessing the degree to which MTSS supports and structures are being implemented across school buildings. In short, determining the effectiveness of an MTSS initiative is possible only with a thorough understanding of the factors associated with implementation fidelity.

MEASURING FIDELITY OF IMPLEMENTATION

Although there have been many advances in our understanding of the dimensions of fidelity and how to best measure these dimensions (Sanetti & Kratochwill, 2009; Sheridan, Swanger-Gagné, Welch, Kwon, & Garbacz, 2009; Zvoch et al., 2007), researchers have also highlighted the challenges to the development and use of research-based tools for measuring fidelity in the context of the delivery of evidence-based academic and behavioral interventions and programs (Gresham, Dart, & Collins, 2017; Noell, 2008; O'Donnell, 2008). The challenges of measuring fidelity of implementation include (a) the identification of core components (i.e., active ingredients) that are logically linked to desired outcomes, (b) the relative weighting of specific core components, (c) the match of measurement tool to intervention components, (d) the technical adequacy (i.e., validity, reliability over time and across multiple measures) of each measurement tool, (e) sensitivity of measures to assess core components (i.e., those that contribute uniquely and in combination to desired outcomes), (f) the appropriate metric that relates empirically to outcomes (e.g., specific items, composite score, or consistency in implementation as a repeated measure), (g) the feasibility of assessment procedures (number of measurements required and ease of completion), and (h) the scope of measurement necessary to capture a representative sample of implementation occasions (Sheridan et al., 2009).

In this section, we will describe practical approaches that can be used to assess implementation fidelity for MTSS initiatives with respect to the challenges listed

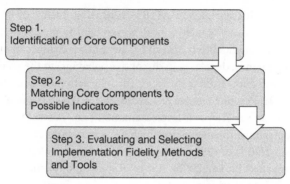

Figure 2.2. Three-Step Process for Measuring Implementation Fidelity

above. It should be clear throughout this chapter that evaluating implementation fidelity should not be approached as a "yes-no" question (Scheirer, 1994). Rather, careful consideration needs to be paid to the local context, the program structures and process, and changes in implementation practices over time as assessed by multiple measures, and in relation to the outcomes achieved. An accurate description of the extent and scope of implementation will inform both program accountability and continuous improvement.

Measuring implementation fidelity involves a three-step process (see Figure 2.2). The first step involves identifying the core components of the program. In the second step, each of the core components of the program are matched to possible indicators with an emphasis on a multimethod, multiinformant approach. The third step involves evaluating and selecting the fidelity methods and tools best suited to measure each indicator. Each of these three steps are described in greater detail in the following sections.

Step 1. Identification of Core Components

The first step in measuring implementation involves operationally defining what the program is intended to look like in practice. The core components are the active ingredients of the program that are logically linked to desired outcomes. The core components are also the nonnegotiables of the program that must be in place (without adaptation) in order for the intended program to truly be implemented with fidelity (Hawkins, Morrison, Musti-Rao, & Hawkins, 2008).

Although identifying the core components of a program is a critical step to measuring implementation fidelity as it relates to the desired outcomes, it is a more challenging and often neglected first step (Durlak, 2010; Fixsen, Blase, Naoom, et al., 2013). Even in established evidence-based programs and practices, there is some question regarding which exact components are critical for achieving positive student outcomes (Harn, Parisi, & Stoolmiller, 2013). The bottom line is that the process of identifying the core components must focus on the intended outcomes. Components that do not represent the active ingredient critical for attaining positive student outcomes do not meet the requirement of a *core* component. Leadership teams need to use their implementation and outcome data over time to affirm or revise what they identify as the core components of their initiative. In Chapter 4, we will describe how a logic model can be used to create a graphic display of the core components and their intended outcomes, which can be very useful for ensuring a shared understanding of the core components.

Fixsen, Blasé, Metz, et al. (2013) established criteria for defining a "usable intervention" with an eye toward measuring its implementation fidelity. The criteria are composed of four parts: (a) a clear description of the program (i.e., clearly stated philosophy, values, and principles that guide all program decision making; clear inclusion and exclusion criteria for defining the target population), (b) a clear description of the core components (i.e., essential functions or active ingredients) that must be present to say a program exists in a given location, (c) operational definitions of the essential functions, and (d) a practical assessment of the performance of teachers and other practitioners who are using the program, which is logically linked to the intended outcomes and can be conducted repeatedly over time to monitor adult implementation practices (Fixsen, Blasé, Metz, et al., 2013). Note that the use of practice profiles are described in the Spotlight on Techniques and Tools: Practice Profiles box in Box 2.2.

The following questions (Metz, 2012) may be helpful in identifying the core components of a program:

- What are the core components (i.e., active ingredients or nonnegotiables) of the program?
- How would we know the program is being implemented as planned (i.e., what does implementation look like in terms of adult practices and program structures)?
- Does the program involve the implementation of an evidence-based practice that has been implemented effectively in other sites? If so, is there a manual, blueprint, protocol, or procedural guide?
- Does the initiative involve the implementation of an evidence-informed approach that has yet to be implemented?
- Is the program being adopted in its final form or is it still being developed during its installment?

Many excellent resources exist for defining the core components of an MTSS initiative, which will eliminate the need for school-based professionals to invest time and energy defining components that are common among MTSS initiatives (e.g., data-based decision making, academic instructional supports and interventions, behavioral supports and interventions). Box 2.3 provides a brief list of organizations that have resources for defining and promoting the critical features of an MTSS framework. In addition to these organizations with national reach, many states, such as Florida, Iowa, Illinois, Colorado, Wisconsin, Kansas,

Box 2.2

SPOTLIGHT ON TECHNIQUES AND TOOLS: PRACTICE PROFILES

Practice profiles are essential tools for operationally defining what the program is intended to look like in practice (Hall & Hord, 2011). Practice profiles describe the "core activities that allow a program to be teachable, learnable, and doable in practice; and promote consistency across practitioners (e.g., teachers and staff) at the level of actual service delivery" (Fixsen, Blasé, Metz, et al., 2013, p. 219). A practice profile is structured around each of the critical components ("nonnegotiables") of a particular focused practice and an outcome for this practice. The National Implementation Research Network's Active Implementation (AI) Hub offers a free 12-minute online module on how to develop a practice profile (http://implementation.fpg.unc.edu/resources/lesson-3-practice-profiles). The focused practice and the outcome for this practice are specified in the header. The critical components are listed in the first column of a table (one component for each row of the table). A model practice profile created by the PBISs: OSEP Technical Assistance Center (see Appendix C) identifies as a focused practice, SWPBISs. The outcome for this practice is to "meet criteria on fidelity measures" (e.g., Team Implementation Checklist, Self-Assessment Survey, Schoolwide Evaluation Tool). The critical components ("nonnegotiables") are: (a) establish commitment, (b) establish and maintain team, (c) self-assessment, (d) establish schoolwide expectations, (e) classroom behavior support systems, (f) establish information systems, and (g) build capacity for function-based support. For each critical component, the team developing the practice profile for a focused practice will need to define "How does this critical component contribute to the outcome?" (the heading of the second column), the "Ideal "Gold Standard" of the Critical Components" (the heading of the third column), what constitutes "Acceptable Variation of the Critical Component" (in the fourth column), and "Unacceptable Variation of the Critical Component" (in the final column). Figure 2.3 provides the basic structure of a practice profile template.

Focused Practice: _____

Outcome for this Practice: _____

Critical Components ("nonnegotiables")	How Does this Critical Component Contribute to the Outcome?	Ideal "Gold Standard" of the Critical Component	Acceptable Variation of the Critical Component	Unacceptable Variation of the Critical Component
Critical Component 1.				
Critical Component 2.				

Figure 2.3. Practice Profile Template

Once developed, a practice profile becomes a valuable tool for making the expected practices explicit to teachers and staff, while providing a rationale for each critical component as it relates to the intended outcome. A practice profile also provides the leadership/implementation team with a means of monitoring the implementation of expected practices specific to the initiative that is directly aligned with the fidelity measures that will be used to assess implementation periodically. Finally, a practice profile has utility for determining targets for professional development and strategic planning.

---

and Missouri, offer excellent resources (e.g., manuals, protocols, checklists) through their state department of educations or an affiliated technical assistance center.

Step 2. Matching Core Program Components to Possible Indicators

In the second step, each of the core components of the program are matched to possible indicators. Each indicator is expected to have a direct impact on an intended outcome. Indicators should also have utility for measuring variance (i.e., higher and lower levels) in implementation fidelity, which is critical for analyzing student outcomes, particularly when the outcomes are mixed or less than desirable (Sheridan et al., 2009). The ability to discern higher and lower levels of implementation will also inform problem solving efforts aimed at improving both adult practices and student outcomes (Durlak, 2010; Gresham, Gansle, & Noell, 1993; Mowbray, Holter, Teague, & Bybee, 2003).

Box 2.3

ORGANIZATIONS WITH RESOURCES FOR DEFINING THE CORE COMPONENTS OF A MTSS FRAMEWORK

Michigan's Integrated Behavior and Learning Support Initiative
https://miblsi.org
National Association of State Directors of Special Education, Inc.
www.nasdse.org
National Center on Response to Intervention
www.rti4success.org
Positive Behavioral Interventions and Supports: OSEP Technical Assistance Center
www.pbis.org
RTI Action Network
www.rtinetwork.org

Another consideration when identifying indicators is the degree to which the indicators represent both structural (adherence, dosage) and process (competence/quality) dimensions of fidelity (Harn, Parisi, & Stoolmiller, 2013; Mowbray et al., 2003). Fidelity indicators based on adherence (e.g., procedural checklist) and dosage (e.g., intervention log) are easier to measure, more reliable, and explicitly linked to the expected program practices of teachers and other practitioners. When using adherence measures, it is important to provide a thorough explanation and rationale for the expected practices. Failure to provide the context and justification can quickly turn valued activities (i.e., "I see the benefit of these activities") into mandated activities ("I'm told I have to do these activities"). Although harder to measure reliably, process dimensions of fidelity (i.e., practitioner competence and the quality of program/intervention delivery commonly measured using a rubric), add valuable information to the assessment of implementation fidelity and are judged by several researchers to be more directly relevant to student outcomes (Gersten et al., 2005; Mowbray et al., 2003). Competence and quality measures of fidelity also enable program decision makers to identify exemplary practices that further advance implementation. For these reasons, a multidimensional approach that combines adherence measures with competence/quality measures of fidelity is recommended for a more thorough understanding of implementation fidelity (Dane & Schneider, 1998; Harn, Parisi, & Stoolmiller, 2013; Mowbray et al., 2003; Odom et al., 2010; Power et al., 2005). To accomplish this, consider using structural measures at regular intervals when the program is initially implemented until the program begins to yield positive outcomes, at which point the structural measures could be administered over extended time intervals and process measures could be incorporated in the evaluation of implementation fidelity (Harn, Parisi, & Stoolmiller, 2013; Mowbray et al., 2003).

The comprehensive evaluation of implementation fidelity will necessarily require a multimethod multiinformant approach to capture desirable and undesirable changes in implementation over time among a variety of classrooms and school settings (Durlak & DuPre, 2008; Fixsen et al., 2005; Odom et al., 2010). Multiple methods might include the use of surveys, rubrics, and/or direct observation of program practices. Given that programs are dynamic and evolve over time, the assessment of implementation fidelity will require the use of some repeated measures (Carroll et al., 2007; Odom et al., 2010; Stoolmiller, Eddy, & Reid, 2000). Multiple informants might involve soliciting feedback from teachers and other practitioners, a member of the school leadership team with oversight responsibilities, or the building principal or district administrator. Single, self-report measure will not suffice to measure implementation fidelity of a complex, multifaceted program, but collecting implementation fidelity data from multiple informants using multiple methods can become cumbersome and unwieldy over time, bogging down the timely analysis of data (Mowbray et al., 2003). Furthermore, as Sheridan and colleagues (2009) have pointed out, the interpretation of data collected from multiple sources can be complicated and there is not an empirically derived approach to integrating data from multiple sources. The careful selection of indicators will require balancing the need for more frequent assessment of fidelity to inform continuous improvement if implementation is lacking, but assessing fidelity should not be so frequent as to surpass a team's ability to use the data meaningfully.

Step 3. Evaluating and Selecting Implementation Fidelity Methods and Tools

A variety of data collection methods are appropriate to measure implementation fidelity. Each of these methods has advantages and disadvantages. In this section we will provide a brief overview of the methods most commonly used to measure implementation fidelity, which are (a) direct observation, (b) **permanent products**, and (c) self-report methods: checklists and surveys. The use of **rubrics** is featured in the Spotlight on Techniques and Tools section (see Box 2.4). Next, we

---

Box 2.4

SPOTLIGHT ON TECHNIQUES AND TOOLS: RUBRICS

Many school-based professionals are familiar with rubrics. A rubric is structured as a grid in which gradations of quality are operationalized for each criterion. The rubric gradations are typically anchored at either end by polar extremes (e.g., highly proficient, not proficient). Rubrics enjoy widespread use in education because they can be developed to measure a variety of teacher and student performances and they are relatively easy to interpret (Andrade, 2000). In the context of program evaluation, rubrics can be used as part of a formative evaluation to measure implementation and outcomes over time or as part of a summative evaluation at the end of the school year. When used as part of a formative evaluation of implementation in progress, rubrics can shape professional practice as well as evaluate it (Reddy & Andrade, 2010). A practice profile, for example, uses a rubric structure to make explicit what constitutes the ideal "gold standard" practice, acceptable variation, and unacceptable variation for each critical component of a focused practice (see Box 2.2, presented earlier in this chapter). As a measure of implementation fidelity, a rubric could be a self-report method or completed by an independent rater.

Rubrics have been found to produce reliable judgments given specific, observable, measurable descriptions for each criteria (Bresciani et al., 2009; Jonsson & Svingby, 2007; Moskal & Leydens, 2000; Silversti & Oescher, 2006; Wald, Borkan, Scott Taylor, Anthony, & Schmuel, 2012). However, others have questioned overall accuracy and quality of rubric assessments (Rezaei & Lovorn, 2010). More recently, Humphry and Heldsinger (2014) called into question the practice of constructing a rubric to have the same number of gradations of quality for each

(continued)

Box 2.4 (Continued)

criterion. Given that there is neither theoretical rationale nor empirical basis for having the same number of graduations across multiple aspects of the performance or product being measured, Humphry and Heldsinger (2014) contended that equal numbers of gradations are chosen for convenience in developing and scoring rubrics, rather than faithfully capturing distinguishable performance levels for separate criteria (i.e., creating more or less categories than is optimal for a given criterion). A promising, practical alternative to the standard rubric struc-

Directions: Place an "X" on the line (◄————►) to indicate your assessment of each expected practice on the continuum of "Highly Proficient" and "Not Proficient."

Skill-based Competency	Highly Proficient		Not Proficient
Expected Practice 1.	*Description provided here*	◄————————►	*Description provided here*
Expected Practice 2.	*Description provided here*	◄————————►	*Description provided here*

Figure 2.4. Half-Naked Rubric Template

ture is the half-naked rubric (Williams, 2013). The half-naked rubric provides operational description for the polar extremes only, stripping out descriptions for the gradations of quality between the extremes (See Figure 2.4). In completing the half-naked rubric, individuals or teams would indicate with a graphical rating scale whether their performance was more similar to one or the other extreme.

describe the technical aspects to consider when evaluating and selecting implementation fidelity measures and provide a list of the most prominent, research-based tools for evaluating MTSS implementation fidelity.

DIRECT OBSERVATION

Direct observation involves the use of "trained observer of prescribed formats and codes for recording in-person or videotaped observations" (Scheirer, 1994, p. 55). Observations are used regularly in schools to assess student performance, the classroom environment, and teacher instruction and managerial behaviors (Cash & Pianta, 2014; Hamre et al., 2013; Hintze, 2005; Shapiro & Heick, 2004; Volpe, DiPerna, Hintze, & Shapiro, 2005). At a systems level, observations play a critical role in the evaluation of teacher performance for the purposes of accountability (Desimone, 2009). Direct observations have an advantage over other fidelity methods in terms of reliability, when comparing data obtained through the use of permanent products and self-report (Gresham et al., 2017). Observations can be used with great accuracy to make

fine distinctions in teacher practice and student performance (e.g., engagement, off-task behaviors) to a degree not possible with measures that rely on
self-report or expert judgment (Cohen, 1990; Hintze & Matthews, 2004; Mayer,
1999; Spillane & Zeuli, 1999). Observation coding systems, such as the Behavior
Observation of Students in Schools (BOSS; Shapiro, 2011), can also be adapted
to meet a wide variety of purposes for use in naturalistic settings. As such, they
have well-established utility for measuring intervention effectiveness and fidelity of implementation (Sheridan et al., 2009; Volpe et al., 2005). The primary
disadvantage of observations is that they require the dedicated time of a trained
observer. As such, they tend to be very resource intensive, particularly when
multiple observations are required to assess various aspects of implementation
fidelity and changes in fidelity over time (Sheridan et al., 2009). With direct
observations, there is also a risk of reactivity among teachers implementing the
program practice. Therefore, the teacher practices observed may not accurately
represent the teacher's day-to-day practices.

Video observations are a cost-efficient alternative to in-person observations.
The appeal of video observations increases with advances in technology that
enable higher quality videos to be recorded with greater ease to produce results
equivalent to those obtain by in-person observations (Brunvand, 2010). A comparison of video and in-person observations conducted using the Classroom
Assessment Scoring System (CLASS; Pianta, La Paro, & Hamre, 2008) to assess
the quality of teacher-child interactions in the classroom yielded equivalent
scores across the two modes (Casabianca et al., 2013). Video observations also
have the advantage of potentially capturing the complexity of interactions,
including small-group interactions that may not be not possible with an observer
(Borko, Jacobs, Eiteljorg, & Pittman, 2008; Stigler, Gallimore, & Hiebert, 2000).
The disadvantages of video observations include (a) challenges in the quality of
information they provide regarding the instructional and classroom context that
may detrimentally affect the precision and reliability of the measure (Erickson,
1986); (b) negative reactions from teachers if teachers anticipate the video
recordings could be used to evaluate their job performance; (c) restrictions ema-
nating from teacher unions on the use of video observations in the classroom;
and (d) the need for parental consent if the images of students are captured in
the video recording.

PERMANENT PRODUCTS
Permanent products are school organizational records (e.g., an activity or participation log) or intervention products (e.g., charts, tokens, home/school notes)
that are generated on site at frequent intervals by teachers or other program
practitioners (Scheirer, 1994). School organizational records and products that
serve as permanent products are maintained routinely by a school for purposes
other than the evaluation. Permanent products are selected to provide tangible
evidence that the intervention or program is being implemented with fidelity. As
such, they are better suited to provide evidence of the structural dimensions of

fidelity (adherence, dosage), than the process dimensions of fidelity (practitioner competence, quality). The primary advantage of a permanent product review is that it capitalizes on existing products of routine activity and therefore may not require an additional burden in terms of time and effort for teachers or other practitioners to create. A permanent product review also enables fidelity data to be gathered at low cost on multiple occasions with minimal reactivity by teachers and practitioners (Sanetti & Collier-Meek, 2014). A disadvantage of a permanent product review is that it is not always the case that a permanent product naturally emerges as evidence of the implementation of an intervention or program. For example, writing interventions generate work samples that can be used as permanent products, whereas an intervention targeting oral reading fluency may not. Furthermore, process dimension of fidelity reflecting teacher competence or judgment in the course of the implementation may be difficult to assess using a permanent product review.

SELF-REPORT METHODS: CHECKLISTS AND SURVEYS

Self-report methods include checklists and surveys completed by an individual teacher/practitioner or a team of practitioners to assess their implementation of the intervention or program components. As measures of adherence, checklists must be structured to narrowly delineate each component. Likewise, surveys designed as self-report measures of fidelity should include narrowly defined, discrete questions regarding specific components of the program and the frequency or duration of time spent engaged in specific practices. The main advantage of self-report methods such as teacher surveys is that they seek behavioral information rather than evaluative information (i.e., questions about what teachers did rather than self-appraisals of how well they did it). These data sources have been shown to compare favorably with direct observations conducted by an independent observer (Mayer, 1999; Porter, Kirst, Osthoff, Smithson, & Schneider, 1993; Ross, McDougall, Hogaboam-Gray, & LeSage, 2003; Sanetti & Kratochwill, 2009). Other studies, however, have called into question teachers' accuracy in self-reporting, noting a tendency to overestimate implementation (Cohen, 1990; Frykholm, 1996; Wickstrom, Jones, LaFleur, & Witt, 1998).

To counter concerns regarding the reliability of self-reporting, the Tiered Fidelity Inventory (TFI), described in the next section, requires the use of a coach or facilitator external to the team to guide the administration and use of the self-assessment (McIntosh et al., 2016). In sum, self-report methods have advantages as cost-efficient, nonintrusive measures of the structural dimensions of implementation fidelity (i.e., adherence, dosage). Checklists and surveys can be used to collect data on a frequent basis and may capture aspects of the intended practice that would be difficult to observe directly. The primary disadvantage of self-report methods is the lingering question of accuracy in self-reporting. As such, self-report methods are best used as one of several sources of data used as part of a multimethod multiinformant approach to measuring implementation fidelity.

FIDELITY OF IMPLEMENTATION TOOLS FOR
A MULTI-TIER SYSTEM OF SUPPORTS INITIATIVE

Many research-based tools are available for assessing the implementation of MTSS initiatives. When selecting the tools best-suited to assess changes in implementation over time, considerations should include: (a) the technical adequacy (i.e., validity, reliability over time and across multiple measures; McGrew, Bond, Dietzen, & Salyers, 1994; Moncher & Prinz, 1991; Teague, Bond, & Drake, 1998), (b) the sensitivity of the tool to assess core components (i.e., those that contribute uniquely and in combination to desired outcomes; Noell, 2008), (c) the appropriate metric that relates empirically to outcomes (e.g., specific items, composite score, or consistency in implementation as a repeated measure), (d) the feasibility of assessment procedures (number of measurements required and ease of completion), and (e) the tool's capacity to capture a representative sample of implementation occasions (Sheridan et al., 2009). The use of multiple repeated measures over time is the best safeguard to counter the psychometric limitations of any one tool. Fortunately, there are many research-based tools for measuring the fidelity of implementation for an MTSS initiative. In this section we will provide an overview of the three most prominent tools for measuring MTSS implementation fidelity.

Schoolwide Positive Behavioral Interventions and Supports *Tiered Fidelity Inventory* (SWPBIS TFI)

The SWPBIS TFI (Algozzine et al., 2014) was designed to measure the extent to which Positive Behavioral Interventions and Supports (PBIS) core features are in place within a school at each tier.

- Tier 1 (universal PBIS: whole school universal prevention)
- Tier 2 (targeted PBIS: secondary, small group prevention)
- Tier 3 (intensive PBIS: tertiary, individual support prevention)

Research (McIntosh et al., 2016) provides support for the reliability of the SWPBIS TFI with regard to test-retest reliability (.98; .99; .99) and interrater agreement (.95; .96; .89). Research has also supported the content validity of the SWPBIS TFI, with validity coefficients of .95, .93, and .91 (McIntosh et al., 2016). The SWPBIS TFI was also judged to be technically adequate with regard to usability (12 of 14 ≥ 80%; 15 minutes per tier; McIntosh et al., 2016). The SWPBIS TFI provides a total score, 3 scale scores (tier 1, 2, 3), and 10 subscale scores (tier 1 teams, tier 1 implementation, tier 1 evaluation, tier 2 teams, tier 2 interventions, tier 2 evaluation, tier 3 teams, tier 3 resources, tier 3 support plan, tier 3 evaluation). By focusing on implementation at each tier, the TFI eliminates the need for separate measures for each tier, as previously provided by the *Benchmarks of Quality* (Cohen, Kincaid, & Childs, 2007), *Team Implementation Checklist* (Sugai,

Horner, Lewis-Palmer, & Rossetto Dickey, 2011), *PBIS Self-Assessment Survey* (Sugai, Horner, & Todd, 2003), *Schoolwide Evaluation Tool* (Horner et al., 2004; Todd et al., 2012; Vincent, Spauling, & Tobin, 2010), *Benchmarks for Advanced Tiers* (Anderson et al., 2012) and the *Individual Student Systems Evaluation Tool* (Anderson et al., 2011; Lewis-Palmer, Todd, Horner, Sugai, & Sampson, 2006).

Reading–Tiered Fidelity Inventory (R-TFI)

The R-TFI was developed to measure the implementation of schoolwide reading systems (St. Martin, Nantais, Harms, & Huth, 2015; St. Martin, Nantais, & Harms, 2015). Elementary-level (53 items) and secondary-level (44 items) editions are available. Each measure includes items related to tier 1, 2, and 3 reading systems organized using the subscales of Teams, Implementation, Resources, and Evaluation. To date, research has been conducted on content validity and response-process validity, with additional research on reliability, construct validity, predictive validity, and consequential validity planned for the future. The R-TFI is the only measure to assess the implementation of reading systems in a way that creates alignment between elementary and secondary schools and aligns with the structure of the SWPBIS TFI.

DECISION, OBSERVATION, RECORDING, AND ANALYSIS (DORA)

DORA was developed by Algozzine, Newton, Horner, Todd, and Algozzine (2012) to assess decision-making practices during schoolwide positive behavior support (SWPBS) meetings. DORA involves the direct observation of adult behaviors with regard to foundation elements (i.e., problem precision, quantitative use of data, solution/decision, action plan) and decision-making thoroughness. As such, DORA can be used to measure fidelity (i.e., adherence and quality) of implementation for SWPBS teams. Interobserver agreement for DORA was calculated by comparing meeting foundation element scores and decision-making thoroughness scores across 20 meetings (Todd et al., 2011). Reliability for meeting foundation scores averaged 94% (range 72–100%) and interobserver agreement for thoroughness scores averaged 88% (range 50–100%).

IMPLEMENTATION DRIVERS AND ACTIVE IMPLEMENTATION FRAMEWORKS

Once you have identified the core components of the program, matched each component to possible indicators logically linked to the intended outcomes, and selected evaluation fidelity methods and tools, you are well on your way to evaluating implementation fidelity. Before moving forward, however, we want to take a step back and provide a big picture of our current understanding of implementation science. Advances in implementation science promoted by the NIRN highlight the critical need to understand the systemic supports that drive the implementation of a new or existing initiative forward. Through research synthesis, NIRN identified commonalities among successfully implemented practices and programs (evidence-based practices or practices within evidence-based programs), which they labeled "drivers" of effective implementation (Fixsen et al., 2005). When in place and functioning at a high level, these drivers can help propel an initiative by increasing its capacity and strengthening its infrastructure to support practitioners' use of high-fidelity behaviors. NIRN's research synthesis resulted in the development of the Implementation Drivers Framework (Fixsen et al., 2005).

The Implementation Drivers Framework is composed of three sets of drivers: Competency Drivers, Organization Drivers, and Leadership Drivers (see Figure 2.5). The Competency Drivers are the mechanisms needed to develop, improve, and sustain practitioners' competent usage of program practices. The Competency Drivers include Selection, Training, Coaching, and Performance Assessment. Selection involves the process of recruiting, interviewing, and hiring practitioners by carefully considering the skills, abilities, and dispositions specific to the initiative. Training requires an understanding and application of adult learning strategies to provide skill-based instruction and support to increase practitioners' competencies. Coaching must be combined with training to increase the likelihood that new learning acquired through training is supported in its use through job-embedded guidance, assistance, and monitoring. Finally, a Performance Assessment process must be in place to ensure practitioners are proficient in their use of program practices.

The Organization Drivers are the mechanisms needed to establish and sustain effective and efficient system structures and processes. The Organization Drivers

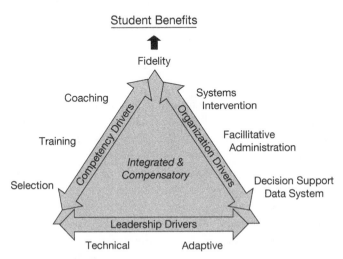

Figure 2.5. The Implementation Drivers Framework
SOURCE: Fixsen, D. L., & Blase, K. A. (2008). Drivers framework. Chapel Hill, NC: The National Implementation Research Network, University of North Carolina. Reprinted with permission from Dean L. Fixsen and the National Implementation Research Network.

include Decision Support Data Systems, Facilitative Administration, and Systems Intervention (Fixsen et al., 2005). A Decision Support Data System is a system for identifying, collecting, and analyzing process data (e.g., fidelity data and student outcome data) over time to provide timely, reliable data to inform decision making. Facilitative Administration pertains to the internal processes, policies, regulations, and structures in place to create a context that is supportive and engaged in learning, continuous improvement, and removing barriers as it relates to the initiative. Systems Intervention is focused on the external systems to ensure the availability of organizational, financial, and human resources required to support the initiative.

The Leadership Drivers focus on the use of effective leadership strategies for different types of leadership challenges: technical challenges and adaptive challenges. Technical challenges respond well to a more traditional management approach where problems are defined and solutions are generated, evaluated, and acted on. Adaptive challenges, in contrast, involve complex, persistent problems that require engaging different, often competing perspectives among stakeholders to address the challenge at many different levels.

Performance assessment (fidelity of implementation) is at the apex of the Implementation Drivers Framework, indicating that efforts of the competency, organization, and leadership drivers are focused on developing a system of support for high-fidelity practitioner behaviors. High-fidelity practitioner behaviors are observable, measureable, and known to all within the initiative (i.e., learnable, teachable, doable).

Perhaps the most appealing feature of the Implementation Drivers Framework is the notion that the drivers relate to one another in a manner that is integrated and compensatory. Each driver facilitates the work of the other drivers and information feeds backward and forward with a focus on increasing implementation fidelity for that initiative. For example, concern regarding an initiative's capacity to provide high-quality training might lead to improvements in the training design and delivery, expanded coaching supports, and attention to the selection of practitioners who will not require as intensive training in the skills required of the initiative.

Recent developments in implementation research have led the Implementation Drivers Framework to be conceptualized as a featured framework within the broader system of Active Implementation Frameworks. Active Implementation Frameworks include usable interventions, implementation stages, implementation drivers, implementation teams, and improvement cycles. NIRN has many resources available on the Active Implementation Hub (http://implementation. fpg.unc.edu/) on each of these five features. Three assessments have been developed to measure the capacity of schools, districts, and regional education agencies to support implementation of effective innovations. An effective innovation is defined as "any set of operationally defined practices used in a defined context (e.g., schools) to achieve defined outcomes" (Ward et al., 2015, p. 4) and certainly includes MTSS and many of the specific practices included underneath the MTSS umbrella. The **Regional Capacity Assessment** (St. Martin, Ward, Harms,

& Russell, 2015) is used by regional education agencies (implementation teams). The **District Capacity Assessment** (Ward et al., 2015) is completed by school districts and the Implementation Drivers: Best Practices Assessment (Fixsen, Blasé, Naoom et al., 2013) is used by school leadership teams. These assessments provide additional valuable information beyond fidelity data because they help evaluators and educators to even further investigate and put into place features that support implementation fidelity and improved student outcomes.

IMPLEMENTATION STAGES

Another major contribution of implementation theory advanced by the NIRN is the notion that implementation proceeds through discernible stages: Exploration, installation, initial implementation, and full implementation (Fixsen et al., 2005; Wallace, Blase, Fixsen, & Naoom, 2008). We focus on this particular active implementation framework here because the implementation stages inform the focus of program activities and program evaluation efforts.

Before an initiative can be installed, a school or school district must demonstrate readiness, evident in a common understanding and shared acceptance, that the program is a good fit that will yield improved outcomes (Fixsen, Blasé, Naoom, et al., 2013). The key outcome of the exploration stage is a collective decision to install the program with the strong support of relevant stakeholders. Fixsen, Blasé, Naoom, et al. (2013) has cautioned against the rush to install a program in cases where the school or district has not demonstrated adequate readiness. The exploration stage can extend 1 to 2 years depending on the resources allocated, access to information, and decision-making authority granted to those engaged in the exploration work. During the exploration stage, program evaluation efforts might focus on needs assessment activities (see Chapter 1) and the development of a theory of change and logic model (see Chapter 4).

The installation stage involves acquiring the resources needed to establish the new program in the local setting. A thorough understanding of the Implementation Drivers Framework is essential for aligning resources needed for competent usage (i.e., staff selection, training, coaching, and performance assessment), organizational structure (i.e., facilitative administration, decision support data system, and systems interventions), and leadership (i.e., technical and adaptive). Without careful consideration of the implementation drivers, the installation stage can quickly serve as a graveyard, the final resting place for yet another appealing initiative that was launched before a school or district had the capacity to install it successfully. Program evaluation activities during the installation stage might include evaluating professional learning (see Chapter 3), the development of practice profiles, and assistance in selecting the implementation and outcome measures incorporated in the decision support data system.

The initial implementation stage marks the point in time when program practitioners are attempting to use newly acquired skills, often in place of longstanding practices, all within a school or district undergoing systems change. Not surprisingly, the initial implementation stage presents many significant challenges, and program leaders can anticipate a strong urge to reject the changes required and return to prior practices. Formative evaluation efforts at the initial implementation stage should focus on assessing fidelity of implementation to guide planning for continuous program improvement.

An initiative is judged to have reached the full implementation stage in a school or district when new practices become the standard approach to supporting teachers' efforts to meet students' needs. Active implementation support is critically important to ensure new and previously trained practitioners have the necessary competence, organizational support, and engaged leadership to maintain and sustain program practices (Fixsen, Blasé, Naoom, et al., 2013). Program evaluation at the full implementation stage involves the use of formative and summative evaluation activities to link program components to their intended outcomes. Timely and ongoing program evaluation is essential at this stage to inform problem solving in instances in which the implementation and/or outcomes are weaker than expected.

BALANCING IMPLEMENTATION FIDELITY AND ADAPTATION

In the 1990 movie *Edward Scissorhands* starring Johnny Depp, suburbanites from nearly identical "cookie-cutter" houses carry out their morning routine in perfect synchrony, backing out of their driveways in unison and heading off to work. This parody of suburban living has little resemblance to the complex, fast-paced, and somewhat fragmented environment of schools and districts. Yet, despite all of the discrete moving parts inherent in a school or district, fidelity of implementation is critical from classroom to classroom and school to school. But how much implementation fidelity is needed, given that teachers do not work in cookie-cutter schools? Box 2.5 expands on what we know about how knowledge spreads within social systems, such as schools and school districts.

Early in this chapter we established that implementation fidelity is essential for (a) determining whether an intervention or program was effective given the quality of its implementation, (b) demonstrating accountability for program implementation, and (c) guiding decisions aimed at continuous improvement. Ultimately, however, implementation fidelity is about attaining student outcomes. Research indicates that evidence-based interventions and programs replicated with higher fidelity achieve better outcomes relative to programs implemented with lower fidelity (Blakely et al., 1987; Drake et al., 2001; Durlak & DuPre, 2008; Paulson, Post, Herincks, & Risser, 2002). Recall the NIRN's formula in Figure 2.1, which shows that positive outcomes for students is the product of an effective intervention that is implemented with fidelity. Research has also shown that when key elements of an established model are omitted, less positive and even contradictory outcomes may result (Bond, Evans, Salyers, Williams, & Kim, 2000).

Box 2.5

SPOTLIGHT ON DIFFUSION THEORY—A KNOWLEDGE-FOR-ACTION THEORY

We have heard it said that schools and districts are like snowflakes: No two are alike. On the contrary, it is our experience that teachers and administrators do not think all schools are unique, but rather they believe that their school alone is distinctly unique and that innovations that are effective in many other schools might not be a good fit for their school. Although an understanding of the unique contextual factors is critical for planning for the implementation of a new innovation, there are predictable patterns to how new unique ideas and practices are adopted, as informed by theory.

Implementation theory is one of several knowledge-for-action theories that serves to explain how knowledge in some form spreads among various stakeholders and contexts to achieve some intended or unanticipated outcomes (Ottoson, 2009). Other knowledge-for-action theories include knowledge utilization, diffusion, transfer, and translation. Ottoson (2009) distinguished among these theories by highlighting the primary question posed by each (p. 8):

- Did learning move as intended from the training site to the community context, or did it morph into alternative, adapted skills (transfer theory)?
- Did intended beneficiaries have the authority or opportunity to use a new skill (implementation theory)?
- Were ideas translated into actionable messages for intended beneficiaries (translation theory)?
- If intended beneficiaries shared but did not use their program experience, does that spread of knowledge count as nonuse or success (diffusion theory)?

Knowledge-for-action theories provide program planners and evaluators valuable insights regarding how individuals will respond to systems change. For example, diffusion is defined as "the process by which an *innovation* is *communicated* through certain *channels* over *time* among the members of a *social system*" (Rogers, 2003, p. 7). From diffusion theory, we can anticipate that teachers and administrators will have different responses to a new innovation. Some educators will adopt an idea or practice right away. Other educators will wait to see outcomes before deciding to adopt. Finally, some teachers and administrators many never adopt the innovation at all. According to diffusion theory, individuals can be classified according to the estimated time it takes them to adopt a new innovation, such that 2.5% of the individuals will likely be "innovators," 13.5% will be "early adopters," the next 34% are considered "early majority" adopters, which are followed by the next 34%, the "late majority" adopters (Rogers, 2003). Remaining are the 16%, classified as "laggards" who avoid the new innovation all together. Furthermore, adopting the innovation also involves adapting the innovation to fit

(*continued*)

Box 2.5 (Continued)

the local school or district context. In contrast to implementation theory, which primarily emphasizes fidelity of implementation with a secondary emphasis on contextual fit, diffusion theory maintains that adapting the innovation to fit the context is critical to its adoption and sustainability.

Diffusion theory has implications for program evaluators in that one can expect selective uptake of an innovation and that the resulting innovation in practice might vary from district to district, school to school, or even classroom to classroom. Also, given that an evaluation of an innovation in its early stages might yield different results than an evaluation conducted once the innovation has been more fully adopted, Ashley (2009) recommended that evaluators carefully attend to the diversity of adopters prior to initiating evaluation activities.

Historically, there has been a tension between advocates of strict implementation fidelity (i.e., replication) of effective programs (Drake et al., 2001; Szulanski & Winter, 2002) and proponents of the need to balance fidelity with adaptation to enhance the contextual fit of the innovation in classrooms, schools, or districts (Bachrach, 1988; Blakely et al., 1987; Fairweather & Tornatzky, 1971; Harn, Parisi, & Stoolmiller, 2013; Hohmann & Shear, 2002). Adaptation, according to the **Instructional Hierarchy model** (Haring & Eaton, 1978), is the fourth and final stage of learning a new skill. First, an individual must acquire the skill and gain accuracy in its use (acquisition stage). In the second stage, an individual gains proficiency in the use of the skill in the context in which it was learned (fluency stage). Once a learner has mastered a skill or practice and is fluent in its use, the individual may seek to perform the skill or practice in new settings and circumstances (generalization stage). Only after the individual has demonstrated mastery of the fluent use of the skill across settings and circumstances is the individual prepared to modify the skill itself for use in novel situations (adaptation stage). Adaptation, therefore, requires that the individual is proficient enough in the skill to be able to identify elements of the skill to fit novel demands or situations.

Adaptation at a systems level more accurately involves mutual adaptation (Datnow, Hubbard, & Mehan, 2002; Hubbard & Mehan, 1999; Stringfield & Datnow, 1998), whereby the program is tailored in light of local circumstances with accompanying changes in the practitioners' practices in the school or district. Adaptation is critical to implementing and sustaining new practices, given consideration to the practice being promoted (e.g., relevance and fit to the target environment, efficiency, and practicality), users (e.g., available time, teachers' instructional philosophy and theoretical orientation, knowledge and skills, teachers' experience, teachers' self-efficacy, mistrust of new initiatives), and organizational factors (e.g., available resources, organizational culture, administrative support, training and coaching). (Supporting references include Carroll et al., 2007; Cook & Odom, 2013; Durlak, 2010; Fixsen et al., 2005; Nelson, Leffler, &

Hansen, 2009; Stein et al., 2008; and Tseng, 2012.) The adaptation of an evidence-based program or practice may enable the program or practice to better suit the social and cultural needs of the students and teachers, increase teacher ownership with the program, and in turn, increase the likelihood of sustainability (Bachrach, 1988; Dearing, 2008; Fairweather & Tornatzsky, 1971). Research has shown that skillful practitioners may adapt an effective intervention or program to achieve superior results (Castro, Barrera, & Martinez, 2004; Luborsky, McLellan, Diguer, Woody, & Seligman, 1997; Webster-Stratton, Reinke, Herman, & Newcomer, 2011). As teachers and administrators adapt established programs to enhance contextual fit, however, it is critical that they have identified the "active ingredients" of the practices to ensure the core components of the program are not fundamentally altered (Harn, Parisi, & Stoolmiller, 2013).

Given this tension between implementation fidelity and adaptation, the question remains: How much fidelity is needed? Although higher levels of implementation fidelity to an evidence-based program or practice are clearly desirable, Durlak and DuPre (2008) identified "implementation thresholds" of fidelity (p. 343), beyond which efforts to increase implementation fidelity did not contribute to more positive student outcomes. According to their research, programs that feature explicitly defined core components may be associated with positive outcomes at lower levels of fidelity, whereas programs with less clearly defined core components require higher levels of implementation fidelity to attain desired outcomes. Thus, Durlak and DuPre (2008) have concluded that expecting near-perfect fidelity is unrealistic and may be unnecessary. Implementation fidelity rates of 60 to 80% may be acceptable if the core components are clearly defined and readily understood by practitioners (Durlak & DuPre, 2008). The SWPBIS TFI authors suggest a criterion threshold score of 70% for tier 1, which is consistent with other measures of PBIS implementation (e.g., Benchmarks of Quality). Until further research is conducted, a criterion threshold score of 80% is suggested for the remaining tiers of the SWPBIS Tiered Fidelity Inventory, Reading–Tiered Fidelity Inventory, District Capacity Assessment, and Regional Capacity Assessment.

Ultimately, determining how much fidelity is needed must be a data-based decision. Table 2.1 provides a matrix we find useful for guiding data interpretation and action planning.

Table 2.1 MATRIX OF FIDELITY AND STUDENT OUTCOMES
FOR DATA-BASED DECISION MAKING

Good	I. Good Fidelity Good student outcomes	II. Good Fidelity Weak student outcomes	
Fidelity	III. Weak Fidelity Good student outcomes	IV. Weak Fidelity Weak student outcomes	
	Good	**Student Outcomes**	Weak

If targeted student outcomes are not being met and fidelity is found to be lacking (cell IV), then greater emphasis should be placed on increasing implementation fidelity to evidence-based practices. However, if targeted student outcomes are being achieved despite moderate levels of implementation fidelity (cell III), both the implementation and outcomes should continue to be monitored and the adaptions contributing to the positive outcomes should be documented.

CASE EXAMPLE

Michigan's Integrated Behavior and Learning Support Initiative works with districts to implement an MTSS for reading and behavior. Participating districts are required to use the following assessments as part of their ongoing evaluation of MTSS:

- **Reach:** District and school stage of implementation and counts of participating schools
- **Capacity:** District Capacity Assessment
- **Fidelity:** Schoolwide PBIS TFI, R-TFI
- **Student Outcomes:** DIBELS Next, Major Discipline Referrals, Early Warning Indicators for Preventing School Dropout (attendance, behavior, course proficiency), Student Risk Screening Scale

Fidelity data are used by school leadership teams to self-assess and then guide ongoing action plans to improve implementation of MTSS. Systems coaches for each school use the SWPBIS TFI and R-TFI to identify areas where schools need to improve. Each coach develops a detailed plan for how they will systematically coach each school to successfully make improvements in the prioritized areas. District implementation teams also look at fidelity data. Rather than examining fidelity scores on a school-by-school basis, they look for trends across all participating schools in the district to find (a) overall levels of implementation, (b) specific subscales/concepts needing improvement, (c) schools' fidelity data compared to student outcomes, and (d) how fidelity and student outcomes relate to the district-level capacity to effectively help schools implement MTSS.

IN CONCLUSION

School-based professionals have long recognized the need for reliable and valid measures to assess student outcomes. It has been only recently, with advances in implementation research, that educators have come to appreciate the need to measure the degree to which the intended practices are being implemented as planned. Attending to adult implementation acknowledges that changes in practices are critically important to achieving the desired goals and that changes do not occur spontaneously without deliberate planning, an investment in professional learning supports, and frequent monitoring over time.

SUMMARY POINTS

- According to the NIRN, even the most effective intervention/innovation will fail to achieve the desired outcomes if not implemented effectively. A poorly implemented effective intervention/innovation is no better than an ineffective intervention/innovation implemented with fidelity.
- Measuring the fidelity of an intervention or innovation requires consideration of structural dimensions and the process dimensions. The structural dimensions of fidelity include determining the degree to which the core components were implemented as intended involves consideration of the exposure (or dosage), or the number, length, frequency, or duration. Process dimensions encompass the quality of intervention delivery as evidenced through the practitioner's competence, decisions, language, timing, choice making, and judgment.
- An MTSS framework is much more than just a continuum of increasingly intensive interventions. The degree to which evidence-based academic and behavioral instruction and interventions are implemented as planned and matched to students' needs is an essential element of an MTSS framework. MTSS implementation also requires systemic change at the classroom, school, and district level. Fidelity of implementation must also consider the system's capacity to implement and sustain MTSS. Both intervention fidelity and implementation fidelity are critical to evaluating an MTSS initiative.
- A three-step process is involved in measuring implementation fidelity:
  Step 1: Identify the core components of the program
  Step 2: Match each of the core components to possible indicators with emphasis on a multimethod, multiinformant approach
  Step 3: Evaluate and select fidelity methods and tools best suited to measure each indicator. Fidelity data can be gathered via direct observation, permanent product review, and/or self-report methods.
- When selecting the tools best suited to assess changes in implementation over time, considerations should include:
  - The technical adequacy (i.e., validity, reliability over time and across multiple measures)
  - The sensitivity of the tool to assess core components (i.e., those that contribute uniquely and in combination to desired outcomes)
  - The appropriate metric that relates empirically to outcomes (e.g., specific items, composite score, or consistency in implementation as a repeated measure)

- The feasibility of assessment procedures (number of measurements required and ease of completion)
  - The tool's capacity to capture a representative sample of implementation occasions
- A practice profile describes the core activities that allow a program to be teachable, learnable, and doable in practice and is designed to promote consistency in practice across educators.
- Research-validated tools for measuring MTSS implementation fidelity includes the SWPBIS TFI and the Reading-TFI at the school level, the District Capacity Assessment at the district level, and the Regional Capacity Assessment at the regional level.
- The Implementation Drivers Framework is composed of three sets of drivers: Competency Drivers, Organization Drivers, and Leadership Drivers.
- Another major contribution of implementation theory advanced by the NIRN is the notion that implementation proceeds through discernible stages: exploration, installation, initial implementation, and full implementation.
- Active Implementation Frameworks include: usable interventions, implementation stages, implementation drivers, implementation teams, and improvement cycles.

QUESTIONS TO FURTHER YOUR UNDERSTANDING

1. Given the notion of implementation thresholds, what would you recommend to a school team with R-TFI data that was just below the criteria for tier 1 implementation but had universal screening data to suggest students were making noteworthy gains? How would you advise the team if their universal screening data were lackluster?
2. Apply the Implementation Drivers Framework to a program or initiative with which you are familiar. How could attention to the drivers lead to improvements in program operations and impact?
3. Does the knowledge of an initiative's implementation stage (i.e., exploration, installation, initial implementation, and full implementation) affect how you will approach measuring implementation fidelity? Why or why not?
4. Under what conditions and to what degree is adaption appropriate when implementing and sustaining a new initiative? That is, when would a school consider customizing implementation to meet the local needs rather than prioritizing strict adherence to the intended plan for implementation?

3

Evaluating Professional Learning

Members of the school leadership team at Central Elementary are in a quandary over how to increase teachers' implementation of multi-tier system of supports (MTSS). They recognize that additional, targeted professional development for teachers will be necessary, but they also anticipate challenges due to the instructional time lost for teachers required to attend one or more training sessions. To be clear, the teachers at Central Elementary are professional and eager to further their own knowledge and skills if they think the professional learning experience will better equip them to have an impact on student learning. Too often, however, the teachers are removed from their classrooms to attend a day-long session that offers very little relevant information—a colossal waste of time! The pressure is on the school leadership team to design and coordinate a high-quality professional learning experience for the teachers and to show that the effort contributes directly to positive student outcomes.

WHAT IS PROFESSIONAL LEARNING?

Professional learning has a long history within the field of education. Traditionally, efforts devoted to increasing the knowledge, skills, and practices of teachers and administrators have been referred to as teacher in-service, staff development, and professional development. Given that the term *development* might have a negative connotation such that it indicates a need for remediation, we prefer the term **professional learning** to emphasize an ongoing investment in improved performance. Learning, as defined by Susan Ambrose and colleagues from Carnegie Mellon University's Eberly Center for Teaching Excellence, is "a *process* that leads to *change*, which occurs as a result of *experience* and increases the potential for improved performance and future learning" (Ambrose, Bridges, DiPietro, Lovette, & Norman, 2010, p. 3). This definition of learning emphasizes that it is a process that unfolds over time. Given that we cannot observe the learning process directly, we can only evaluate whether learning has occurred by examining the products or practices of the adult learner. Finally, this definition accentuates the experiences of the learner as an active agent in the professional learning process.

The emphasis on professional learning within education reflects a recognition that education is a dynamic professional field and that teachers and administrators need to further their knowledge and skills as advances in teaching and learning shape the educational landscape (Guskey, 2000). It should, therefore, not be surprising that developing teachers' capacity to improve their instructional practices has been shown to be key to achieving systemic goals for improving student achievement above all other school-level characteristics (Aaronson, Barrow, & Sander, 2007; Darling-Hammond, Wei, Andree, Richardson, & Orphanos, 2009; Goldhaber, 2002; Rivkin, Hanushek, & Kain, 2005; Rockoff, 2004). In fact, most school improvement efforts target teacher professional learning to improve student outcomes (Desimone, 2009), and systemic and sustained improvements in education almost never take place in the absence of professional learning efforts (Guskey, 2000).

In order to evaluate professional learning initiatives, there needs to be a clear understanding of what constitutes a high-quality, evidence-based professional learning program. In this chapter, we review the research regarding the principles and strategies for optimizing adult learning. Next, we describe approaches to evaluating professional learning initiatives for teachers and administrators.

CHARACTERISTICS OF EFFECTIVE ADULT LEARNING METHODS

Malcolm Knowles used the term *andragogy* to refer to methods and principles used in adult education and in doing so brought attention to the unique characteristics of adult learners. In more recent years, Carol Trivette and Carl Dunst's pioneering work on adult learning methods and strategies has led to advances in efforts designed to improve professional learning. In their research synthesis of 79 empirical studies of professional learning programs and their outcomes, Trivette, Dunst, Hamby, and O'Herin (2009) identified six characteristics of adult learning methods that were the most highly associated with positive learner outcomes. Learner outcomes in this research synthesis were organized into four categories: (a) knowledge; (b) skills; (c) attitudes/satisfaction with the professional learning experience; and (d) self-efficacy, which is an individual's judgment regarding one's own capabilities to use a skill or practice effectively.

The six characteristics of adult learning methods were structured according to the three key elements of learning identified by Donovan, Bransford, and Pellegrino (1999): planning, application, and deep understanding. The element of planning represents the notion that information is learned with greater ease when it is related to existing learner knowledge. The element of application emphasizes that the mastery of information requires application of the knowledge in the context of a conceptual, procedural, or practical framework. Finally, the element of deep understanding highlights the notion that ongoing monitoring and self-assessment of learning are critical for advancing a deeper understanding and continued application of newly acquired knowledge or skills.

Table 3.1 Characteristics of the Adult Learning Methods

Features/Characteristics	Definition
PLANNING	
Introduce	Engage the learner in a preview of the material, knowledge, or practice that is the focus of instruction or training.
Illustrate	Demonstrate or illustrate the use or applicability of the material, knowledge, or practice for the learner.
APPLICATION	
Practice	Engage the learner in the use of the material, knowledge, or practice.
Evaluate	Engage the learner in a process of evaluating the consequence or outcome of the application of the material, knowledge, or practice.
DEEP UNDERSTANDING	
Reflection	Engage the learner in self-assessment of his or her acquisition of knowledge and skills as a basis for identifying "next steps" in the learning process.
Mastery	Engage the learner in a process of assessing his or her experience in the context of some conceptual or practical model or framework, or some external set of standards or criteria.

SOURCE: Trivette, C. M., Dunst, C. J., Hamby, D. W., & O'Herin, C. E. (2009). Characteristics and consequences of adult learning methods and strategies. *Winterberry Research Synthesis, 2*(2), 1–33. Reprinted with permission.

Within the element of *planning*, Trivette and associates (2009) identified two characteristics of adult learning methods (see Table 3.1). Introduce, the first, involves engaging the learner in a preview of the content that is the focus of instruction or training. The use of out-of-class activities and self-instruction, warm-up exercises, and preclass quizzes are adult learning strategies that epitomize the characteristics of Introduce. Illustrate, the second, involves demonstrating the use of new knowledge or skills. Real-life demonstrations and role plays have been found to be effective strategies for illustrating new knowledge and skills. Despite the obvious advantage of providing an opportunity to role play a new skill and receive feedback during a training session, role playing as an adult learning strategy has not been consistently used in teacher professional learning initiatives.

Relevant to the element of *application*, Trivette and associates (2009) identified two characteristics of adult learning methods: Practice and Evaluate. Practice involves engaging the learner in the use of the material, knowledge, or skills featured in the professional learning experience. Real-life application, problem-solving tasks, and role plays have been shown to provide effective practice opportunities. Evaluate, as a characteristic of adult learning methods, involves engaging the learner in a process of judging their own learning outcomes (e.g., reviewing learner's solutions to problem-solving tasks, having learners assess their own strengths and weaknesses in the application of new knowledge or skills).

Corresponding to the element of *deep understanding*, Trivette and associates (2009) identified two characteristics of adult learning methods: Reflection and Mastery. Reflection involves engaging the learner in determining the next steps of the learning process given the individual's self-assessment of his or her knowledge and skill acquisition. Strategies to promote reflection include journaling, the provision of instructor or peer feedback, and group reflection on instructor or peer feedback. Mastery, the final characteristic of adult learning methods, involves having individuals assess his or her learning attainment with regard to an established set of standards of external criteria.

The results of the research synthesis support the importance of the six characteristics (i.e., Introduce, Illustrate, Practice, Evaluate, Reflection, and Mastery) in relation to the learner outcomes: knowledge, skills, attitudes/satisfaction, and self-efficacy (Trivette et al., 2009). The influences of the adult learning method characteristics on the outcome measures were evident in moderate effect sizes (presented in order of effect size magnitude along with the confidence interval [CI]; Trivette et al., 2009) for skill acquisition ($d = .66$ [CI $= .43, .88$]) and attitudes/satisfaction ($d = .68$ [CI $= .40, .96$]), learner knowledge ($d = .49$ [CI $= .29, .69$]), and learner self-efficacy beliefs ($d = .47$ [CI $= .28, 65$]). Furthermore, the research synthesis demonstrated that the influence of the six characteristics were additive, such that professional learning programs that featured a greater number of characteristics yielded larger effect sizes than programs that used fewer. Studies of professional learning programs with none or only one of the characteristics had little or no effect on learner outcomes. Studies that included two, three, or four characteristics were associated with an average effect size of about 0.75 (Trivette et al., 2009). Among the studies of professional learning programs that featured five or all six characteristics, the average effect size was almost 1.25!

The findings from the research synthesis of adult learning methods have significant implications for designing and evaluating professional learning programs. First, although the association between the adult learning methods and the study outcomes were consistent regardless of the setting (classroom vs. work site), learners (college students vs. practitioners), sample size (9–34 learners, 35–75 learners, or 76–300+ learners) and length of training (1–10 hours, 11–40 hours, 40+ hours), adult learning methods were more effective when used with a relatively small number of learners (i.e., 34 or fewer learners) and where the learning experience occurred for 10 or more hours (Trivette et al., 2009). Within the context of education, previous researchers have advocated for the need for more than 40 hours of professional learning on a given topic for teachers over a school year (Yoon, Duncan, Lee, Scarloss, & Shapley, 2007).

Second, whereas each of the six characteristics of adult learning methods were moderately to highly related to study outcomes independently and in combination with one another, the characteristics that required the learner to be more actively involved in assessing their own learning (evaluate, reflection, and mastery) demonstrated a stronger positive relationship to the learner outcomes. A final implication of the research synthesis is that high-impact professional learning programs feature instructors that actively facilitate learner engagement and content mastery, in contrast to professional learning approaches that promote learner self-discovery in the absence of instructor guidance and feedback (Trivette et al., 2009).

The *Observation Checklist for High-Quality Professional Development Training* (Noonan, Gaumer Erickson, Brussow, & Langham, 2015) can be used to assess the degree to which each of these six characteristics of adult learning methods are evident in a training session. A copy of this instrument is provided in Appendix B. We find it useful to analyze the results of the *Observation Checklist for High-Quality Professional Development Training* separately for (a) items that related to the content (and therefore the content development process) and (b) items that relate to the delivery.

SEVEN PRINCIPLES OF TEACHING ADULT LEARNERS

Susan Ambrose and associates from Carnegie Mellon University's Eberly Center for Teaching Excellence developed seven research-based principles for teaching adult learners in the university setting that apply equally well to teacher professional learning initiatives (Ambrose et al., 2010). The seven research-based principles compliment the six characteristics of adult learning methods previously described (see Table 3.2 for a list of the seven research-based principles cross-referenced with the six characteristics of adult learning methods). For our purposes, we have replaced references to (university) *students* in the seven principles with the term *learners*. Each principle is described briefly in this section along with implications for evaluating professional learning.

Principle 1: Learners' Prior Knowledge Can Help or Hinder Learning

According to the first principle, instructors need to "deliberately activate relevant prior knowledge to strengthen appropriate associations" (Ambrose et al., 2010, p. 23). Instructors seeking to facilitate associations between prior knowledge and the new content need to identify the requirements for prior knowledge (i.e., what do learners need to know to perform this skill?). In doing so, instructors should differentiate between declarative (knowing what and knowing why) and procedural knowledge (knowing how and knowing when). Diagnostic assessments and learner self-assessments can yield valuable information regarding a learner's prior knowledge.

Principle 1 holds several implications for the evaluation of professional learning programs. First, in evaluating changes in learners' knowledge and skills, there

Table 3.2 SEVEN RESEARCH-BASED PRINCIPLES FOR TEACHING ADULT LEARNERS CROSS-REFERENCED WITH SIX CHARACTERISTICS OF ADULT LEARNING METHODS

	Planning		Application		Deep Understanding	
	Introduce	Illustrate	Practice	Evaluate	Reflection	Mastery
1. Learners' prior knowledge can help or hinder learning.	✓	✓				
2. How learners organize knowledge influences how they learn and apply what they know.	✓	✓			✓	
3. Learners' motivation determines, directs, and sustains what they do to learn.	✓	✓	✓	✓	✓	✓
4. To develop mastery, learners must acquire component skills, practice integrating them, and know when to apply what they have learned.			✓	✓		
5. Goal-directed practice coupled with targeted feedback enhances the quality of participants' learning.			✓	✓		
6. Learners' current level of development interacts with the social, emotional, and intellectual climate of the course to affect learning.	✓			✓	✓	
7. To become self-directed learners, participants must learn to monitor and adjust their approaches to learning.				✓	✓	✓

must be sufficient time allowed for learners to correct inaccurate knowledge and misconceptions. Changes in conceptual understanding will likely occur gradually over time and not be immediately observable and measurable (Ambrose et al., 2010). Learners may be correcting for inaccuracies in their prior knowledge that do not yet translate into changes in their professional practices (Alibali, 1999; Chi & Roscoe, 2002). Furthermore, given the distinction between declarative and procedural knowledge, a learner may be able to demonstrate knowledge of facts or concepts but not yet know how to use this new knowledge, just as a learner may know how to perform a new practice but not understand what he or she is doing and why (Ambrose et al., 2010).

Principle 2: The Ways in Which Learners Organize Knowledge Influences How They Learn and Apply What They Know

According to the second principle, expertise in a given topic or domain involves deep conceptual understanding that is reflected in dense connections to other related topics. Experts see the big picture, but they also see how other concepts interrelate. Learners seeking to develop a deeper understanding of the content will need an instructor to monitor periodically how well they are processing what they are learning (Ambrose et al., 2010). As reinforced by the research synthesis on characteristics of adult learning methods, learners need instructors to engage them in a process of evaluating their experiences in the context of some framework, model, or operationally defined performance standards or expectations (Henry, McTaggert, & McMillan, 1992; Otis-Wilborn, Winn, & Ford, 2000; Trivette et al., 2009).

The implication of Principle 2 for the evaluation of professional learning is that frequent and periodic assessment of how well the learner is progressing is critical. Ongoing, formative assessment of learners' knowledge and skill acquisition, application, and mastery enables the instructor to ascertain whether the learners are making the expected gains in knowledge and skills relative to the learning objectives. Where the expected gains are not evident, the instructor can tailor his or her approach accordingly.

Principle 3: Learners' Motivation Determines, Directs, and Sustains What They Do To Learn

Given the critical importance of motivation in the context of learning, it is crucial to attend to factors that may increase to decrease learners' motivation. Ambrose and associates (2010) pointed to three concepts that are central to understanding a learner's motivation:

1. The subjective value of a goal
2. The expectancies, or expectations for successful attainment of that goal
3. The perception that the learning environment is supportive

When learners find value in a learning goal, expect to successfully achieve a desired learning outcome, and perceive support from their environment, they are likely to be strongly motivated to learn (Ambrose et al., 2010). Research shows that learners who hold goals for their own learning (mastery goals) are more likely to invest the time and energy to deepen their understanding of the content, pursue more challenging tasks, seek help when needed, and persist when faced with difficulty. They are more likely to seek out and feel comfortable with challenging tasks than learners who simply seek to demonstrate their competence relative to others participating in the session (performance-approach goal) or seek to avoid appearing incompetent (performance-avoidance goal). (Supporting references include Barron & Harackiewicz, 2001; Harackiewicz, Barron, Taucer, Carter, & Elliot, 2000; McGregor & Elliot, 2002; Miller, Greene, Montalvo, Ravindran, & Nichols, 1996; and Somuncuoglu & Yildirim, 1999). In addition to learners' goals aligning with the learning objectives of the professional learning experience, the learners must also hold positive expectations that the effort will lead to the desired outcome (Carver & Scheier, 1998), as well as expectations in their own capabilities (self-efficacy) to bring about the outcome (Bandura, 1997). A supportive learning environment is needed to facilitate learners' positive expectations in pursuit of their goals for learning mastery.

The implications for the evaluation of professional learning programs that stem from Principle 3 are twofold. First, the evaluation of professional learning must attend to learners' satisfaction with the professional learning experience in terms of (a) the degree to which the learning objectives were stated explicitly, (b) the degree to which the learning objectives were aligned with the instructional strategies and assessments used, (c) the importance and relevance of the learning objectives, and (d) the perception that the learning environment was supportive and conducive to learning. Second, a measure of teacher self-efficacy may be useful for evaluating teachers' learning of new knowledge and skills (Guskey, 2000).

Principle 4: To Develop Mastery, Learners Must Acquire Component Skills, Practice Integrating Them, and Know When to Apply What They Have Learned

Explicit instruction in the key component skills of a complex task with ample opportunities to practice these skills to the point where they can be performed fluently is a cornerstone of Trivette and Dunst's adult learning method characteristics and most prominent instructional frameworks (Archer & Hughes, 2011). According to the **instructional hierarchy model** (Ardoin & Daly, 2007; Haring & Eaton, 1978), practice is crucial for advancing a learner through a learning progression that begins with the skill acquisition stage, where the learner first acquires the component skill and gains accuracy in its use (acquisition stage). In the fluency stage, the learner practices using the skill in the context in which it was learned. In the generalization stage, the learner needs to practice the skill in new settings and circumstances. Only after the individual has demonstrated mastery of the fluent use of the skill across settings and circumstances is the individual prepared to practice modifying the skill itself for use in novel situations (adaptation stage).

The implication of Principle 4 for evaluating professional learning is that professional learning should be skill-based in part or in whole. Individuals evaluating a professional learning program need to determine whether the program provides (a) practice in component skills that are anchored by specific goal or criterion for performance, (b) an appropriate level of challenge relative to a learner's current performance within an instructional hierarchy (i.e., acquisition, fluency, generalization, and adaptation), and (c) practice opportunities of sufficient quality, frequency, and duration (Ambrose et al., 2010). Data literacy refers to a set of skills central to the implementation of MTSS that may be appropriate targets for professional learning in promoting MTSS implementation (see Box 3.1).

Box 3.1

Spotlight on Data Literacy as a Target for Professional Learning

The implementation of a multi-tier system of supports (MTSS) framework represents a fundamental shift in how educators gather, monitor, and respond to data (Daly, Martens, Barnett, Witt, & Olson, 2007; Kratochwill, Volpiansky, Clements, & Ball, 2007). Despite the critical importance of data-based decision making, many teachers do not have the data literacy knowledge and skills they need for instructional decision making within a MTSS framework. Data literacy is defined as the "ability to understand and use data effectively to inform decisions" (Mandinach & Gummer, 2013, p. 30). Mandinach and Gummer (2013) identified the following knowledge, skills, processes, and practices that teachers need that are often underdeveloped in educator preparation programs:

- Differentiate instruction to meet the needs of all students
- Formulate hypothesis about students' learning needs and instructional strategies
- Collect and use multiple sources of data
- Use formative, summative, interim, benchmark, and common assessments, as well as student classroom work products to make decisions
- Modify instructional practice according to the data collected
- Drill down to the item level to gain a deeper understanding of performance
- Use student work, not just tests, and other sources of data
- Monitor outcomes
- Focus on all children, not just the "bubble kids"
- Look for causes of failure that can be remediated
- Work in data teams to examine data

Professional learning for a MTSS initiative should incorporate a focus on building and advancing educators' data literacy skills.

Principle 5: Goal-Directed Practice Coupled with Targeted Feedback Enhances the Quality of Students' Learning

Explicit, frequent, and timely feedback that communicates how well a learner has performed relative to a specific target criterion is an essential element of teaching adult learners (Ambrose et al., 2010). The implication of Principle 5 for evaluating professional learning is that professional learning must incorporate feedback opportunities in the learning experience. Feedback can be provided at the individual or group level and it can take the form of instructor feedback or peer feedback.

Principle 6: Learners' Current Level of Development Interacts with the Social, Emotional, and Intellectual Climate of the Course to Affect Learning

Principle 6 emphasizes the importance of the climate within the learning environment. Whereas a positive climate can engage and energize learners, a negative climate may impede learning and close the door to future professional learning experiences (Ambrose et al., 2010). Ambrose and associates (2010) have recommended strategies to promote a positive, productive climate that include (a) making uncertainty safe; (b) resisting a single right answer; (c) incorporating evidence into performance criteria; (d) reducing anonymity; (e) modeling inclusive language, behavior, and attitudes; (f) establishing and reinforcing ground rules for interaction; (g) using the session agenda to establish the climate during the introduction; (h) anticipating and preparing for potentially sensitive issues; and (i) addressing tensions early. Teacher teams and professional learning communities may help foster a productive and supportive learning environment, as highlighted in Box 3.2.

The primary implication of Principle 6 is that the climate in the learning environment is an important consideration as part of the evaluation of a professional learning experience. The degree to which the learners were satisfied the professional development they received is the first consideration in the evaluation of a professional learning program. Learners' level of satisfaction serves as an early indicator of the likelihood the learner will acquire the knowledge and skills, use the new knowledge/skills, and have the desired impact on student outcomes (Guskey, 2000).

Principle 7: To Become Self-directed Learners, Individuals Must Learn To Monitor and Adjust their Approaches to Learning

Frequent, formative assessment of learners' performance and progress toward mastery of the learning objectives is a critical element of research-based instruction for adult learners. Instructor-facilitated performance-based assessment

Box 3.2

PROMOTING PROFESSIONAL LEARNING THROUGH TEAMING AND PROFESSIONAL LEARNING COMMUNITIES

Experts in professional learning and systems change have long recognized that sustained embedded support for new knowledge and skills is essential for teachers to make substantial changes to their existing practices (Coburn, 2004; Johnson & Stefurak, 2013; McDonald & Viehbeck, 2007). Professional learning initiatives are most effective when they provide opportunities for teachers to interact with each other, receive feedback from their colleagues on their developing practices, and determine how the practice will be implemented in their school (Sun, Loeb, & Grissom, 2017; Sun, Penuel, Frank, Gallagher, & Youngs, 2013). Examples of professional learning activities that promote professional learning through teaming include team attendance at an intensive, multiweek professional learning seminar (Lieberman & Wood, 2003), protocol-driven discussions of student work among peers (Horn & Little, 2010), peer observation of classroom instruction, and peer instructional coaching (Darling-Hammond, Wei, Andree, Richardson, & Orphanos, 2009). A number of studies point to the potential role of teacher teams and professional learning communities in schools in supporting sustained systems change through increased teacher collaboration and collective learning (e.g., Horn & Little, 2010; McLaughlin & Talbert, 2003; Scribner, Sawyer, Watson, & Myers, 2007; Sun et al., 2013). District and building leadership teams are also essential for determining the professional learning needs of educators and developing an action plan to further implementation efforts.

Learning communities is the first of the seven *Standards for Professional Learning* promoted by Learning Forward (2012). Information regarding Learning Forward's Standards for Professional Learning can be found at www.learningforward.org.

and learner self-assessments can be used to provide information to learners for reflection.

Principle 7 informs the evaluation of professional learning programs by emphasizing the need to assess learners' changes in knowledge and skills as a result of their participation in the professional learning experience. In the next section, we will present options for assessing participants' learning relative to specific, well-crafted learning objectives.

Concluding Remarks: Principles of Teaching Adult Learners

Taken together, the characteristics of adult learning methods and the seven principles of teaching adult learners provide a solid foundation for understanding the "what" of high-quality, evidence-based professional learning. Evaluators of professional learning programs need to have a deep understanding of the research on effective professional learning program design and delivery in order to frame their evaluation and provide actionable recommendations. In the next section, we will present two comprehensive approaches for evaluating professional learning.

FRAMEWORKS FOR EVALUATING PROFESSIONAL LEARNING FOR EDUCATORS

Evaluating professional learning is complex, multilayered, and multifaceted, given that the direct impact of the program on educators' practices must also account for the impact of changes in educator practices on student learning and behavioral outcomes. Several frameworks have emerged that are invaluable for planning a comprehensive evaluation of professional learning for educators. In this section, we will present Guskey's (2000) framework for evaluating professional development for educators and compare his framework to the contributions of Kirkpatrick and Kirkpatrick (2007) and Desimone (2009).

Guskey's (2000) framework for evaluating professional development is composed of five critical levels (see Figure 3.1):

1. Participants' reactions/perceptions of satisfaction
2. Participants' learning
3. Organization support and change
4. Participants' use of new knowledge and skills
5. Student learning outcomes

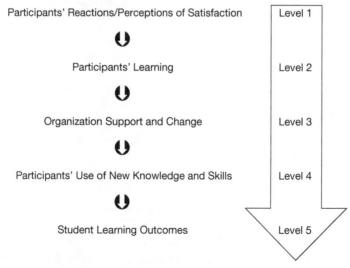

Figure 3.1. Guskey's (2000) Framework for Evaluating Professional Development

These critical levels are sequential and progressive, such that successful out-comes in earlier levels need to be evident before one would expect to see the desired outcomes in subsequent levels. In other words, if educator participants are largely dissatisfied with the professional learning program, they are not likely to benefit from the session in terms of gains in knowledge or skills targeted by the learning objectives. Likewise, if a professional learning program cannot show that educators experienced gains in the knowledge and skills targeted, then it is highly unlikely that the educators would be able to use the new knowledge and skills in their classrooms and, in turn, have a measurable impact on student learn-ing. Therefore, the evaluation must determine whether the professional learning experience has had the intended direct effect on educators' knowledge and skills and whether resulting changes in educators' knowledge and skills had an impact on student outcomes (Wayne, Yoon, Zhu, Cronen, & Garet, 2008). Following this logic, the evaluation of professional learning involves building a "compelling chain of evidence" linking the professional learning experiences to the longer-term impact on bottom-line outcomes (Kirkpatrick & Kirkpatrick, 2007, p. 123). A comprehensive framework for evaluating professional learning enables school-based professionals to examine short-, medium, and long-term outcomes for-matively to inform problem solving and continuous improvement planning and document successes.

Guskey's (2000) five critical levels for evaluating educator professional devel-opment build on earlier versions of Kirkpatrick and Kirkpatrick's (2006) four levels for evaluating training programs in business and industry. The four levels are (a) reaction, (b) learning, (c) behavior, and (d) results. Beyond the field of education, Kirkpatrick and Kirkpatrick's (2006) four-level system is the dominant framework for evaluating training and includes considerations relevant to busi-ness and industry, such as a training program's return on investment.

Unlike the frameworks developed by Guskey (2000) and Kirkpatrick and Kirkpatrick (2006) for use in evaluating professional learning, Desimone's (2009) framework was developed to guide the design of research on teacher profes-sional learning programs. Desimone's four steps serve to test both the theory of teacher change (i.e., that professional development brings about changes in teacher knowledge and/or practice) and a theory of instruction (i.e., that changes in teacher's practices affect student learning). The four steps in Desimone's framework include: "(1) Teachers experience effective professional development. (2) The professional development increases teachers' knowledge and skills and/or changes their attitudes and beliefs. (3) Teachers use their new knowledge and skills, attitudes, and beliefs to improve the content of their instruction or their approach to pedagogy, or both, and (4) The instructional changes foster increased student learning" (Desimone, 2009, p. 184).

A comparison of these three prominent frameworks for evaluating professional learning is presented in Table 3.3. Guskey's unique contribution is reflected in the third level of his framework, Organizational Support and Change. An overview of Guskey's critical levels will be provided in this section along with the evaluation methods and measures appropriate for gathering data at each level.

Table 3.3 COMPARING PROMINENT FRAMEWORKS FOR EVALUATING PROFESSIONAL LEARNING PROGRAMS

Guskey's Five Critical Levels (2000)	Kirkpatrick & Kirkpatrick (2006)	Desimone (2009)
1. Participants' reactions/satisfaction	✓	✓
2. Participants' learning	✓	✓
3. Organizational support and change		
4. Participants' use of new knowledge and skills	✓	✓
5. Student learning outcome	✓	✓

Table 3.4 illustrates how Guskey's (2000) five critical levels can be applied to a professional learning program targeting reading instructional supports and interventions within an MTSS framework.

Table 3.4 AN ILLUSTRATION OF MULTI-TIER SYSTEM OF SUPPORTS READING PROFESSIONAL LEARNING PROGRAM COMPONENTS ASSOCIATED WITH GUSKEY'S FIVE CRITICAL LEVELS

Professional Learning Program Components	Guskey's Five Critical Levels
Educators learn research-based instructional strategies for increasing literacy skills through the use of instructional supports (tier 1) and interventions (tiers 2 and 3) that are perceived to be relevant and effective for use in their classroom setting.	1: Participants' reactions/satisfaction 2: Participants' learning
Educators practice/rehearse research-based instructional strategies during the professional learning session and receive feedback.	2: Participants' learning
Educators have access to the featured instructional and intervention materials required for implementation in their classrooms.	3: Organizational support and change
Educators have individual and team planning time each week to design new lessons and instructional materials for integrating the new techniques in their classrooms.	3: Organizational support and change
Educators apply research-based instructional strategies in their classrooms.	4: Participants' use of new knowledge and skills
Educators receive feedback through coaching and reflect on their instruction.	4: Participants' use of new knowledge and skills
Gains in reading achievement are evident from the universal screening assessments administered three times a year for all students and from progress monitoring assessments for students receiving tier 2 and tier 3 interventions.	5: Student learning outcome

Level 1: Participants' Reactions/Satisfaction

The seven principles of teaching adult learners emphasize the critical importance of engaging teacher participants actively in the context of a supportive learning environment (Ambrose et al., 2010). The learning climate matters. Measuring teachers' satisfaction is an important early indicator in a comprehensive evaluation both as a prerequisite for adult learning and to guide improvements in the design and delivery of future professional learning sessions (Guskey, 2000).

Participants' reactions are assessed effectively and efficiently by using a questionnaire distributed at the end of each session or via an online survey posted shortly after each session. Postsession questionnaire items typically address the organizational structure of the session, the presenter's expertise and delivery style, the presence of the characteristics of evidence-based professional learning, and the relevance of the content. Sample items for each category include:

Organizational Structure

- The objectives of the professional development session were clearly stated in the beginning.
- The learning activities were appropriate and aligned with the objectives.

Presenter's Expertise and Delivery Style

- The presenter was knowledgeable of the topic/process.
- The presenter used techniques related to the session's information.
- The presenter engaged me in learning.

Characteristics of Evidence-Based Professional Learning

- This session provided me with an opportunity to practice the new skills presented (e.g., through a small-group or individual activity).
- This session provided me with an opportunity to receive feedback as I practiced the new skill (e.g., observation by the presenter or a peer).
- This session provided me with an opportunity to reflect on what I was learning (e.g., through a written reflection or conversation in a small group).
- This session was interactive, providing me multiple cycles of presentation and reflection.

Relevance

- The session activities were aligned with my goals for learning.
- This session further developed my knowledge and skills for a practice that will likely produce direct results in my classroom or school.
- The session was worth spending the time away from my typical work responsibilities.

Postsession questionnaires typically end with two or three open-ended questions to solicit participants' reactions. Specific questions, rather than a generic query for comments, is preferable as a general prompt for comments tends to lead to an abundance of comments on the physical features of the facility (i.e., temperature of the room, acoustics). Open-ended questions we have used include:

- What new knowledge and skills did you acquire?
- How do you intend to use that knowledge and those skills?
- What additional information/support do you need to fully implement knowledge and skills learned at this session?

Postsession questionnaires are valuable as an early indicator of whether the professional learning experience is effectively engaging learners to the degree that the intended changes in knowledge, skills, and practices are even possible. For example, following a recent professional learning session on leadership skills in schools and districts in which the presenter often speaks about the importance of doing the "right work," a participant commented in writing, "used the word 'right' 273 times in 132 minutes of talk time." Certainly, if the participant was tallying the presenter's use of a particular word, little to no new learning occurred for that individual. Fortunately, the vast majority of the comments reflected a high degree of satisfaction with the presenter and the session as a whole, as indicated by the participants' ratings. In this way, postsession questionnaires can be invaluable for understanding how participants, individually and collectively, are connecting with the content provided in a professional learning session. Participant's reactions can be gathered formatively throughout the session using audience response systems, such as the Poll Everywhere app, or summatively at the end of the session using online surveys, paper questionnaires, or participant focus groups.

The evaluation of participants' reactions can also be supplemented with direct observations of the professional learning session. The *Observation Checklist for High-Quality Professional Development Training* (Noonan et al., 2015) assesses the degree to which the training session features the characteristics of effective adult learning methods. A copy of the *Observation Checklist for High-Quality Professional Development Training* is provided in Appendix B. This tool and other valuable resources for evaluating the impact of professional learning can be accessed through the SIGNetwork (see Box 3.3).

Level 2: Participants' Learning

Level 2 examines the professional learning program's theory of teacher change—that the professional learning activities had the intended impact on gains in teachers' knowledge and skills/practices (Desimone, 2009). The first step in assessing changes in teacher participants' learning is identifying the learning objectives. Although the learning objectives should drive the selection of appropriate teaching and learning activities (Miller, 1987), too often the learning objectives are added to the top of an agenda once the session has been planned. To be functional,

Box 3.3

Spotlight on the SIGnetwork

The U.S. Department of Education, Office of Special Education Programs provides funding to state education agencies and their partners to improve systems of professional development as a means for improving outcomes for students with disabilities. Funding is provided to state departments of education in the form of State Personnel Development Grants (SPDGs). The State Personnel Development Network, better known as the SIGnetwork, was developed by the Office of Special Education Programs to support states' efforts in designing and implementing their SPDG-funded projects. Projects funded by SPDGs must demonstrate accountability in accordance with the SPDG program measures, which focus on the use of evidence-based professional development components, direct measures of implementation, and funding for follow-up professional learning activities. The SIGnetwork hosts a national meeting annually and a series of webinars designed to disseminate knowledge about best practices in evidence-based professional learning. The archives from the national meeting and access to the webinar series as well as other useful resources for planning and evaluating professional learning for teachers serving students with disabilities can be found at the SIGnetwork website (www.SIGnetwork.org). As such, the SIGnetwork is an excellent resource for school-based professionals involved in planning and evaluating professional learning.

learning objectives should (a) be learner-centered (i.e., stated as "participants should be able to . . ."), (b) break down desired practices into discrete component skills, (c) use action verbs based on Bloom's (1956) taxonomy (see Table 3.5), and (d) include measurable indicators of their attainment (Ambrose et al., 2010).

Table 3.5 A Sample of Action Verbs from Bloom's Taxonomy

Remember	Understand	Apply	Analyze	Evaluate	Create
Arrange	Classify	Calculate	Break down	Appraise	Assemble
Define	Compare	Construct	Combine	Argue	Build
Identify	Contrast	Demonstrate	Compare	Assess	Compose
Label	Describe	Develop	Contrast	Check	Construct
List	Differentiate	Employ	Debate	Conclude	Design
Locate	Discuss	Estimate	Diagram	Critique	Formulate
Name	Explain	Examine	Examine	Detect	Generate
Recall	Infer	Execute	Extrapolate	Judge	Integrate
Recognize	Interpret	Implement	Illustrate	Justify	Produce
Reproduce	Paraphrase	Modify	Organize	Monitor	Propose
Select	Restate	Solve	Predict	Rate	Rearrange
State	Summarize	Use	Question	Recommend	Set up

NOTE: This table includes revisions from Anderson, L. W., & Krathwohl, D. R. (Eds.) (2001). *A taxonomy for learning, teaching, and assessing: A revision of Bloom's taxonomy of educational objectives.* New York: Longman.

Once the learning objectives have been identified, the next step in assessing participants' learning is to determine the methods by which the progress toward the attainment of the objectives will be measured. For learning objectives requiring participants to remember and understand, a pretest/posttest approach to content mastery may be appropriate. The use of case studies or performance-based assessment (i.e., problem-solving tasks) may be well suited to assess gains on learning objectives requiring participants to apply, analyze, or evaluate. An authentic assessment (i.e., portfolio) may be used to evaluate gains relative to learning outcomes requiring adult learners to create.

Self-assessments can be used as part of a pretest/posttest approach to assess knowledge and skills that may not be readily observable and measurable in the course of a professional development session or series of sessions. When designing a self-assessment, Ambrose et al. (2010) recommended defining response options that are tied to specific concepts or behaviors and using a scale that represents a learning progression. The following three examples based on the work of Ambrose et al. (2010) illustrate this approach to self-assessment.

1. How familiar are you with XYZ?
   - I have never heard of XYZ.
   - I have heard of it but don't know what it is.
   - I have some idea of what XYZ is but don't know when or how to use it. (Or: I have some idea of what XYZ is but am not too clear.)
   - I have a clear idea of what XYZ is but haven't used it. (Or I know what it is and could explain what it's for.)
   - I can explain what XYZ is and what it does, and I have used it. (Or: I know what it is and when to use it and could use it to . . .)
2. Have you designed or built an ABC?
   - I have neither designed nor build an ABC.
   - I have designed an ABC but have never built one.
   - I have built one but I have not designed one.
   - I have both designed and built an ABC.
3. How familiar are you with App 123?
   - I have never used it, or I have tried but couldn't really do anything with it.
   - I can use simple edit functions, such as . . .
   - I can perform more advanced functions, such as . . .
   - I can easily use . . . to create . . .

A major concern with pretest/posttest self-assessments is that participants are unable to assess themselves accurately, especially prior to a professional development experience (Eva, Cunnington, Reiter, Keane, & Norman, 2004; Pratt, McGuigan, & Katzev, 2000). Participants may, for example, overestimate their knowledge prior to the professional learning session (i.e., they do not know what they do not know). To counter for this situation, the retrospective pretest method developed by Campbell and Stanley (1963) has been recommended by Lamb and

Tschillard (2005) and Siegel and Yates (2007). The retrospective pretest method involves asking participants to "look back" and assess their level of knowledge and performance prior to the professional development experience. In this manner, the retrospective pretest method controls for situations (coined "**response-shift bias**" by Howard [1980]) in which the participants might have self-rated their knowledge as higher prior to the professional development only to self-rate their knowledge lower on the posttest measure, thus generating a negative gain score. Consequently, response-shift bias can contribute to underestimating the effects of a professional development presentation (Lamb & Tschillard, 2005). The presence of response-shift bias has been supported by Hyman (1993), but was not detected in a more recent study by D'Eon, Sadownik, Harrison, and Nation (2008).

Despite the appeal of self-assessments, both the pretest/post-test self-assessment approach and the retrospective pretest method should be used judiciously and in combination with other measures. It should be clear that self-assessments are not direct measures of learning (i.e., test of knowledge acquisition, evaluation of skill performance), but instead assess participants' perception of growth in knowledge and/or skill. Both the pretest/posttest and retrospective pretest approaches have been found to yield a moderately greater effect size than the scores obtained from trained raters (D'Eon et al., 2008).

The learning objectives will also dictate the interval of time one might expect to see the changes in teacher participants' knowledge, skills, or attitudes. Gains in knowledge and discrete skills may be expected to occur over a relatively short period of time. The development of more complex combinations of skills to form new instructional practices will likely take an extended period of time and require embedded (onsite) and sustained support in the form of coaching (Killion, 2008). Research shows that significant changes in attitudes and beliefs are a product of teachers' observing improvements in student learning resulting from their implementation efforts (Guskey & Huberman, 1995; Huberman & Miles, 1984). In other words, although teachers must be somewhat receptive toward learning a new practice (and that shift in attitude may be the result of the professional learning experience), significant attitude and belief changes occurred only when professional learning and implementation were combined to provide evidence of positive student outcomes (Guskey, 1982, 1984). The use of an assessment of attitude and belief changes conducted immediately following a professional learning session, but prior to implementation, is short-sighted as it will not likely capture changes that may occur over time (Guskey, 2000).

Teacher self-efficacy is a potential target for change in a professional learning program. Teacher self-efficacy refers to a teacher's belief in their capabilities to influence valued outcomes (Soodak & Podell, 1996; Tschannen-Moran, Hoy, & Hoy, 1998; Tschannen-Moran, Wheatley, 2005; Tschannen-Moran & Woolfolk Hoy, 2001). Self-efficacy is a belief about what an individual can do specific to a particular skill, task, or domain (Bong, 2006; Bong & Skaalvik, 2003; Zimmerman & Cleary, 2006). Teacher self-efficacy has been shown to predict teachers' goals and aspirations (Muijs & Reynolds, 2002), attitudes toward innovation and change (Fuchs, Fuchs, & Bishop, 1992; Guskey, 1988), use of teaching strategies

(Allinder, 1994; Woolfolk, Rosoff, & Hoy, 1990), and teachers' referral rates for special education services for students (Meijer & Foster, 1988; Soodak & Podell, 1993). Research also provides evidence of the relationship between teacher self-efficacy and student motivation and achievement (Ashton & Webb, 1986; Midgley, Feldlaufer, & Eccles, 1989; Ross, 1992). Although teacher self-efficacy measures are most valuable to the evaluation of professional learning when they focus on the specific instructional practices addressed in the learning objectives, a general measure of teacher self-efficacy developed by Skaalvik and Skaalvik (2007) may be of interest in the context of teacher professional learning (see, for example, the Norwegian Teacher Self-Efficacy Scale in Appendix C).

Level 3: Organization Support and Change

Far too often teachers participate in a high-quality professional learning program and return to their school with new knowledge and skills only to have their enthusiasm quelled by a school culture indifferent or resistant to innovation. Noting the powerful influence schools and districts can have on supporting or stifling professional learning efforts, Guskey (2000) identified organization support and change as a critical level of focus for a comprehensive evaluation of a professional learning program. Aspects of organizational support and change that can shape teachers' opportunities to implement and promote new practices include principal and district administrators' leadership and support; organizational policies; resources; provision of time and protection from intrusions; and a staff culture reflecting collegial support, an openness to experimentation, and recognition of success (Guskey, 2000). This concept of organizational support and change also relates to implementation capacity as previously discussed in Chapter 2.

One way in which the culture of a school plays out is through the social networks established among teachers. Research shows that social networks characterized by high levels of expertise, high-depth substantive interactions, and a culture of mutual trust and respect enable instructional improvements targeted by professional learning efforts to be sustained over time (Bryk & Schneider, 2002; Bryk, Sebring, Allensworth, Luppescu, & Easton, 2010; Coburn, Russell, Kaufman, & Stein, 2012). These social networks translated into supportive practices in which teachers collaborate frequently, receive meaningful feedback about their instructional practices, and are recognized for their efforts (Kraft & Papay, 2014).

A supportive school and district culture can also maximize the likelihood of the **spillover effect** of professional learning participation (De Grip & Sauermann, 2012). Spillover effects are defined as the effects of professional learning that extend above and beyond the direct effects on the teachers who participated in the experience (Sun, Loeb, & Grissom, 2017; Sun, Penuel, Frank, Gallagher, & Youngs, 2013). Research indicates that the degree to which teachers can benefit from professional development programs through interacting with professional learning participants can be equivalent to the effect of direct participation (Sun et al., 2013). As such, the evaluation of professional learning that focuses solely on the participants without accounting for possible spillover effects may underestimate the true impact on a school (Angelucci & Di Maro, 2010). An analysis of the organizational supports that mediate and moderate the implementation of new practices targeted by professional learning programs is a critical component of a comprehensive evaluation and will necessarily require multiple methods engaging multiple informants based on the unique context of the school or district. Furthermore, the development of leadership teams at the building and district level whose members understand the local context and organizational culture and share a vision for where a school needs to go in terms of implementation is an essential early step in the installation of an MTSS framework.

Coaching is an essential organizational support to promote professional learning. You will recall from Chapter 2 that coaching is an implementation driver that facilitates competent usage of a new practice within the Implementation Drivers Framework (Fixsen, Naoom, Blase, Friedman, & Wallace, 2005). A variety of coaching models exist to meet the needs of a school or district from instructional coaching at a classroom level (Killion, Harrison, Bryan, & Clifton, 2012; Knight, 2007) to process coaching at a systems level (Blase, Fixsen, Van Dyke, & Duda, 2013). Readers interested in learning more about effective coaching strategies are encouraged to read Joellen Killion's work (see Box 3.4).

Box 3.4

SPOTLIGHT ON JOELLEN KILLION AND LEARNING FORWARD

Throughout this book we have sought to highlight individuals and organizations whose work advancing evidence-based practices incorporates an emphasis on evaluation. As a Senior Advisor for Learning Forward (formerly known as the National Staff Development Council) and the previous Executive Director of the National Staff Development Council, Joellen Killion has a passion for results-driven staff development. She led the revision process for the 2012 *Standards for Professional Learning* (http://learningforward.org/standards-for-professional-learning) and has authored or coauthored four books on professional development and coaching. An evaluative focus permeates every aspect of the design, delivery, and continuous improvement of professional development, as described in her book, *Assessing Impact: Evaluating Staff Development* (Killion, 2008). Killion contends that a thoughtfully designed evaluation increases and extends the impact of the professional development process itself. In other words, professional development is more effective when data are generated and analyzed in response to carefully crafted evaluation questions to promote successes and inform future planning and problem solving. Thus, professional development and its evaluation are inseparable and together ensure that professional learning remain focused on its ultimate goal of impacting student learning.

Of Guskey's (2000) five critical levels, the evaluation of organization support and change presents the greatest challenges. Surveys of teachers may provide information regarding the degree to which teachers feel that the school or district supports their professional learning efforts. Focus groups may also provide insights regarding teachers' perceptions of support and change. Coaching supports can be evaluated using the *Implementation Drivers—Best Practices for Coaching* checklist available from the National Implementation Research Network (Blase et al., 2013). At a district level, the *District Capacity Assessment* (Ward et al., 2015) can be used to evaluate district- and building-level factors that contribute to educators' successful implementation of new practices targeted by the professional learning sessions.

Level 4: Participants' Use of New Knowledge and Skills

The degree to which participants in a professional learning program actually use the new knowledge and skills in the classroom is the critical link in the program's theory of teacher change. The evaluation plan needs to address the question: How can you tell if what participants learned is being used and being used well? (Guskey, 2000, p. 84). Assessing teachers' use of new knowledge and skills involves identifying specific, measurable practices that are expected to be implemented with fidelity as a result of the professional learning experience. As presented in Chapter 2, implementation fidelity has structural dimensions that include program adherence and dosage in terms of the number, length, frequency, or duration intervention or instructional sessions provided by the teacher (Dane & Schneider, 1998; Durlak & DuPre, 2008; Gersten et al., 2005; Power et al., 2005).

Implementation fidelity also has process dimensions, which encompass the quality of intervention delivery as evidenced through the teacher's competence, decisions, language, timing, choice making, and judgment in implementing an intervention (Dane & Schneider, 1998; Durlak, 2010; Justice, Mashburn, Hamre, & Pianta, 2008; Kaderavek & Justice, 2010; O'Donnell, 2008). Evaluating teachers' use of the targeted knowledge and skills requires expertise in the instructional or intervention practices being accessed in the classroom setting to discern whether the practices are being implemented as intended (i.e., implementing the core components with a moderate degree of adaptation and customization). Evaluating teachers' use of new knowledge and skills has implications for planning professional learning to include on-site coaching and consultation. Follow-up assessment of teachers' implementation will need to occur over time and on multiple occasions given that changes in practice is often a gradual and uneven process (Guskey, 2000; Joyce & Showers, 1995). The data collection methods described in Chapter 2 are applicable to evaluating changes in teacher practices as a result of professional learning.

A final consideration when evaluating changes in teacher practices in the context of a professional learning program is a determination of whether changes can be attributed directly to the professional learning experience. Typically, evaluations of system initiatives focus on the degree to which practitioners implemented core components with fidelity regardless of how they came to adopt those practices. Professional learning evaluations, however, must account for the direct (and spill-over) effects of the professional learning experience. In many cases, highly effective teachers may already be using the targeted skills in their daily practices, such that their implementation of the targeted skills does not reflect a change in practice. Effective teachers or early adopters may also have pursued other professional learning opportunities that may have contributed to their use of new knowledge and skills. Attributing measurable changes in practice to the professional learning experience involves assessing practices before and after the professional learning sessions or asking teachers explicitly about changes in their instructional practices (i.e., how is this different from what you have been doing all along?; Guskey, 2000).

Level 5: Student Learning Outcomes

Ultimately, the merit and worth of a professional learning program is based on the degree to which changes in teachers' targeted instructional practices result in increases in student achievement. As straightforward as this might seem, linking teacher professional learning to its impact on student learning outcomes requires careful consideration of a number of factors. First, the measures of student learning need to be aligned with the focus of the professional learning program and other aspects of the classroom instructional environment (e.g., curriculum content, pedagogy/instructional practices, instructional resources, and other assessment tools in use) (Killion, 2008). Secondly, the measures of student achievement need to be sensitive to incremental changes in student learning. Ideally, student learning measures should be able to be evaluated formatively to allow for changes in the professional learning content and delivery to maximize its impact on student learning. For all of these reasons, state-mandated achievement tests may not be well suited for measuring the impact of a professional learning program on student outcomes.

Despite their appeal as a readily accessible, objective measure for accountability in education, state-mandated achievement tests have a broad focus on grade-level content acquisition, which might not align well with the targeted focus of a professional learning program. Although standardized achievement tests, particularly norm-referenced achievement tests, are typically psychometrically sound in terms of reliability and validity, they are not designed to be sensitive to incremental changes in student learning. A curriculum-based evaluation approach (Hosp, Hosp, Howell, & Allison, 2014) to measuring student growth has advantages over state-mandated achievement tests in that curriculum-based measures are able to do the following: (a) focus on the specific skills addressed by the professional learning, (b) measure incremental gains in student achievement in response to intervention, and (c) provide formative assessment data to inform instructional planning in the classroom and the need for midcourse corrections to the professional development program design and delivery. The primary limitation of curriculum-based evaluation is that teachers may be unfamiliar or inexperienced with curriculum-based measures, such as those offered by DIBELS Next or the

Formative Assessment System for Teachers (FAST), and may require an additional investment in professional learning to advancing teachers' skills in their use.

Linking professional learning programs to targeted student outcomes also requires thoughtful consideration of the amount of time one can reasonable expect for changes in teacher practices to occur and have their intended impact on student learning outcomes. According to Loucks-Horsley, Hewson, Love, and Stiles (1998), "It is foolhardy to either expect or focus on measuring student learning when teachers have just begun to learn and experiment with new ideas and strategies" (p. 222). Consequently, the evaluation of the impact of professional learning programs needs to be realistic about the degree of change required and the amount of time needed to bring about changes in teachers' knowledge, skills, attitudes/self-efficacy, practices, and gains in targeted student outcomes (Desimone, 2009).

In the event that a professional learning program is able to document measurable gains in student achievement among students taught by the teacher participants, it may be very difficult to make the claim that the professional learning program was solely responsible for the gains. Killion (2008) makes the distinction between claims of **attribution** and **contribution**. Attribution claims the program being evaluated caused the observed changes in outcomes. Claims of attribution require the use of an internally valid research design (i.e., the random assignment of participants to groups as in a randomized control trial) to isolate the influence of the professional learning program from all other factors that affect learning, such as a new curriculum, student abilities and characteristics across cohorts, prior teacher knowledge and skills on the content targeted by the program, and the influence of other concurrent professional learning experiences.

High-quality evaluations of professional learning are best suited to test claims of contribution. Claims of contribution, for example, might assert that changes in student learning outcomes occurred among the students taught by teachers participating in the professional learning program and even compare the student outcomes for teachers with high levels of implementation versus teachers with low levels of implementation, while acknowledging other factors that might have also influenced adult implementation and student outcomes. As such, an evaluation may be able to document outcomes that occurred with the implementation of a professional learning program (contribution) but may not be able to claim that the program is solely responsible for the students' gains (Killion, 2008). We will revisit the distinction between attribution and contribution in Chapter 4 as we see it as one of the most critical, yet poorly understood, concepts in program evaluation in education.

PROFESSIONAL LEARNING AS A FOCUS FOR PROMOTING MULTI-TIER SYSTEM OF SUPPORTS IMPLEMENTATION STATEWIDE

Statewide efforts to promote the implementation of an MTSS framework in districts and schools focus predominately on creating a state and regional professional learning support system for the provision of training, coaching, and technical assistance/consultation. For example, Michigan's Integrated Behavior and Learning Support Initiative (MIBLSI) identifies itself as an intensive technical assistance program for the implementation of an integrated reading and behavior MTSS framework that focuses on research from Positive Behavioral Interventions and Supports and the National Reading Panel, as well as implementation science to ensure sustainability and scalability. MIBLSI provides the statewide structure to create local school and district capacity for MTSS implementation. This statewide structure, known as the cascading model in Michigan (see Figure 3.2), calls for supports from the state department of education to the classroom (Russell & Harms, 2016). Each layer (e.g., regional education agency, district, school) provides support to the layer underneath and communicates successes, needs, and barriers to the layers above on the cascade. Within this cascading model, MIBLSI provides MTSS-focused professional learning for regional education agencies, local school districts, and K–12 schools via a strategically designed 4-year scope and sequence.

MIBLSI's professional learning is designed to build competencies over time and result in durable, sustainable implementation of MTSS because educators and agencies across the cascade learn and support implementation together. Topics include the development of implementation capacity and the use of reading and behavior supports at tiers 1, 2, and 3. Individuals in specific roles are developed to provide specialized layers of support. For example, systems coaches for schools attend coaching

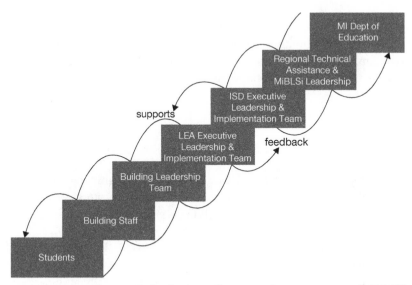

Figure 3.2. Michigan's Integrated Behavior and Learning Support Initiative (MIBLSI)'s Cascading Model for the Systemic Support of Multi-tier System of Supports Professional Learning
SOURCE: Michigan's Integrated Behavior and Learning Support Initiative. (2017). Statewide cascading structure of support. Holland, MI: Author. Available at: https:// miblsi.org/miblsi-model/cascading-systems. Reprinted with permission from the author.

support sessions without the rest of their school leadership team so that they can deepen their background knowledge and develop plans for how they will coach their teams beyond initial training. MTSS coordinators at the district and regional levels preview professional learning materials and analyze data to target their coordination supports and plan activities to keep their respective implementation teams moving forward. MIBLSI staff members provide coaching to regional and district partners. Professional learning is evaluated in multiple layers, using Guskey's model (2000). At the end of each training session in the standard scope and sequence, participants complete a two-part evaluation. The first part is a retrospective self-assessment where participants rate their knowledge and skills related to the learning objectives at the end of the session. Then, they do the same ratings, retrospectively thinking back to their knowledge and skills before the training session started. Participants also respond to a set of eight general questions on the quality of the training. These data are then entered into the project database and available for MIBLSI project staff, regional, and district teams to review in reports for use as they (a) continuously improve the training content and delivery and (b) feed the information forward to identify areas that will need strategic follow-up coaching. The impact of training is then further evaluated by examining (a) follow-through on action items, (b) regional and district-level capacity assessment data, (c) school-level implementation fidelity data, and (d) student outcomes.

IN CONCLUSION

As we recognized in Chapter 2, changes in adult practices in schools do not happen spontaneously. The current emphasis on professional learning stems from the recognition that the development of innovative practices requires the provision of equally innovative professional learning support for educators in order to meet students' needs.

SUMMARY POINTS

- The emphasis on professional learning reflects a recognition that education is a dynamic professional field and that educators need to further their knowledge and skills to keep pace with advances in teaching and learning.
- The six characteristics of adult learning methods (i.e., Introduce, Illustrate, Practice, Evaluate, Reflection, and Mastery) related to valued learner outcomes (i.e., changes in knowledge, skills, attitudes/satisfaction, and self-efficacy) provide a blueprint for the design and delivery of high-quality professional learning opportunities.
- Data literacy, otherwise known as data-based decision making, and teaming are two key targets for professional learning when promoting the implementation of an MTSS framework.

- Guskey's (2000) framework for evaluating professional development is composed of five critical levels to be evaluated: (a) participants' reactions/perceptions of satisfaction, (b) participants' learning, (c) organization support and change, (d) participants' use of new knowledge and skills, and (e) student learning outcomes.
- Statewide efforts to promote the implementation of an MTSS framework in districts and schools focus predominately on creating a state and regional professional learning support system for the provision of training, coaching, and technical assistance/consultation.

QUESTIONS TO FURTHER YOUR UNDERSTANDING

1. In thinking about the language we use to describe adult learning, why is it preferable to *engage* educators in professional *learning* than provide educators with professional development?
2. Consider a recent experience attending in a professional workshop, seminar, or taking a college course. To what degree did the presenter/instructor incorporate the six characteristics of adult learning methods (i.e., Introduce, Illustrate, Practice, Evaluate, Reflection, Mastery)?
3. What are the advantages and disadvantages of using an online survey to gather participants' reactions/satisfaction and participants' learning relative to a paper questionnaire administered at the conclusion of the session?

4

Developing an Evaluation Plan

Recognizing they need to formalize their plan for evaluating the outcomes of their multi-tier system of supports (MTSS) initiative, the members of the school leadership team at Central Elementary organize a series of meetings for developing an evaluation plan. The team members know they need goals and a timeline for data collection activities, but there is some confusion about determining the best outcomes to measure. The team is very interested in capitalizing on data that are readily available and not piling on additional or redundant measures, but they also do not want to find at the end of the year that critical information has been overlooked. They need to craft a detailed and comprehensive evaluation plan that is feasible to follow.

"Evaluations should be issues driven, not methods driven" (White, 2013, p. 61). As such, educators need to be very clear about what they want to measure and how the information they seek will better inform their decision making before they consider what methods and measures are available and feasible. We assume that educators seeking to drive innovation in their schools have a deep understanding of the pressing issues, local context, and the program to be evaluated. We also assume that they do not work in isolation when engaged in program planning and evaluation. Therefore, we begin the evaluation planning process with a focus on establishing measurable goals and objectives developed collaboratively among a team of educators.

Collaboration is key to effective evaluation planning. According to the *Program Evaluation Standards*, "Evaluations should devote attention to the full range of individuals and groups invested in the program and affected by its evaluation" (Joint Committee on Standards for Educational Evaluation, Yarbrough et al., 2011). Similarly, the *Guiding Principles for Evaluators* states that, "When planning and reporting evaluations, evaluators should include relevant perspectives and interests of the full range of stakeholders" (American Evaluation Association, 2004). Once the team collaborates on establishing measurable goals and objectives, the team members will continue the evaluation planning process by articulating the **theory of change**, designing the **logic model**, identifying the evaluation questions, and developing the evaluation plan.

ESTABLISHING MEASURABLE GOALS AND OBJECTIVES

The very first step in developing an evaluation plan is determining what is being evaluated. If the program does not have specific, measurable goals already, the evaluation team will need to help establish or refine goal statements that represent the program's overall purpose. A goal is a statement that identifies the intended outcome of the program (e.g., increase the percentage of students at or above the benchmark in reading fluency). A goal could also pertain to the process through which the program will operate to improve student outcomes (e.g., increase the number of teachers completing all eight modules of the professional learning series of evidence-based, phonics instruction). Regardless of whether the goal focuses on outcome or process, there are several criteria that are required of a well-written goal. These criteria are known by the acronym S.M.A.R.T., which originated in business management (Doran, 1981; Meyer, 2003) and has widespread use in education. **S.M.A.R.T. goals** are **S**pecific, **M**easurable, **A**ttainable (or **A**chievable), **R**elevant, and **T**ime-bound (see Table 4.1).

In most cases, broad goals will need to be broken down into specific objectives in order to operationalize the changes the program is expected to impact. Objectives should use precise verbs (e.g., increase rather than improve), state only one aim per objective, specify a single-end product or result, and be time-bound (i.e., by when?; Rossi & Freeman, 1982).

For goals and objectives to be measurable, there must be a realistically ambitious criterion or expected level of performance designated by which the program's progress will be gauged. There are several approaches to establishing a criterion. The criterion could be determined by examining data regarding performance levels at present and over the past 3 years retrospectively. Depending on the goal, an expected level of performance could be defined based on the performance trends of similar districts or schools. State-mandated standards for student achievement based on standardized tests could also serve as a relevant and valued criterion for a goal. Defining an expected level of performance in terms of both status (i.e., percentage at or above a criterion) and gain/growth (i.e., progress toward a criterion) might be more realistic and fair, especially for schools whose current level of performance is well below the criterion for a given goal. For goals and objectives that are judged to be rather ambitious, the team might consider extending the timeline and, for example, redefining the goal as a 3-year goal (rather than a 1-year goal) and setting annual targets for achieving that goal. In many cases, extending the timeline to make an ambitious goal more realistic is preferable to writing a goal with a very modest, uninspiring expected level of performance.

Table 4.1 CRITERIA FOR JUDGING THE QUALITY OF A GOAL STATEMENT

Criteria	Description of the Criteria
Specific	Goals state what the program is expected to do clearly while avoiding vague platitudes. The team can determine if the goal is specific by asking, "Is the change we expect to see clear to everyone who reads the goal statement?" *Specific goal:* The **percentage of grade 2 students at or above benchmark on the oral reading fluency measure** will increase to at least 85% by the end (May) benchmark. *Nonspecific goal:* All students will read by the end of the school year.
Measurable	Goal statements provide criteria for measuring progress toward the attainment of the goal. The team can determine if the goal is measurable by asking, "How will we know when this goal is accomplished?" *Specific goal:* The percentage of grade 2 students at or above benchmark on the oral reading fluency measure will **increase to at least 85%** by the end (May) benchmark. *Nonspecific goal:* The percentage of grade 2 students at or above benchmark on the oral reading fluency measure will improve.
Attainable (or Achievable)	Goals are realistic and achievable. They need to be ambitious enough to motivate a team to pursue it, without being out of reach. Goals reflecting a substandard level of performance do a disservice to the program. The team can determine if the goal is attainable by asking, "Can this goal be accomplished?" *Specific goal:* The percentage of Grade 2 students at or above benchmark on the oral reading fluency measure will increase to at least 85% by the end (May) benchmark. *Nonspecific goal:* The percentage of grade 2 students at or above benchmark on the oral reading fluency measure will increase to 100%.

Relevant	Goals need to reflect the priorities and realities of the conditions in the school. The team can determine if the goal is relevant by asking the questions, "Is the effort required to reach this goal worthwhile?" "Is this the right time to pursue this goal?" "Does this goal align with our other priorities?"
Time-bound	Goal statements establish a time frame for their attainment. By designating a target date, the team can then consider milestones for what needs to be accomplished in the interim to reach the goal within the timeframe. The team can determine if the goal is time-bound by asking, "When does this goal need to be accomplished?" *Specific goal:* The percentage of Grade 2 students at or above benchmark on the oral reading fluency measure will increase to at least 85% **by the end (May) benchmark.** *Nonspecific goal:* The percentage of Grade 2 students at or above benchmark on the oral reading fluency measure will increase to at least 85%.

Compiled from Meyer, P. J. (2003). *What would you do if you knew you couldn't fail? Creating S.M.A.R.T. Goals. Attitude is Everything: If You Want to Succeed Above and Beyond. Beyond.* Meyer Resource Group, Inc.

ARTICULATING THE THEORY OF CHANGE

Once measurable goals have been established, the next step in the evaluation planning process is to articulate the theory of change. A theory of change is defined as, "the process through which program components are presumed to affect outcomes and the conditions under which these processes are believed to operate" (Donaldson, 2007, p. 22). In other words, the theory of change establishes the logical, causal linkages between the program's strategies or actions (the "WHAT"), intervening or mediating factors, and the goals the program is seeking to attain. The theory of change is the hypothesis for the program (i.e., "If we do . . ., we will see changes in [adult implementation and student outcomes defined by the goals]). For example, a theory of change might state, "If we implement positive behavioral interventions and supports with fidelity (i.e., explicit behavioral expectations, a positive student recognition system, evidence-based interventions matched to student need, and data-based decision making), then we will see a decrease in the number of monthly office discipline referrals." The emphasis on the causal linkages differentiates a theory of change from an implementation plan.

A theory of change has several benefits that make its development a top priority in the evaluation planning process (Killion, 2008; Scheirer, 1994). First, a theory of change puts a spotlight on the hypothesized causes and effects of program practices that underlie the program's strategies thus encouraging the program team to examine critically the research support for their assumptions or search for alternative program strategies (Scheirer, 1994). Second, a theory of change creates a common understanding of the program's assumptions, strategies, and intended outcomes among the program team, stakeholders, and participants (Killion, 2008). Third, a theory of change will help determine what measures are needed to assess implementation and what outcomes should be examined at what points in time (Scheirer, 1994). Fourth, in the process of clarifying the theory of change, potential implementation problems and unsupported inferences can be identified and corrected (Killion, 2008). Finally, articulating a theory of change contributes to an understanding of program effectiveness that can be valuable for developing more effective program strategies in the future (Scheirer, 1994). The illustration of the components of an MTSS Reading Professional Learning Program presented in Chapter 3, Table 3.4 provides an example of a theory of change (see Figure 4.1).

Evaluation planning, beginning with the theory of change, needs to be a collaborative effort that includes a variety of stakeholders (Preskill & Jones, 2009). Stakeholders may include collaborators within a school building, within a district, parent or community representatives, or consultants providing coaching and/or technical assistance to the school leadership team. One can expect articulating a theory of change to be an iterative or cyclical process with changes and refinements made in response to input from valued stakeholders. Once the theory of change has taken shape, the school leadership team can critically review their work and solicit feedback from stakeholders using the criteria for judging the quality of a theory of change put forth by Connell and Klem (2000; see Table 4.2).

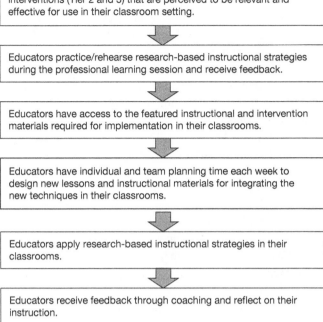

Figure 4.1. An Example of a Theory of Change for a Multi-tier System of Supports Reading Program

Table 4.2 CRITERIA FOR JUDGING THE QUALITY OF A THEORY OF CHANGE

Criteria	Description of the Criteria
Plausible	Evidence and common sense support the hypothesis that the program strategies will lead to the intended outcomes.
Doable	The program has adequate organizational, technical, leadership, financial, and human resource support.
Testable	The pathways of change are specific, complete, and reflect sound inferences. Specific preconditions and relevant, measurable indicators are identified for tracking progress.
Meaningful	Stakeholders perceive that the intended results are important and that the magnitude of change the program will likely bring about is worthwhile.

Compiled from Connell, J. P., & Klem, A. M. (2000). You can get there from here: Using a theory of change approach to plan urban education reform. *Journal of Educational and Psychological Consultation, 11*, 93–120.

DESIGNING A LOGIC MODEL

A theory of change is commonly accepted to be the starting point in the evaluation planning process that will lead to the development of a logic model and evaluation questions (Ravallion, 2009; Rogers, 2009; White, 2010). Logic models provide a graphic display of the theory of change and further help articulate the program's goals, activities, and intended outcomes. Logic models are widely used in program planning and evaluation and are often required by sponsors of programs that support students in schools in order to be competitive for grant funding (Fitzpatrick, Sanders, & Worthen, 2011).

Logic models reflect a flow chart connecting program resources (inputs) and the activities or strategies described in the theory of change that are designed to generate changes in outputs and outcomes over time (see Figure 4.2). The components of a logic model are identified in Table 4.3 and a template we find useful for developing a logic model is provided in Appendix D.

Although the components of a logic model are displayed in sequential order from inputs to outcomes, Millar, Simeone, and Carnevale (2001) recommended designing a logic model by thinking backward through the intended change process to identify how best to achieve the desired results. In doing so, Millar et al. (2001) suggested teams begin with a focus on the intended outcomes using the following series of questions:

1. What is the current situation that we intend to affect?
2. What will it look like when we achieve the desired situation or outcome?
3. What behaviors need to change for that outcome to be achieved?
4. What knowledge or skills do people need before the behavior will change?
5. What activities need to be performed to cause the necessary learning?
6. What resources will be required to achieve the desired outcome?

More than one logic model may be needed to represent all of the core program components captured by the theory of change. The team may decide to design one logic model for each goal or broad component of the program. They may also decide to revisit the theory of change and make revisions or refinements based on the evolution of their planning. Although developing a theory of change and logic model may seem tedious at times, this is a critically important step in program planning and evaluation. A theory of change and logic model must be plausible,

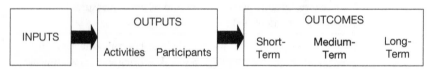

Figure 4.2. Basic Components and Sequence of a Logic Model

Table 4.3 COMPONENTS OF A LOGIC MODEL

Component	Description of the Logic Model Component
Inputs	The resources used to support the program activities. Inputs may include personnel, materials, technology, facilities, and partners.
Activities (Outputs)	The strategies, action steps, or services/supports provided by a program that are the core components of the program designed to bring about the intended results. Activities for an MTSS program may include the provision of professional learning (e.g., training sessions or on-line modules); coaching/consultation support; use of a decision-support data system; and the design and delivery of universal, strategic, and intensive interventions and supports.
Participants (Outputs)	Participant outputs identify who was served (e.g., educators, students) as the intended participants and quantify the extent of the program's reach (e.g., number or percentage of educators attending professional learning sessions, hours of professional learning provided to educators, number of students receiving intensive intervention).
Short-term Outcomes	Reasonable short-term outcomes include changes in adult learning in terms of gain in knowledge and skills. For an MTSS program, short-term outcomes might include increased knowledge and skills in: (a) engaging and explicit instruction; (b) evidence-based intervention; (c) data-based decision making in teams; and (d) universal screening and progress monitoring.
Medium-term Outcomes	Expected medium-term outcomes include changes in adult behaviors, practices, or decision making. For an MTSS program, medium-term outcomes might include adult implementation of the critical components of the program with fidelity.
Long-term Outcomes	Long-term outcomes include the changes in conditions that represent the ultimate goal of the program. Long-term outcomes include measurable gains in students' achievement (e.g., percentage of students at or above benchmark) and/or improvements in students' behavior (e.g., decrease in office discipline referrals, suspensions, or expulsions).

NOTE: MTSS = multi-tier system of supports.

doable, testable, and meaningful as they will serve as the hypothesis(es) to be tested by the evaluation. Programs can fail to achieve their goals for two different reasons: (a) programs may not be implemented as intended; or (b) programs may be implemented with fidelity, but the theory of change and logic model tested was faulty (Donaldson, 2007). A well-developed theory of change and logic model are key to distinguishing between implementation challenges and a faulty hypothesis regarding how and why the program will meet its goals.

IDENTIFYING THE EVALUATION QUESTIONS

Evaluations should always be conducted in ways that increase the likeli-hood that the findings will be used for learning, decision-making, and tak-ing action . . . When we ask good questions and design an evaluation using rigorous and culturally appropriate methods, instruments, and data analysis procedures, then we can anticipate more useful, relevant and credible evalu-ation findings. (Preskill & Jones, 2009, p. 6)

Evaluation questions provide the structure and focus of the evaluation. Written as broad, overarching questions directly aligned to the program's goals and objectives, evaluation questions establish the boundaries and scope of the evaluation in terms of what will and will not be addressed (Preskill & Jones, 2009). Evaluation questions also set the stage for future evaluation planning by establishing what can be measured and how, given opportunities and constraints related to data collection and available resources (Wingate & Schroeter, 2015). As such, evaluation questions must be specific in their focus on measurable indicators of program performance and how those indicators will be measured (Killion, 2008).

We described the distinction between process evaluation and impact evaluation in Chapter 1. That distinction can also be represented by the evaluation questions. Process evaluation questions focus on the degree to which the core components of the program are being implemented as planned. Examples of process evaluation questions relevant to an MTSS program might include:

- To what extent did the teachers of students in preschool to grade 3 implement early literacy and language core instruction using (specified literacy framework) with fidelity, as assessed by an instructional coach using the (specified literacy framework) implementation checklist?
- To what extent did specialists provide instructional coaching in the use of the (specified literacy framework), as documented by the instructional coaching logs?
- To what extent did the teachers of students in preschool to grade 3 use data literacy skills to implement screening, progress monitoring, and instructional decision making with fidelity, as assessed by the **Reading–Tiered Fidelity Inventory** (R-TFI)?

In contrast, impact evaluation questions will focus on changes in specified out-comes as they relate to the program's goals. Examples of impact evaluation ques-tions relevant to an MTSS program include:

- To what extent did students in preschool to grade 3 demonstrate gains in indicators of basic early literacy skills relative to national benchmarks, as assessed by DIBELS Next?

- To what extent did the implementation of the MTSS initiative result in an increase in the percentage of students whose instructional and behavioral needs were being met with universal supports (tier 1) and a decrease in the percentage of students requiring strategic (tier 2) and intensive (tier 3) interventions?
- To what extent did the implementation of the MTSS initiative contribute to a decrease in the suspension and expulsion rate?

In developing an impact evaluation question, the team should be careful to avoid suggesting a causal link between the program's components and the intended outcomes. This involves precise wording to ensure that the question (and subsequent findings) are not presented in such a way as to imply the program *caused* the desired student outcomes (Killion, 2008). Establishing causality requires a rigorous research design (e.g., randomized control trial) that isolates the effects of the program's components and controls for extraneous factors such that the changes that are observed can be attributed to the program and nothing else. Such research designs are typically not feasible in schools (Killion, 2008). Joellen Killion (2008) offered a useful distinction between attribution and contribution. Unlike attribution claims, which assert that the implementation of the program activities alone brought about the changes in the valued outcomes, contribution claims assert only that the implementation of the program may have likely contributed to the changes in the desired outcomes, but other factors (e.g., new curriculum, new principal, new teachers, professional learning opportunities on different or related topics) might also have contributed to the positive outcomes during that program year. A successful evaluation will be able to identify the changes *reasonably* associated with the implementation of the program (contribution) without necessarily claiming that the program was solely responsible for the changes (attribution; Killion, 2008). In other words, an evaluation can inform decisions regarding how an MTSS program contributes to changes in student learning and behavior outcomes without asserting that the MTSS program alone caused these changes.

Evaluation questions will be derived from the logic model. As such, a simple logic model has advantages over one that is dense and convoluted. A complicated logic model can yield more evaluation questions than can be reasonably addressed. The team should solicit input from stakeholders regarding the evaluation questions to be prioritized when there are competing priorities, given that each question will likely require a different data source, data collection methods, and analysis. Considerations for prioritizing evaluation questions include selecting questions that capture the essential components of the program, yield meaningful findings to support decision making on a timely basis, and reflect the practical opportunities and constraints of the team's evaluation capacity (e.g., knowledge, skills, time, resources, and data availability) (Weiss, 1998).

DEVELOPING THE EVALUATION PLAN

Developing the evaluation plan involves matching data collection methods to each of the evaluation questions. A planning template, such as the one provided in Appendix E, can be very useful for identifying the data source (i.e., to be recruited or from existing records) and the data collection method and procedures for each evaluation question. A clear understanding of how the data will be analyzed once they are collected is a critically important, but often overlooked, aspect of the evaluation plan. This planning template guides the team members in their planning of the criterion to be used for the data analysis and expectations for the timely reporting of the results (i.e., to whom, how, and when). Several other templates useful for planning an evaluation are highlighted in Box 4.1.

Much can be said about choosing a research design to address the evaluation questions and yield types of information that will serve as the basis for the conclusions that may be possible. **Experimental designs**, such as the randomized control trial, involve the random assignment of participants to groups (i.e., an intervention group and a control group) to test inferences regarding the degree to which it can be stated with confidence that changes in the outcomes observed

---

Box 4.1

SPOTLIGHT ON EVALUATION PLANNING TEMPLATES

In addition to the evaluation planning template provided in Appendix E, two other templates may be helpful for teams as they set a course for evaluating a MTSS initiative. An Assessment Schedule identifies all of the data collection tools that will be used as part of the evaluation. For each tool, the team will determine the month or months in which the data collection will take place, creating a year-at-a-glance schedule of data collection activities. The Assessment Schedule template is provided in Appendix F.

A Responsibility Matrix provides an overview of the roles and responsibilities of key contributors to the evaluation. The major evaluation tasks are listed in the first column of the matrix. The date to accomplish the task is provided in the second column. Then the key contributors are identified by name or by role in the heading of the subsequent columns. Under each heading for each task listed in the matrix, a code is assigned representing their level of engagement in the task. The code "E" designates the individual or individuals who are responsible for Executing the task. The code "C" indicates the individual(s) who must be Consulted; and with whom there is two-way communication. Individuals who need to be Informed of evaluation activities through regular updates (i.e., one-way communication) are assigned a code of "I" and the individual(s) charged with giving final Approval for each task is indicated with a code of "A." A Responsibility Matrix template is provided in Appendix G.

---

were caused by the implementation of the innovation. Widely held to be the gold standard for basic research, the random assignment of struggling students to "intervention" and "no intervention" groups is not generally feasible, ethical, or desirable in the context of a school-based program evaluation.

Experimental designs can also involve the use of time-series data whereby baseline data gathered over a span of time are compared to outcome data to determine the effects of the program. Using the logic of a **multiple-baseline design**, the baseline and program outcome data could be compared across three different classrooms, as illustrated in Figure 4.3.

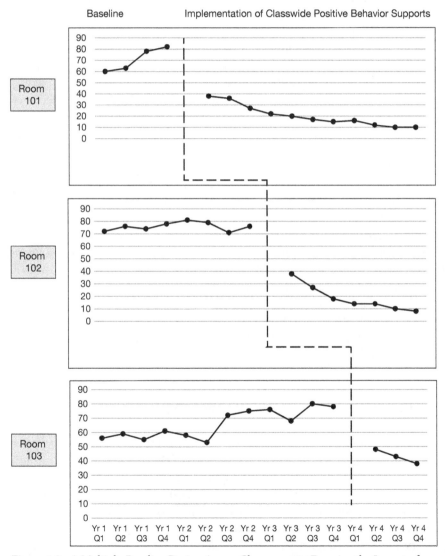

Figure 4.3. A Multiple-Baseline Design Across Classrooms to Examine the Impact of a Classwide Positive Behavior Support Initiative on Office Discipline Referral Rates

Quasi-experimental designs provide a valuable alternative to experimental designs in their use of comparison groups. Comparison groups can be formed based on existing classroom or school assignments (e.g., comparing students participating in the intervention with similar students from a different classroom or school who have not yet participated in the intervention). Given that random assignment of students to groups is not in place, a concerted effort must be made to ensure the comparison groups are as similar as possible. For example, the matched comparison groups should have similar academic achievement levels or similar discipline rates prior to the implementation of the initiative.

The vast majority of school-based program evaluation questions can be addressed with descriptive research methods. Descriptive research methods are used to summarize the outcomes of the program using statistics that are very familiar to educators (i.e., number [count], percentage, mean, range). Program outcomes can be presented overall and disaggregated by grade level or subgroup status (i.e., students with disabilities, race/ethnicity, socioeconomic status). Student outcomes can be compared to national benchmarks, district performance, or state standards. Implementation outcomes can be compared to the established criterion for the given measure.

Qualitative data are often used to give meaning to quantitative data. Qualitative data can be gathered through the use of interviews, focus groups, or questionnaires using short-answer or extended response questions. An evaluation is enhanced by the use of multiple methods that use both quantitative and qualitative data. The use of both qualitative and quantitative data is sometimes referred to as a **mixed-methods approach**. This is not necessarily accurate. Mixed-methods include philosophical assumptions that guide every aspect of the evaluation regarding the nature of ethics, the nature of reality, the nature of knowledge, and the nature of systematic inquiry (Creswell & Plano Clark, 2007). These philosophical assumptions drive the design, selection, and sequence of the research methods. Given this understanding of mixed-methods, we prefer the use of "multiple methods" rather than "mixed methods" to describe the evaluation approaches most often used in schools.

STUDENT LEARNING AND BEHAVIORAL OUTCOMES

Student learning and behavior can be assessed using a variety of means that could be incorporated into the evaluation of a school-based program. In this section, we will describe the student outcomes to be addressed in an evaluation of an MTSS initiative, according to Shapiro and Clemens (2009). Their approach is structured according to three indicators linked to the key components of the MTSS/Response to Intervention process: universal screening, response to tiered intervention and support, and special education decision making and related long-term outcomes.

Indicator 1: Monitoring Risk Levels Across Benchmark Periods and Movement Between the Tiers

Indicator 1 involves examining the percentage of students who scored at or above, below, and well below at each benchmark period. With the implementation of an effective MTSS initiative, students should move increasingly from the at-risk trajectory to a lower risk category so that the initiative meets the expected targets of at least 80% of students falling within a low-risk (at or above benchmark) category, 15% or less of students at a category of some risk (below benchmark), and 5% or less of students falling a within an at-risk (well below benchmark) category (e.g., Batche et al., 2005). For districts with a large population of students experiencing socio-economic disadvantage, Shapiro and Clemens (2009) recommend adjusting these targets based on a baseline screening, so that the targets are more realistic and attainable, yet still represent the majority of students in the low-risk category with an emphasis on increasing this proportion of students over time.

A **universal screening** system is required for Indicator 1. Typically, this would involve the use of **curriculum-based measurement** for screening for academic concerns. Curriculum-based measures are short-cycle, formative assessment measures of academic skill fluency that have empirically-derived cut points that represent categories of relative risk (Good, Simmons, & Kame'enui, 2001; Shapiro, Solari, & Petscher, 2008). Curriculum-based reading measures, such as DIBELS Next and aimsweb, are well-suited for use within a proactive, MTSS framework because they are aligned with curriculum, sensitive to instruction, repeatable (to enable progress monitoring weekly, monthly, or at least three times a year, based on the learner's need), and criterion-referenced so that they could be used to determine when a student has mastered a task (Hosp, Hosp, & Howell, & Allison, 2014). Curriculum-based measures of reading have been shown to be a reliable and valid indicator of overall performance in reading (Deno, 1985; Deno, Mirkin, & Chiang, 1982; Fuchs, Fuchs, Hosp, & Jenkins, 2001; Fuchs, Fuchs, & Maxwell, 1988; Good & Kaminski, 2002; Good, Simmons, & Kame'enui, 2001; Hintze & Silberglitt, 2005; Hosp & Fuchs, 2005; Rouse & Fantuzzo, 2006; Shapiro et al., 2008; Shinn, 1989, 1998; Shinn, Good, Knutson, Tilly, & Collins, 1992; Wheldall & Madelaine, 1997).

Universal screening for behavioral concerns involves monitoring **office discipline referral** (ODR) data and/or the use of a behavioral screening measure. An ODR is "an event in which (a) a student engages in a behavior that violated a rule/social norm in the school, (b) a problem behavior was observed by a member of the school staff, and (c) the event resulted in a consequence delivered by administrative staff who produced a permanent product defining the whole event" (Sugai, Sprague, Horner, & Walker, 2000, p. 96). ODR data include minor infractions that do not result in a suspension (i.e., in-school, out-of-school) or expulsion.

The process for universal screening for behavioral concerns parallels the process used for screening for academic skills. Quarterly data reviews are used to monitor risk levels across benchmark periods and track students' movement from at-risk to low-risk categories. ODRs can be used to identify specifics about frequent problem behaviors (what, when, where, and who) and show where behavioral supports are needed.

Research supports the use of office discipline referrals as a universal screening system to identify students in need of more intensive positive behavioral interventions and supports and as an outcome to evaluate schoolwide efforts to implement and sustain a multitiered behavioral framework (e.g., Irvin, Tobin, Sprague, Sugai, & Vincent, 2004; McIntosh, Frank, & Spaulding, 2010; Predy, McIntosh, & Frank, 2014; Sugai et al., 2000). ODRs have been shown to be a reliable and valid indicator of a school's behavioral climate (e.g., general student misbehavior, school attendance, student and teacher perceptions of safety, classroom orderliness, students' experiences of academic success/failure) when used in a consistent, standardized manner (Irvin et al., 2004; McIntosh et al, 2010).

In addition to ODRs, several screening tools are available that have demonstrated reliability, validity, and utility for identifying students who are at risk for future social-emotional difficulties. When selecting a behavioral screening measure, Severson, Walker, Hope-Doolittle, Kratochwill, and Gresham (2007) recommended careful consideration of the following characteristics: (a) cost efficient, (b) able to accurately identify a high proportion of students requiring support (sensitivity), (c) able to accurately identify students not requiring support (specificity), (d) capable to identifying students early, (e) able to provide information useful for guiding interventions, and (f) usable by various raters.

The Student Risk Screening Scale (SRSS; Drummond, 1994) is a behavioral screening tool in which the classroom teacher provides a rating for each student on seven behavioral descriptors. The SRSS is formatted as a matrix. The first column of the matrix is used to list students' names. Seven externalizing behavioral descriptors appear across the top of the rating form: (a) steal; (b) lie, cheat, sneak; (c) behavior problem; (d) peer rejection; (e) low academic achievement; (f) negative attitude; and (g) aggressive behavior. Five internalizing behavioral descriptors are listed next: (a) emotionally flat; (b) shy, withdrawn; (c) sad, depressed; (d) anxious; and (e) lonely. The classroom teacher rates each student on all 12 items based on the behaviors they have observed. Every student is assigned a rating, ranging from 0 = "never" to 3 = "frequently," for each of the 12 descriptors. The ratings are summed for each student to yield an externalizing total score ranging from 0 to 21 and an internalizing total score ranging from 0 to 15 (elementary) or 0 to 18 (secondary). The total score is then used to identify students' risk level using research-derived cut scores. When used as part of a universal behavioral screening system, the SRSS is administered three times a year: in the fall (4–6 weeks after the school year has begun), in the winter (2–3 weeks before winter break), and in the spring (6–8 weeks before the end of the school year). Research supports the use of the SRSS as a reliable and valid tool for universal screening at the elementary school level (Menzies & Lane, 2012; Oakes et al., 2010), middle school level (Lane, Parks, Kalberg, & Carter, 2007), high school level (Lane, Kalberg, Parks, & Carter, 2008), in early childhood settings (Lane et al., 2015), and for use with English Language Learners (Lane, Richards, Oakes, & Connor, 2014).

The SRSS served as a model for two other universal screening tools for behavior. The Student Internalizing Behavior Screening Scale (SIBS; Cook et al., 2011) was designed to identify students at risk for internalizing behavior disorders. Developed as a companion scale to the SRSS, the SIBS is composed of seven behavioral descriptors: (a) nervous or fearful, (b) bullied by peers, (c) spends time alone, (d) clings to adults, (e) withdrawn, (f) seems sad or unhappy, and (g) complains about being sick or hurt. Research supports the use of the SIBS as a reliable and valid measure at the elementary school level (Cook et al., 2011).

The Student Protective Factors Screening Scale (SPF-7; Morrison, 2015) also employs the same matrix system used by the SRSS. Unlike the SRSS, however, which gathers a teacher's ratings on seven behavioral risk factors, the SPF-7 involves teacher ratings of individual students on seven protective factors identified in the research literature on social/behavioral competence and resiliency as strong correlates of positive developmental outcomes. The seven behavioral descriptors include (a) demonstrates competence, is optimistic, and has a sense of purpose; (b) has effective social skills, relates well to others, and has good friendship skills; (c) shows respect and concern for others and empathy; (d) identifies with a prosocial peer group; (e) is engaged and motivated to do well in school; (f) is connected with teachers and school, and (g) has a family that is supportive and invested in student's school success. Initial research supports the use of the SPF-7 as a reliable and valid measure at the elementary school level (Morrison, 2015).

Other behavioral screening tools that have demonstrable technical adequacy include the Behavioral and Emotional Screening System (BESS; Kamphaus & Reynolds, 2007) and the Social and Academic Behavior Risk Screener (SABRS; Kilgus, Chafouleas, & Riley-Tillman, 2013).

Indicator 2: Students' Response to Instructional Supports and Interventions Across Benchmark Periods

The second indicator to be examined in the evaluation of an MTSS initiative involves assessing students' response to core instruction and universal supports, targeted interventions, and intensive interventions (Shapiro & Clemens, 2009). For academic outcomes, a rate of improvement is calculated for each student by determining the gain on each curriculum-based measure divided by the number of weeks between two benchmark periods. Students' rates of improvement overall and for students receiving targeted and intensive intervention should be compared to (a) normative growth rates available from a national database, such as that provided by DIBELS Next (Dynamic Measurement Group), and/or (b) empirically derived expected rates of improvement available in the research literature (Hasbrouck & Tindal, 1992, 2005) overall and by the level of tiered instruction or intervention. Individual students' rate of improvement can be analyzed at the classroom level and/or grade level or by subgroup status (i.e., students with disabilities, race/ethnicity, socioeconomic status). An analysis of students' rates of improvement can reveal gains that are meaningful in terms of the impact on the individual learner despite not being large enough to advance the students from a high-risk to a lower-risk category (Shapiro & Clemens, 2009).

For behavioral outcomes, assessing students' response to universal supports, targeted interventions, and intensive interventions is accomplished through the visual analysis of graphed time-series data with regard to changes in trend, level, and variability (Cooper, Heron, & Heward, 2007; Fisher, Piazza, & Roane, 2011; Kazdin, 2011). Single-case design intervention data can also be aggregated across groups of students to show overall outcomes and inform the continuous improvement of the program (Burns, 2015). In Chapter 6, we describe how summary statistics, such as **effect size** and the **percentage of nonoverlapping data**, can be used to quantify intervention outcomes from single-case design data.

Indicator 3: Long-Term Student Outcomes

With a proactive MTSS framework, students receive timely, evidence-based interventions on a continuum of low- to high- intensity based on students' individual needs to prevent more serious academic and behavioral concerns (Vaughn, Wanzek, Woodruff, & Linan-Thompson, 2007). For most students, the intervention support they receive will be sufficient to address their needs. However, a small proportion of students who receive targeted (tier 2) or intensive (tier 3) intervention will continue to struggle and may be found eligible for supplementation special education services due to an underlying disability rather than a lack of success due to inadequate instruction. An evaluation of an MTSS initiative should therefore examine the percentage of students referred for a multifactored evaluation due to limited success in response to intervention that are indeed found to be eligible for special education services. If the MTSS framework is implemented with fidelity, the proportion of students experiencing significant academic and behavioral challenges will decrease over time as students' needs are met proactively. Consequently, resource-intensive special education services will be dedicated to a smaller percentage of students who are truly in need of these services (Shapiro & Clemens, 2009).

Student performance on state-mandated achievement tests might also be included as a summative measure of academic performance. They are considered an important and consequential outcome in the eyes of many educators and their inclusion in the evaluation plan may give weight to the initiative as a whole. For criterion-referenced tests, the results are reported by classroom, grade level, and/or school as the percentage of students at or above a criterion or proficient level for each subject area tested.

Suspension and expulsion data are another valued outcome of an MTSS initiative. Suspension and expulsion data can be reviewed quarterly as a formative measure or at the end of the school year on a summative basis. In addition to the number and rate (per 100 students) of in-school suspension, out-of-school suspension, and expulsions, suspension and expulsion data can yield (a) the number and percentage of students receiving a suspension or expulsion, and (b) the number of days out due to suspensions and expulsions.

IN CONCLUSION

Schools are complex environments with an array of student, teacher, and building variables at play. The challenge for an evaluation team is to gather the evidence needed to answer evaluation questions regarding the program's contribution to valued student outcomes. Isolating the effects of a program is usually not critical to a school-based evaluation team who understands and appreciates the many factors that interrelate to influence student learning and behavior (Killion, 2008). A tightly controlled research study is needed to determine whether a clearly delineated program implemented with fidelity caused the intended outcome. In contrast, school-based evaluation efforts focus on gathering information that can be used to inform continuous program improvement by ascertaining whether the implementation efforts are contributing to improved student outcomes. As such, Daniel Stufflebeam, a leading force in advancing evaluation as a professional field emphasized that "Evaluation's most important purpose is not to prove, but to improve" (Stufflebeam, 2004, p. 262) and "Unless there are important decisions to be made, we ought not to be wasting money on it" (Stufflebeam in an interview with Brandt, 1978, p. 253).

Program evaluation planning must focus on the best, most feasible methods available to answer the evaluation questions to inform future decision making. In the words of Patton (2008), another leading figure in the field of evaluation, "Our aim is modest: reasonable estimations of the likelihood that particular activities have contributed in concrete ways to observed effects—emphasis on the word *reasonable*. Not definitive conclusions. Not absolute proof" (p. 217). In this chapter, we outlined an evaluation planning process complete with useful planning templates and relevant outcome measures that we believe will equip school-based evaluation teams with the knowledge, skills, and tools they need to inform continuous program improvement.

SUMMARY POINTS

- A goal is a statement that identifies the intended outcome of the program (e.g., increase the percentage of student at or above the benchmark in reading fluency). A goal could also pertain to the process through which the program will operate to improve student outcomes (e.g., increase the number of teachers completing all eight modules of the professional learning series of evidence-based, phonics instruction).
- The theory of change establishes the logical, causal linkages between the program's strategies or actions (the "WHAT"), intervening or mediating factors, and the goals the program is seeking to attain.

- A logic model is a graphic display that connects program resources (inputs) and the activities or strategies described in the theory of change to intended changes short-, medium-, and long-term outcomes.
- A theory of change and logic model must be plausible, doable, testable, and meaningful as they will serve as the hypothesis(es) to be tested by the evaluation.
- Process evaluation questions focus on the degree to which the core components of the program are being implemented as planned.
- Impact evaluation questions focus on changes in specified outcomes as they relate to the program's goals.
- Developing the evaluation plan involves matching data collection methods to each of the evaluation questions.
- Three indicators that are key to evaluating the student learning and behavior outcomes of an MTSS initiative include (a) monitoring risk levels across benchmark periods and movement between the tiers, (b) students' responses to instructional supports and interventions across benchmark periods, and (c) long-term student outcomes evidencing a reduction in the risk of more serious learning and behavioral needs (Shapiro & Clemens, 2009).

QUESTIONS TO FURTHER YOUR UNDERSTANDING

1. What are some of the benefits of articulating a theory of change and creating a logic model when working in a school struggling to meet students' needs?
2. Is it possible to ever conduct an evaluation that is exclusively a process evaluation or exclusively an impact evaluation? Why or why not?
3. Attribution claims assert that the implementation of the program activities alone brought about the changes in the valued outcomes, whereas contribution claims assert only that the implementation of the program may have likely contributed to the changes in the desired outcomes, but other factors (e.g., new curriculum, new principal, new teachers, professional learning opportunities on different or related topics) might also have contributed to the positive outcomes during that program year. Why is this distinction important when evaluating the results of an MTSS initiative?

5

Communicating Evaluation Findings

With the most recent review of the data, the school leadership team at Central Elementary is starting to see some results they like. The percentage of second grade students at or above benchmark on their early literacy measures is the highest it has been since Central Elementary started universal screening. Expectations for appropriate behavior are in place schoolwide, giving educators a common language and structure for addressing student behavior. The number of office discipline referrals has markedly decreased. It is too early to tell if these positive outcomes can be maintained, but the school leadership team is hopeful. The team members know they need to recognize their school's collective efforts publically. Other schools in the district have considered adopting Central Elementary's multi-tiered system of supports (MTSS) initiative, and they are eager to know if it is making a difference. The topic on the agenda for today's meeting is the way to communicate outcomes to the staff, students, and parents at Central Elementary to sustain our efforts and to encourage district leaders, educators in other schools, and community members to get on board.

The question of how to most effectively communicate research and evaluation findings to teachers, parents, and key stakeholders in order to facilitate meaningful change has been a perennial question in education (e.g., Cook, Cook, & Landrum, 2013; Heibert, Gallimore, & Stigler, 2002; Hood, 2002; Winton, 2006; Winton & Turnbull, 1982). Efforts to attain positive outcomes through the implementation of evidence-based practices will be more likely to reach their maximum impact and be sustained over time when activities, accomplishments, and barriers are communicated effectively.

Unfortunately, evaluation findings have been communicated traditionally in the form of a written report that is heavy in technical detail but light on likely impact (Volkov, 2011b). This approach to disseminating evaluation findings is based on the generally faulty assumption that individuals conducting an evaluation need only to make their findings available. Providing access to information for others to locate, interpret, and act on has been the typical method of distribution. On the contrary, ample experience has shown that this passive approach to dissemination is not effective in supporting systems change (Cook et al., 2013). Individuals and teams must actively disseminate the program's efforts and outcomes in order to inform continuous improvement and scale-up (adoption, installation, and implementation) at new sites.

Contemporary approaches to reporting place individuals engaged in evaluation in the role of change agents. When evaluators communicate in a way that ignites excitement around results and leads stakeholders to action-based analysis, they are positioning themselves as change agents. Active dissemination involves planned, systematic efforts designed to facilitate the adoption of a program or innovation (Dearing & Kreuter, 2010; Owen, Glanz, Sallis, & Kelder, 2006). Chapter 5 explores strategies for the effective communication of evaluation findings through with the school-based evaluator cast in the role of a change agent.

DEVELOPING A COMMUNICATION PLAN

Ideally, the evaluation planning process presented in Chapter 4 incorporates decisions around how data will be stored, displayed, summarized, and used. In this section we provide guidance about how to develop a communication plan for sharing evaluation findings, emphasize the value of data-driven communication, provide some basic pointers on data visualization, and share some tips for linking results to proposed actions.

Whether one is creating a quarterly monitoring report or a more comprehensive annual evaluation report, the very first step in communicating evaluation findings should be the development of a communication plan. This communication plan will be most effective when established early in implementation and in the context of communicating about an MTSS in general, and not just communicating evaluation findings. A school's communication plan should include the following elements (State Implementation and Scaling-Up of Evidence-Based Practices, 2016; St. Martin, 2016):

- Who (or what group) needs communication and for what purpose
- What information needs to be communicated
- Designee to carry out communication
- Format for gathering information
- Agreed-on timelines for communication and necessary responses
- Format for responding to challenges
- Frequency and method for evaluating the effectiveness of communication

Effective communication is critical for getting administrators, staff, and other stakeholders invested in a school's efforts to implement MTSS. The details specified in a communication plan will help ensure that others in the school and district are clear about what to expect in term of how MTSS is being implemented, with communication provided at regular intervals and in a designated format. A communication plan will help ensure that (a) there is awareness of MTSS implementation and impact and (b) regular prompts are in place for leaders to make decisions that will promote and sustain accomplishments and remove barriers impeding implementation. All four of the capacity and fidelity assessments highlighted in Chapter 2 (i.e., Regional Capacity Assessment, District Capacity Assessment, Schoolwide PBIS Tiered Fidelity Inventory, and the Reading-Tiered Fidelity Inventory) call for three features of communication. These three features include: (a) a data-driven focus, (b) the ability to link current results to proposed actions, and (c) the provision of written communication at least twice per year. An example of a district-level communication plan for an MTSS initiative is presented in Appendix H.

DATA-DRIVEN FOCUS TO COMMUNICATION

Sharing data gives us the opportunity to elevate communication from a mere set of activities or requests to a dynamic story punctuated with fact and figures. As school systems have become more data-oriented and educators more data savvy, it is common to see graphs and data tables featured in communications, on websites, and in the hallways of schools. A data-driven focus to communication featuring graphs and tables offers greater efficiency and clarity than what can be accomplished with words alone when trying to communicate patterns, trends, accomplishments, and areas of need. Graphic displays generated from a data dashboard can be highly effective in bringing the data to life in concrete, visual terms (Lipkus & Hollands, 1999).

Web-Based Data Systems and Data Dashboards

In order to communicate evaluation findings, individuals responsible for evaluating school-based initiatives must have timely access to relevant data and other critical implementation information. The growing prevalence of web-based data systems and data dashboards reflects this demand for timely data entry, analysis, and communication to inform decision making.

Data systems with the capacity to analyze data and generate visual displays have become increasingly common in education. In the past couple of decades, we have seen software-based files (e.g., Microsoft Excel) designed for a particular initiative give way to web-based systems. An example of this is the School-Wide Information System (SWIS) Suite, designed by PBISApps for data-based decision making within a schoolwide Positive Behavioral Interventions and Supports (PBIS) framework. Under the guidance of a local facilitator, schools and school districts can subscribe to PBISApps and have access to a highly functional, confidential, web-based data system to collect, analyze, and display student behavior data. Similarly, schools and districts can subscribe to DIBELS net, a data reporting service developed by Dynamic Measurement Group, for analyzing and communicating DIBELS Next data or Fast Bridge Learning web-based data system for

Box 5.1

Spotlight on the MIBLSI Database for Data-Driven Communication of a Statewide MTSS Initiative

Michigan's Integrated Behavior and Learning Support Initiative (MIBLSI) Database (Harms & Oskam, 2014) is an example of a system that functions to facilitate the communication of evaluation findings. Within the MIBLSI Database, the home screen provides a dashboard display of key indicators essential for regional and district implementation teams to monitor multi-tier system of support (MTSS) implementation and impact. Users need not click through several dropdown menus of reporting options to get what they need. Graphic images can be saved for use in communicating with teachers, staff, administrators, and other stakeholders. The MIBLSI Database was designed with four unique features to enhance the system's value for communicating evaluation findings efficiently and effectively. First, the dashboards and reports are designed for alignment with the MIBLI's data review process at the regional, district, and school levels. Second, the system provides a place to enter and analyze fidelity and capacity data not hosted in other web-based systems. Third, the system provides a single point of entry at the school level that aggregates data up to the district, regional, and state levels. Finally, data dashboards have been designed using principles for effective display of data and information processing.

collecting, analyzing, and displaying universal screening and progress monitoring data using curriculum-based and other forms of assessment.

Many school systems and initiatives have set out to create a data dashboard to integrate data collected from web-based data systems with relevant data collected locally (e.g., fidelity data, capacity data, attendance, grades). For example, Michigan's Integrated Behavior and Learning Support Initiative (MIBLSI) data system for managing and displaying data is described in Box 5.1. Modeled after the function of a dashboard on a vehicle, data dashboards provide timely feedback on a small number of indicators using simple and concrete visual displays (Few, 2013).

Although specific guidance about how to create a data dashboard and other visualizations is not the intent of this chapter, a few suggestions are warranted. When designing data dashboards with reporting features, we have seen many school systems and developers lean toward "smorgasbord reporting," which enables users to generate any number and variety of reports based on different filters and custom options. This approach can be appealing for those enamored with data and keen on the idea of being able to answer any potential evaluation question with the click of a mouse. However, a system will hold more value to educators when it is designed to answer specific questions, namely the ones outlined in the evaluation plan. Rather than overwhelming a user with endless possibilities, automating data analysis and visualization to focus on answering the evaluation questions can positively impact a team's ability to translate data analysis into effective communication. Figure 5.1 provides a side-by-side

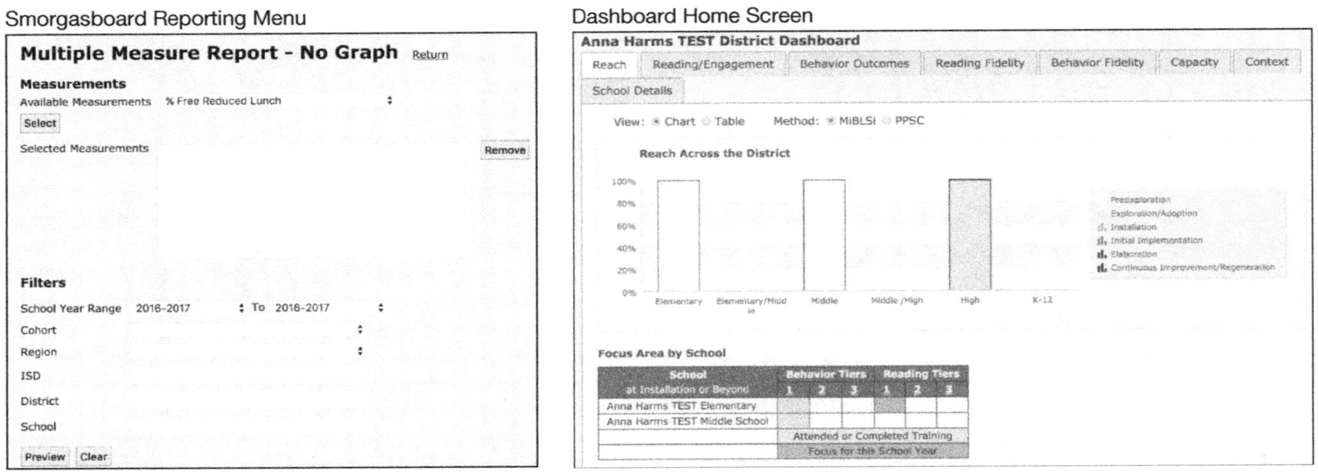

Figure 5.1. Contrasting Reporting Features: A Menu for "Smorgasbord Reporting" and a Dashboard Home Screen

comparison of a menu for "smorgasbord reporting" and a dashboard home screen, both from the MIBLSI Database (Harms & Oskam, 2014). The reporting menu option requires users to consider what question they want to answer, select the correct report options, and then possibly further organize and summarize the resulting data file. In contrast, the dashboard home screen starts with highly relevant data views that are designed to answer questions about reach and school participation in training.

If a team must spend considerable effort organizing, analyzing, and summarizing continuously updated data, less time and energy are available to focus on how to translate that information into critical actions and talking points for team members. The use of data dashboards for monitoring MTSS implementation and outcomes highlights a current trend emphasizing monitoring systems to identify "hot spots" that may require more in-depth evaluations in place of extensive, exhaustive "wall to wall" evaluations (Volkov, 2011b). Monitoring systems in the form of dashboards can be effective as they can be targeted and nimble, while still retaining their accountability function (Love, 2003). An effective data and reporting system must provide immediate and automated views of the most important data needed to answer common evaluation questions. These data views can then be easily pulled into other communications, such as reports and presentations. For example, the dashboard image from Figure 5.1 could be embedded into a formal or informal communication about schools' stage of implementation.

Data Visualization

Recent advancements in data visualization emphasize the critical importance of well-conceived graphics to enable the intended recipient of the communication to understand the data-driven message, regardless of their level of data literacy. Consider, for example, the use of pictographs. Pictographs are grids of icons or figures (e.g., a 10×10 grid of 100 faces), in which a portion is shaded or colored to show changes over time as a result of an intervention within a specified population (see Figure 5.2). Pictographs have been shown to reduced significantly the influence of misleading anecdotal information (Fagerlin, Wang, & Udel, 2005) and resulted in faster and more accurate processing of risk information in comparison with bar graphs (Zikmund-Fisher, Fagerlin, & Ubel, 2008).

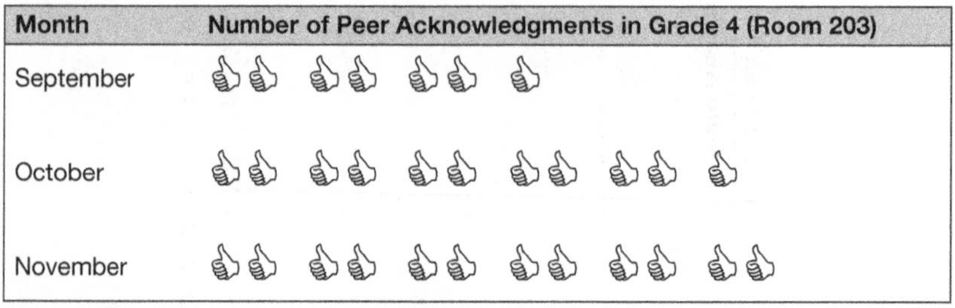

Month	Number of Peer Acknowledgments in Grade 4 (Room 203)
September	👍👍 👍👍 👍👍 👍
October	👍👍 👍👍 👍👍 👍👍 👍👍 👍
November	👍👍 👍👍 👍👍 👍👍 👍👍 👍👍

Figure 5.2. Acknowledgment System Data for Grade 4

Effective data visualization provides a context or frame of reference by which the consumer can make sense of the patterns in the data. Adding visual boundary lines and corresponding evaluative category labels (e.g., poor = 0–60, fair = 61–70, good = 71–80, excellent = 81–100) to horizontal bar graphs, for example, can increase consumers understanding of the data. The title of a graph can be used to describe the data pattern presented in the graph, rather than just containing information regarding the data sources and the period of time represented by graph. Similarly, a graph can be paired with one to two brief sentences to highlight key findings.

Other graphic aides that have been shown to increase understanding of outcome data presented over time in a line graph include the use of goal lines, aim lines, and trend lines (Van Norman, Nelson, Shin, & Christ, 2013). A goal line provides the visual context for the expected or desired level of performance and an aim line connects the baseline data (typically the median data point) to the goal line over a specified period of time (e.g., 12 weeks) (see Figure 5.2). Trend lines represent the best fit line representing the trend in a set of data points. Taken together, goal lines, aim lines, and trend lines facilitate the interpretation of time-series outcome data presented in a line graph (Van Norman et al., 2013). A simple chart can be equally as effective, depending on the data, to communicate current outcomes as compared to the expected or desired outcomes.

Broad suggestions for how to visualize data depending on the purpose of the communication are presented in Table 5.1. Whole books have been devoted to

Table 5.1 SUGGESTION FOR DATA VISUALIZATIONS GIVEN
THE COMMUNICATION PURPOSE

Purpose	Suggestions for Data Visualization
Demonstrate a need for the new initiative or a need to make a change	• Line or bar graphs that show either that the data are not improving over time or that conditions are worsening
Demonstrate improvements over time	• Line or bar graphs that show movement in a desirable direction. • Stacked bar graphs that show how parts of a whole shift over time
Demonstrate how implementation fidelity relates to student outcomes	• Multiple lines on the same graph • Scatterplot
Demonstrate improvement in relation to a major change or event	• Include vertical phase/intervention lines on the graph to separate data prior to and after the event
Compare outcomes from schools that are implementing with fidelity compared to schools that are not	• Line graph with each line representing outcomes for a different group (schools implementing with fidelity, schools not implementing with fidelity)
Demonstrating sustained outcomes	• Line graph that shows outcomes with markers for when initial training ended, when leadership changed, and when/how demographics changed

Box 5.2

Spotlight on Stephanie Evergreen and Effective Data Visualization

Stephanie Evergreen, a teacher and then researcher/evaluator by training, has been inspiring organizations to improve their communication of evaluation findings from formal reports, to website content, to research presentations at professional conferences. Evergreen consults with a wide variety of organizations and is among a group of leading experts in the area of effective data visualization. Her blog can be accessed at http://stephanieevergreen.com/category/blog/. One of the most influential suggestions she has shared in consultation work with these authors is the idea of flipping the typical sequence of presentations and reports. The general idea is that a research manuscript or evaluation report nearly always starts with contextual and input information such as a description of participants, measures, and methods used. The results and implications typically appear last. To capture the attention of the intended recipient and emphasize the most critical information, Evergreen advocates for beginning with the evaluation findings. Flipping the typical sequence to feature the data-driven message is a concept that Evergreen has also promoted within the American Evaluation Association via the Potent Presentations initiative (http://p2i.eval.org/).

these principles and should be referenced for comprehensive guidance on selecting appropriate data visualization methods (Evergreen, 2017; Knaflic, 2015; Wong, 2013). Box 5.2 highlights the contributions of Stephanie Evergreen to the field of data visualization. The careful selection of the right graphic to communicate evaluation findings helps ensure that the message is clear and concrete and not obscured by extraneous information. Figure 5.3 provides an example of how a poor chart selection could obscure a critical message about the relationship between implementation fidelity and student outcomes. In the bar graph, it is difficult to know what to compare—schools or measures. The use of a scatterplot draws focus to the relationship between Reading-Tiered Fidelity Inventory scores and DIBELS Next results. The additional inclusion of an interpretive title further focuses the audience on the intended message.

Linking Current Results to Proposed Actions

For communication to be maximally effective, educators, staff, and administrators must be able to process the information, interpret it accurately, and then link information to recommendations for future action. Meaningfully organizing results will increase the likelihood for action. One way to organize data-driven communication is to cluster information into three categories: accomplishments, challenges and barriers, and next steps.

Potentially Confusing Display of Data

Improved Visualization and Description of the Message

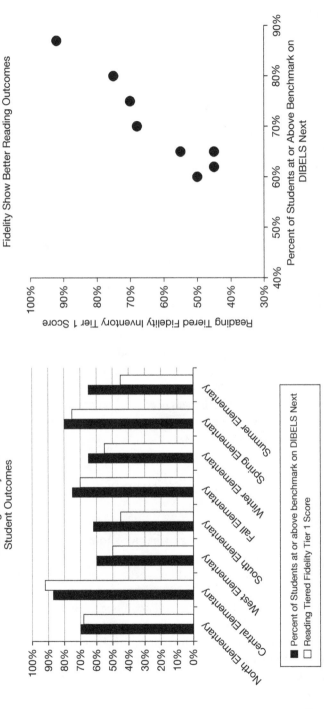

Figure 5.3. Communicating with Effective Data Visualization

Accomplishments recognize the hard work of administrators, staff, and students. Showcasing accomplishments at a classroom, school, district, or even regional level can ignite a spread of the work to other classrooms, schools, districts and regions. Toward the end of this chapter, we will highlight what diffusion theory tell us about how communication regarding the successful implementation of an innovation can help promote further adoption and implementation over time and across sites. Communication focused on a problem-solving process can be used to address challenges and remove barriers through the development of plans for future action. To be sure, addressing challenges and removing barriers is a reality of systems change. We have yet to evaluate an initiative in schools that can boast a 100% success rate. With all communication, sufficient detail should be provided so that an individual or team accountable for next steps is clearly identified and should be linked to sustaining, expanding, or improving on implementation.

Written Communication at Least Twice per Year

Although an annual report is standard practice in evaluation as established by the *Program Evaluation Standards* (Yarbrough et al., 2011), research-based measures of MTSS implementation fidelity and capacity call for the written communication of findings at least twice a year (i.e., interim and final report). Adding interim reporting allows for the opportunity for a midcourse correction if the initiative is not achieving its intended goals and objectives at key milestones. A final report provides the opportunity for a comprehensive review of what was accomplished during the year and what challenges need to be rectified. Brief monitoring reports can also be shared following more regular data reviews to maintain a data-driven focus to all communications.

TARGETED, TAILORED COMMUNICATION AS INFORMED BY DIFFUSION THEORY

In this final section, we will revisit what we know about **diffusion theory**, first introduced in this book in Chapter 2, to describe how communication can be tailored to meet the needs of individuals as they progress from adoption to implementation over time. Diffusion is "the process by which an *innovation* is *communicated* through certain *channels* over *time* among the members of a *social system*" (Rogers, 2003, p. 7). Although initially conceptualized as a model of change for individual decision making and the factors associated with the adoption (or rejection) of new products, practices, programs, policies, or ideas, diffusion theory has been applied to organizations as well. Diffusion and other knowledge-for-action theories and processes have forced evaluators to consider how they can devise a communication plan to affect change through timely, tailored, and varied communications (Ashley, 2009; Ottoson & Hawe, 2009), such as the type of plan

Box 5.3

SPOTLIGHT ON CONCEPTS: THE DISTINCTION BETWEEN DISSEMINATION AND
DIFFUSION

Although the terms **dissemination and diffusion** are often used interchangeably,
the terms are distinct. With dissemination there is an emphasis on the spread
of an innovation that maintains its fidelity. As such, dissemination leans more
heavily toward the replication of an existing model or evidence-based practice
(Langberg & Smith, 2006). Diffusion, in contrast, describes the process by which
an innovation is adopted and likely adapted to fit the local context. Although
fidelity is critical to the implementation of an MTSS framework, the contextual
fit is also an important consideration for successful implementation. We find that
diffusion theory is highly relevant to understanding how innovations take hold
over time and how communication can be structured to meet the needs of the
potential user and consumers.

---

discussed earlier in this chapter. The distinction between diffusion and dissemination is highlighted in Box 5.3.

Diffusion theory has identified five characteristics of an innovation that influence whether an innovation is adopted by potential users (see Table 5.2). These five
characteristics are highly relevant to promoting the use of an MTSS framework
within a school or district. The first characteristic is relative advantage. **Relative
advantage** is the extent to which the innovation is perceived to have significant
advantages over the status quo or current alternatives (Rogers, 2003). Educators
will be more likely to adopt and implement an MTSS initiative if they judge it to
be superior to their school's current practices.

Compatibility, the second characteristic, refers to the degree to which the
innovation is seen to be a good fit within the local context in terms of its consistency with past practices, prevailing values, and current needs (Rogers,
2003). Educators will be more inclined to implement evidence-based practices
within an MTSS framework if the initiative is viewed as compatible within the
school context.

Complexity is the third characteristic. Diffusion theory holds that the more
complex an innovation is, the less likely potential users will adopt and implement
it (Rogers, 2003). The core components of an MTSS framework need to be communicated in a manner that is readily understood and relevant to educators; this
increases the likelihood that it will be implemented.

Trialability is the fourth characteristic of an innovation, which determines
whether an innovation is adopted. Trialability refers to the extent to which components of an innovation can be tried out before a potential user decides to
adopt it (Rogers, 2003). Early exposure or an opportunity to test-drive components of an MTSS framework will increase the likelihood that they will adopt and
implement it.

Observability is the final characteristic. It is the degree to which the use and benefits of an innovation made visible to others (Rogers, 2003). Communicating classroom, grade level, or school's outcomes will increase the likelihood that other educators will adopt and implement MTSS practices in their classrooms. These five characteristics of innovations that influence the adoption and implementation of an innovation are valuable when planning the initial introduction to the innovation and for making sense of why some educators embrace the changes as early adopters while others lag behind (Ashley, 2009).

Similar dimensions are also outlined by the National Implementation Research Network in the Hexagon Tool (Blase, Kiser, & Van Dyke, 2013), designed for use in the strategic selection of effective innovations. Additional considerations include an analysis of the evidence/research to support an innovation and the school or district's capacity to implement it well given the necessary resources. We place diffusion theory's characteristics that influence program adoption alongside the hexagon components in Table 5.2.

Diffusion theory accounts for the fact that diffusion is a process that progresses over time. As such, individuals will vary in their time of adoption. According to diffusion theory, adoption follows a rather predictable pattern (Mahajan & Peterson, 1985; Rogers, 2003). The first individuals to adopt a new innovation are known as the "innovators." Innovators compose approximately 2.5% of the target population. The "early adopters" represent the next group of individuals to adopt the innovation. They represent approximately 13.5% of the target population. Early adopters are often in the position to become opinion leaders, whereby they increase the likelihood of adoption among their peers by modeling their own use of the innovation (Dearing, 2008). The early adopters are followed by the "early majority" (34%) and then the "later majority" (34%). Individuals who remain the last to adopt an innovation (or fail to adopt it altogether), are known as the "laggards." Laggards constitute approximately 16% of the target population. This notion that diffusion is a process in which, predictably, a small proportion of individuals will adopt early in the diffusion process and that adoption will continue at a faster pace as more individuals are exposed to the innovation has implications for how evaluation findings are communicated.

Communications need to be tailored to the intended audience per the communication plan. Not all stakeholders need to know the same type and detail of information, with the same frequency. As districts work to support MTSS, it is common to try to get all schools to begin training and implementation at the same time. However, not all schools are at the same level of readiness to begin the implementation process. Starting with the innovators and early adopters allows for the development of model demonstration schools and creates an opportunity for the schools and districts to work through the challenges on a small scale, with less fear of creating a false start across the entire district. Communicating frequently and strategically about the activities and impact in model demonstration schools is important for how MTSS is perceived and subsequently adopted in other district schools.

Table 5.2 CHARACTERISTICS THAT INFLUENCE SELECTION/ADOPTION

Characteristics That Influence Adoption	Hexagon Categories
Relative Advantage The extent to which the innovation is perceived to have significant advantages over the status quo or current alternatives	Need
Compatibility The degree to which the innovation is seen to be a good fit within the local context in terms of its consistency with past practices, prevailing values, and current needs	Fit
Complexity The degree to which the innovation is seen as straightforward and easy to implement	Resources
Trialability The extent to which components of an innovation can be tried out before a potential user decides to adopt it	Readiness for Replication
Observability The degree to which the use and benefits of an innovation made visible to others	Research
	Capacity to Implement

Adapted from: Blase, K., Kiser, L., & Van Dyke, M. (2013). The Hexagon Tool: Exploring Contex. Chapel Hill, NC: National Implementation Research Network, FPG Child Development Institute, University of North Carolina at Chapel Hill.Rogers (2003). *Diffusion of innovations* (5th ed.). New York: Free Press.

Diffusion theory has implications for evaluation of an MTSS initiative and the design of a communication plan that is targeted to the changing needs of the intended audience. Consistent with implementation research (see Chapter 2), we know that a variety of individual and systemic factors contribute to educators' adoption of new practices and process. Communication regarding the implementation and outcomes of an MTSS initiative has a greater impact to the degree they are able to show that MTSS is superior to the status quo or alternative practices and a good fit within the school culture. Evaluation findings should highlight key outcomes, rather than a lengthy, exhaustive list of indicators. Simplifying the message can help avoid perceptions that MTSS is too complex and burdensome. Understanding where individual educators are within the diffusion process will make it possible for program coordinators and evaluators to encourage the early majority and late majority to gain more exposure to and experiences with MTSS practices and processes through collaboration with innovators and early adopters.

Box 5.4

SPOTLIGHT ON THE SUCCESs MODEL FOR MAKING MESSAGES "STICK"

Within the special education literature, Cook, Cook, and Landrum (2013) have urged researchers to overcome the research-to-practice gap by applying six communication strategies developed by Heath and Heath (2008) to researchers' efforts to disseminate their findings. These six strategies, represented by the acronym SUCCESs explain why some messages "stick"—that is, are understood, remembered, and have a lasting impact on opinions and behavior—and others quickly fade away (Heath & Heath, 2008). The six strategies for enhancing dissemination identified in the SUCCESs model include: Simple, Unexpected, Concrete, Credible, Emotional, and Stories. These highly effective strategies are critically important and yet often run counter to the traditional means by which evaluation outcomes are reported.

Diffusion theory focuses on communication for the purposes of getting others to adopt an effective innovation (see Box 5.4). However, there are other critical reasons for effectively and regularly communicating MTSS efforts and impact with a variety of stakeholders. Regular communication with executive leaders in the district is essential for continuing to leverage resources for sustained implementation and for addressing barriers to implementation. A personal narrative can be particularly powerful way of conveying a message that is intended to have a meaningful impact. Although the research is mixed with regard to whether narratives are more persuasive than other modes of information sharing (e.g., statistics) for promoting adult behavior change (Hinyard & Kreuter, 2007), narratives may be especially effective for use with individuals who are not influenced by a report on research findings or other standard modes of information sharing (Gersten, 2001). Within education, storytelling is more effective in promoting meaningful change among educators to the degree that the educators identify with the individuals in the story in terms of relevant teaching experiences, values, and goals (Cook et al., 2013). Stories are a critical part of initial training on MTSS. In a similar vein, Cook et al. (2013) recommended fostering an emotional connection among educators by focusing on the impact of the innovative practices on one student. Creating a forum for educators to make a personal connection to the information being shared is critical for educators to willingly adopt and implement the practices being promoted (Bartunek, 2007).

EDUCATORS AS OPINION LEADERS FOR PROMOTING INTERVENTION IMPLEMENTATION

The diffusion of innovative practices follows a predictable pattern in which, according to diffusion theory, a small proportion of innovators and early adopters adopt the new practices and in turn serve as opinion leaders to help facilitate the engagement of their peers. Research has shown that educators can play a critical role in affecting changes as opinion leaders in an MTSS initiative. Atkins et al. (2008) examined the influence of educators serving as opinion leaders on classroom educators' self-reported use of interventions for students with attention-deficit/hyperactivity disorder (ADHD) in high-poverty schools in Chicago. In order to identify influential, credible educators to serve as opinion leaders, educators of students in grades 1 to 5 were asked to list up to three teacher colleagues at their school from whom they sought advice regarding academic concerns, behavior concerns, and/or curriculum issues. The resulting group of 12 educators serving as opinion leaders were similar to their peers in gender, race, and educational attainment but had significantly more years of teaching experience overall and at their school. The opinion leaders were then trained in the use of school-based assessment and intervention strategies for students with ADHD and deployed alongside mental health providers in 6 of the 10 schools. The results indicate that over the course of 2 years, classroom educators' self-reported use of target behavioral interventions was higher in the schools served by a trained opinion leader relative to schools receiving support from an external mental health provider only. The study by Atkins et al. (2008) provides further support for the positive role an opinion leader or highly regarded coach can play in communicating expected practices, encouraging implementation on an ongoing basis, and providing feedback to change adult behaviors individually and systemically.

IN CONCLUSION

In this chapter, we presented practical strategies for providing timely, tailored communications to targeted audiences within the school community and beyond with the goal of promoting the implementation of an MTSS initiative. With so many digital platforms available, educators functioning as evaluators have many options to consider when developing their communication plan. The use of a communication plan will ensure timely, tailored, data-driven communications regarding evaluation findings to facilitate engagement, implementation, and the continuous improvement of the initiative.

SUMMARY POINTS

- A communication plan helps stakeholders expect and know what to do with communication that includes evaluation findings.
- Data dashboards and the strategic selection of data visualizations can enhance communication.
- Communication of evaluation findings needs to occur several times per year for formative and summative purposes.

- Diffusion theory provides a framework for ensuring communication of evaluation findings addresses factors that influence what stakeholders do with the information and results.

QUESTIONS TO FURTHER YOUR UNDERSTANDING

1. What features should be specified in a communication plan to ensure stakeholders can expect and attend to communication regarding program evaluation findings?
2. Describe some strategies for maximizing the effect of graphs and other visualized data and information.
3. Is producing a comprehensive evaluation report sufficient for impacting change as an evaluator? Why or why not?
4. How can attention to the factors that influence adoption or selection of an effective innovation be addressed in communication stakeholders?

Case Studies Using Program Evaluation to Drive Evidence-Based Practices

It should be clear by now that we see program evaluation as an ideal vehicle for driving systems change in schools and school districts. Throughout this book, we have sought to equip school-based professionals with the content knowledge and skills they need to engage in fundamental program evaluation activities in their schools. In this final chapter, we present three case studies to illustrate how the evaluation models, methods, techniques, and tools featured in this book can be incorporated into practice.

The first case study describes an evaluation of the Dyslexia Pilot Project, a statewide MTSS initiative targeting early literacy. In this evaluation, special attention was paid to the evaluating the cost-effectiveness of serving students in kindergarten to grade 2 proactively.

The second case study features the use of single-case designs and corresponding summary statistics to evaluate the collective impact of more than 500 academic and behavioral interventions provided within an MTSS framework as part of the annual statewide evaluation of an internship program in school psychology. **Goal attainment scaling** and summary statistics, such as the **percentage of nonoverlapping data (PND) points** and **effect size**, were used to aggregate intervention outcomes across school settings to determine the impact of this program—overall and by tier and to inform its continuous improvement.

The third case study focuses on efforts to evaluate the fidelity of implementation for teacher teams' use of a five-step process for data-based decision making and instructional planning. Evaluating the effectiveness of teacher teams could help identify targets for future professional learning that would advance teachers' use of data-driven problem solving and build the school's capacity for meeting the needs of all learners. Each of these case studies provides a window into the use of program evaluation expertise to facilitate meaningful change in schools that have a direct and measurable impact on students.

CASE STUDY 1: EXAMINING COST-EFFECTIVENESS
IN THE EVALUATION OF THE DYSLEXIA PILOT PROJECT

An analysis of cost-effectiveness enables decision makers to evaluate the impact of an initiative on the system as a whole, beyond the effects measured at an individual student level (Barrett & Scott, 2006; Scott & Barrett, 2004). This may be particularly appealing to educators who are trying to ascertain the value of the primary prevention practices incorporated in MTSS and to school and district leaders who may use fiscal savings as a means for communicating the systemic outcomes in simple and concrete terms in order to shore up support for MTSS.

The Dyslexia Pilot Project

Case Study 1 focuses on the Dyslexia Pilot Project, an MTSS Reading Initiative designed to promote early screening and intervention services for children with risk factors for dyslexia. The primary goal of the Dyslexia Pilot Project was to evaluate the effectiveness of early screening and reading assistance programs for children at risk for reading failure, including those students exhibiting risk factors associated with dyslexia. A secondary goal of the Dyslexia Pilot Project was to evaluate whether effective early screening and reading assistance programs could reduce future special education costs.

Eight school districts were selected by the state department of education for participation in the Dyslexia Pilot Project based on the merit of their proposals. To be considered for participation in the Dyslexia Pilot Project, school districts were required to address the following: (a) identify a method of screening children for low phonemic awareness and other risk factors for dyslexia, (b) design and implement a tiered model of reading instructional support that utilized a multisensory structured language approach to instruction, and (c) include a methodology for evaluating the reading program's effects on the children's identified risk factors. Participation in the Dyslexia Pilot Project involved a 3-year commitment from school districts to invest in teacher professional learning and infrastructure supports for universal screening, a tiered model of reading instructional support that utilized a multisensory structured language approach to instruction (e.g., Orton-Gillingham), and ongoing progress monitoring to inform data-based decision making. Funding for two school districts was discontinued at the end of year 1 due to a failure to implement the core components of the Dyslexia Pilot Project. The six school districts continuing in the Dyslexia Pilot Project in years 2 and 3 included one large urban, one suburban, and four rural school districts. Among the six school districts, the total number of elementary schools increased from 9 schools (year 1) to 11 schools (year 2) and 16 schools (year 3) as the urban district scaled up from 2 to 3 schools and the suburban district scaled up from 1 to 7 schools.

Description of Interventions Provided

Dyslexia Pilot Project schools provided descriptive information for each student receiving early literacy intervention through the project. The descripting information included the type of intervention (e.g., Orton Gillingham, Corrective Reading, Read Naturally), start and end dates, minutes per week, number of weeks, the interventionist (e.g., classroom teacher, reading specialist, intervention specialist), setting (e.g., classroom whole group, classroom small group, pull-out small group, pull-out individual), and the ratio of interventionist to students in that setting.

Impact on Student Outcomes

The design of the Dyslexia Pilot Project evaluation was consistent with the approach established by Shapiro and Clemens (2009), as described in Chapter 4. Student learning outcomes were assessed using standardized curriculum-based assessments of phonological processing (e.g., phoneme blending, deletion, substitution, and segmentation), rapid naming skills (e.g., letter naming fluency), and oral reading fluency. National norms were used to determine the number and percentage of students whose needs were best served by the core instruction (tier 1); core instruction plus strategic intervention (tier 2); or core instruction plus intensive, individualized intervention (tier 3). Where multiple measures of early literacy skills were used, students were classified as in need of intensive intervention if they performed within the intensive range on any of the measures administered during that screening period. Local norms were used in instances where the percentage of kindergarten students in need of intensive intervention according to the national norms exceeded 50%. Hit rates were calculated to represent the percentage of students who were selected for strategic, small group reading intervention (tier 2) and individualized, intensive reading intervention (tier 3) appropriately.

The effects of the reading intervention on student progress were evaluated by calculating individual student growth or rates of improvement over time compared to expected rates of growth based on empirically based benchmarks. The performance of students who received strategic and intensive interventions were compared to expected rates of growth for students in need of tier 2 and tier 3 interventions. Rates of improvement for students served by the core instruction were compared to expected rates of improvement for students in tier 1. Mean rates of improvement were calculated for each measure at each grade level for each school. An example of the visual display is provided in Figure 6.1.

Cost-Effectiveness Analysis

The objective costs of a multitiered reading intervention program consist of any objectively measurable resource (i.e., time and money) consumed as a result of

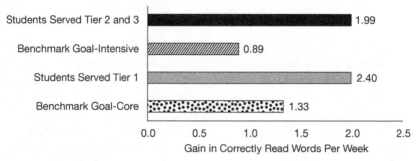

Figure 6.1. Mean Rate of Improvement on DIBELS Next: Oral Reading Fluency for Grade 1 Students Served in the Pilot Project Relative to Expected Rates of Improvement

implementing an intervention. Cost analysis of schoolwide systems of positive behavior support have used two time-based indices of cost (i.e., instructional time saved and school personnel time saved) to evaluate the cost-effectiveness of positive behavior support (Barrett & Scott, 2006; Scott & Barrett, 2004). For the Dyslexia Pilot Project, teacher time, or the amount of time a teacher is being diverted from other activities to provide intensive, individualized (tier 3) intervention, was used as an objective metric of a resource used. Teacher time meets the characteristics of a metric for determining hard costs as it is (a) objectively based, (b) easy to measure and quantify, (c) relatively easy to assign monetary value to, and (d) has credibility with administrators (Phillips & Stone, 2002). As such, teacher time has been recommended as a metric to calculate the hard costs of academic and behavioral interventions in the intervention research literature (Noell & Gresham, 1993).

In the evaluation of the Dyslexia Pilot Project, teachers' salaries (and the number of calendar days under contract) were obtained from the state treasurer's website for kindergarten to grade 2 teachers, intervention specialists, and Title I teachers listed on each school's website. A day rate and an hourly rate were calculated for each teacher and the median hourly rate was determined for each school district participating in the Dyslexia Pilot Project. The median hourly rate for teachers' salaries ranged from $38.87 per hour (for a 183-day contract) for teachers in one rural school district to $50.14 per hour (for a 191-day contract) for teachers in the large urban school district. The teacher time cost metric was used to calculate cost based on the median hourly rate multiplied by the number of minutes (converted to hours) of intervention provided weekly multiplied by the student unit (i.e., number of students served divided by the student-teacher ratio for small group interventions). The teacher time metric was calculated for tier 3 interventions at each grade level. For students receiving tier 2 interventions who demonstrated a rate of improvement that exceeded the expected rate of improvement based on DIBELS benchmark goals, the reduction in risk precluded the need for more intensive (and costly) tier 3 interventions. To evaluate the cost-effectiveness of the Dyslexia Pilot Project, an analysis of the effectiveness of the school districts' capacity over the 3 years of the Dyslexia Pilot Project to meet students' needs (see Figure 6.2) was coupled with the projected cost savings in year 3 (see Table 6.1).

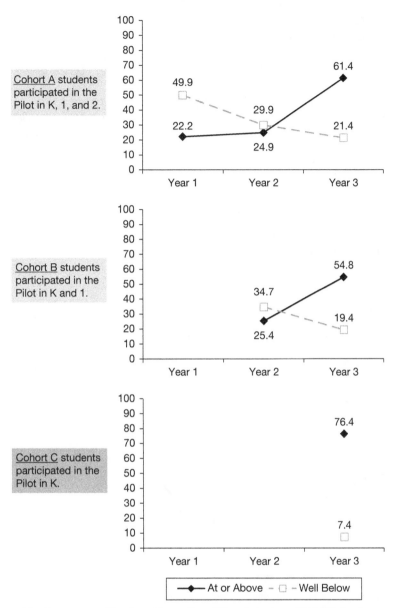

Cohort A students participated in the Pilot in K, 1, and 2.

Cohort B students participated in the Pilot in K and 1.

Cohort C students participated in the Pilot in K.

—◆— At or Above – ☐ – Well Below

Figure 6.2. Percentage of Students "At or Above" Benchmark and "Well Below" Benchmark at the End of Each School Year Over the Course of the Three-Year Dyslexia Pilot Project

NOTE: Outcomes represent the performance of students in the five school districts with adequate implementation fidelity. Cohort A counts were 595 (year 1), 598 (year 2), and 569 (year 3). Cohort B counts were 710 (year 2) and 697 (year 3). The Cohort C count was 639 (year 3).

Table 6.1 PROJECTED COST SAVINGS OF PRECLUDING THE NEED FOR INTENSIVE, INDIVIDUALIZED INTERVENTIONS FOR STUDENTS EXCEEDING THE EXPECTED RATE OF IMPROVEMENT WITH STRATEGIC INTERVENTIONS (I.E., THE DIFFERENCE IN COSTS BETWEEN TIER 2 AND TIER 3 INTERVENTIONS)

	Number and Percentage of Students with a Measureable Reduction of Reading Failure Risk at Tier 2		Costs Savings (in Teacher Time) of Tier 3 Interventions Not Incurred
Large Urban			
Kindergarten	15	93.8%	$16,922.25
Grade 1	67	72.8%	$75,586.05
Grade 2	8	47.1%	$9,025.20
			$101,533.50
Small Rural #1			
Kindergarten	7	100%	$10,857.00
Grade 1	21	100%	$32,571.00
Grade 2	12	80.0%	$18,612.00
			$62,040.00
Small Rural #2			
Kindergarten	18	85.7%	$23,078.88
Grade 1	58	74.4%	$74,365.28
Grade 2	28	66.7%	$35,900.48
			$133,344.64
Small Rural #3			
Kindergarten	10	100%	$4,372.88
Grade 1	26	83.9%	$11,369.48
Grade 2	13	68.4%	$5,684.74
			$21,427.09
Small Rural #4			
Kindergarten	4	100%	$2,803.20
Grade 1	10	62.5%	$7,008.00
Grade 2	1	10.0%	$700.80
			$10,512.00

Assuming meaningful gains in student rates of improvement are sustained with the initial Dyslexia Pilot Project investment, all of the school districts over time will have cost savings that exceed the initial investment in teacher professional development, intervention materials, and infrastructure for a tiered system of reading interventions and supports.

Case Study 1 Takeaway

The use of evaluation methods, including the analysis of cost-effectiveness, can help district and building leaders make data-based decision regarding the effective use of prevention and early intervention practices on the system as a whole. By analyzing the cost effectiveness of their school's tiered intervention services, educators can advocate for strengthening and sustaining their building's MTSS efforts in the face of tight budgets and public exchanges regarding the effectiveness of MTSS (Balu, Zhu, Doolittle, Schiller, Jenkins, & Gersten, 2015; VanDerHeyden et al., 2016).

This approach to analyzing cost-effectiveness isolated the cost savings of having more effective tier 2 interventions in place for students who were at risk for reading failure. It did not account for the impact of strengthening the core curriculum and instruction (tier 1), which would preclude the need for more costly strategic (tier 2) interventions. This approach to quantifying costs also focused exclusively on teacher time as a hard cost of providing tiered interventions. In doing so, this cost analysis did not account for the soft costs, which can be more difficult to measure directly and convert into monetary values. The soft costs for evaluating intervention cost-savings might include students' increases in self-efficacy for meeting academic or behavior expectations, decreases in absenteeism, as well as teachers' increases self-efficacy for teaching, decreases in absenteeism, and decreases in teacher burnout and turnover.

CASE STUDY 2: SUMMARIZING ACADEMIC AND BEHAVIOR INTERVENTION OUTCOMES USING SINGLE-CASE DESIGNS

At its very core, an MTSS framework involves measuring students' progress in response to evidence-based interventions matched to each student's needs and implemented with fidelity. An evaluation of an MTSS framework must be designed to assess the outcomes obtained by the academic and behavioral interventions delivered throughout the program year. Given the diverse needs of students, a continuum of supports and increasingly intensive interventions are needed to ensure that no students fall through the cracks. One challenge of evaluating an MTSS initiative is finding a way to capture and all of the outcomes for a variety of academic and behavioral interventions provided across the three tiers. In this second case study, we highlight how single-case designs can be used to evaluate and aggregate intervention outcomes across schools in a state-wide evaluation.

Single-case designs are widely considered to be one of the best methods for evaluating intervention effectiveness and linking educators' efforts to student growth over time (Bloom, Fischer, & Orme, 2005). When used in practice in schools, single-case designs (i.e., A-B designs) involve repeated measures to establish a student's baseline level of performance. A minimum of three baseline data points is considered desirable to document that the performance of the behavior or skill being targeted is stable. Once the baseline level of performance is established, an intervention is implemented and ongoing progress monitoring data are gathered (Steege, Brown-Chidsey, & Mace, 2002). Single-case design data are displayed visually in a line graph to discern whether there have been changes in trend, level, or variability.

An important distinction needs to be made between single-case designs (e.g., A-B designs, also known as accountability designs) used in practice to document intervention outcomes and more rigorous single-case designs (e.g., A-B-A or A-B-A-B designs) used in research. In research, rigorous experimental designs are required to establish the internal validity of a novel intervention approach if the new intervention is to be disseminated as evidence-based (Brown-Chidsey, Steege, & Mace, 2008). By contrast, accountability for practice involves document-ing the delivery of well-established, research-based intervention approaches and assessing their effectiveness. To illustrate this distinction, consider the primary care physician who is expected to show that her recommended treatments had the desired effects over time for a variety of concerns for professional account-ability purposes. She is not obligated, however, to conduct double-blind randomly controlled trials with her patients as part of her professional practice (Morrison, 2013). As such, single-case accountability designs play an important role in the overall framework of evidence-based practices (Kazdin, 1981). Furthermore, aggregating single-case design outcome data can be aggregated across a number of interventionists (Burns, 2015), which can be particularly valuable for program evaluation.

The Statewide Internship Program in School Psychology

The Internship Program in School Psychology is a collaboration among the state department of education and nine school psychology graduate preparation pro-grams. Nearly 100 school psychology graduate students complete their internships each year in the state-funded Internship Program. Emphases in accountability for school psychological services and shifts toward evidence-based intervention deci-sions led to the development of a model of the evaluation of the state-wide intern-ship experience with regard to outcomes for schools and students (Morrison et al., 2011; Morrison, Graden, & Barnett, 2009).

A primary component of the evaluation of the Internship Program involved determining the impact of intervention services on student outcomes using a standard single-case design approach. Each intern submitted data for six interventions—that is, three academic interventions (tiers 1–3) and three social/behavior interventions (tiers 1—3), judged by the intern to be exemplars of the support services provided during their internship year. Goal attainment scaling was the primary method used for summarizing intervention outcomes for stu-dents supported by school psychology interns. The PND points and effect size served as supplements to goal attainment scaling.

Description of Interventions Provided

Nearly 100 interns annually provided descriptive information regarding the six interventions they selected to include in the statewide evaluation of the Internship

❑   Direct instruction, which may include modeling and prompting

❑   Improving the quality of instructional materials

❑   Improving the quality of the instructional context
      (i.e., modifications to the instructional environment)

❑   Establish/review rules + reinforcement

❑   Practice/increase productive practice

❑   Strengthen reinforcement contingencies (positive reinforcement)

❑   Contingency contracting/behavioral contracting

❑   Self-management

❑   Differential reinforcement of appropriate behaviors

❑   Response cost procedures for inappropriate behaviors

❑   Group contingencies

❑   Token economy

❑   Other (please specify): _____

Figure 6.3. Checklist for Identifying the Core Components of an Intervention

Program. For each intervention, interns were asked to identify the core components of the intervention by selecting as many as applied from among those provided in a checklist (see Figure 6.3). Interns were also asked to provide the name of the school, agency, or clinic in which the intervention was delivered, the intervention provider (e.g., classroom teacher, school psychology intern, school psychologist, paraprofessional/teacher aide, tutor, parent), the number of students served (for tier 1 and tier 2 interventions and supports only), the grade level(s) of the target student(s), the number of weeks of implementation, and the average number of hours per week. In addition, interns were asked to report on the intervention adherence for each intervention. Interns reported the method they used to assess intervention adherence, give the following options: (a) procedural checklist: self-reported by interventionist, (b) procedural checklist: independent observer, (c) permanent product review, or (d) intervention adherence was not measured. Interns also identified how often intervention adherence was measured and provided a brief description of their evidence of intervention adherence.

Impact on Student Outcomes

Standard methods for aggregating single-case design outcome data were used to evaluate the impact of more than 500 academic and behavioral interventions provided each school year by school psychology interns participating in the Internship in School Psychology. All interns were required to summarize and report their intervention outcomes using goal attainment scaling. Summary statistics, namely the PND points and effect size, were used to supplement the goal attainment scaling ratings. Additional information regarding goal attainment scaling ratings, the PND points, and effect size is provided in this section.

Goal Attainment Scaling

The goal attainment scaling process involved the development of a five-point scale for measuring goal attainment based on the work of Kiresuk, Smith, and Cardillo (1994). The basic methodology of goal attainment scaling involves (a) the selection of the target behavior; (b) a specific, observable, measurable description of the desired intervention outcome; and (c) the development of five descriptions of that target behavior scaled to approximate varied levels of attainment of the desired outcome (Sladeczek, Elliott, Kratochwill, Robertson-Mjaanes, & Stoiber, 2001). In this application of goal attainment scaling, the scale was anchored on the descriptor of "No Change" with positive ratings reflecting a positive change in the target behavior (i.e., "Somewhat More Than Expected" and "Much More Than Expected") and negative ratings reflecting a change in an undesired direction for the target behavior (i.e., "Somewhat Less Than Expected" and "Much Less Than Expected").

The guidelines used for goal attainment scaling of intervention outcomes in this evaluation are provided in Boxes 6.1 and 6.2. Sample scale descriptors for

---

Box 6.1

GUIDELINES FOR DEVELOPING AND SCALING INTERVENTION GOALS USING GOAL ATTAINMENT SCALING

STEP 1. **Identify the Current Level of Performance for the Target Behavior and Specify "No Change"**
- The current level of performance should be based on baseline data.
- Given the current level of performance, determine how the student will likely perform if no intervention is provided or if an intervention had no impact.

STEP 2. **Specify a "Somewhat More" than Expected Level of Outcome**
A "Somewhat More" than Expected Level should be:
- Based on expected rates of improvement given the baseline data, number of weeks of intervention, and benchmark or empirically derived goal
- Realistically ambitious, based on what the student will likely achieve by the end of the intervention
- Take into consideration the usual outcomes of this intervention, the resources of the student, the amount of time planned for intervention, and the skills of the intervention specialist/change agent
- Socially valid (i.e., acceptable to teachers, parents, and the student)
- Stated in the positive (i.e., promoting replacement behaviors)

Box 6.1 (Continued)

Consider also the following:
- Relevance: Is the goal relevant to the student's present situation?
- Availability of Services: Are the intervention services necessary to attain this goal available?
- Scale Realism: Is the expected level of outcome realistic for this student at this time with this intervention?

STEP 3. **Specify the "Somewhat Less" Than Expected Level of Outcome**
- Provide an observable, measurable description of an outcome that is less favorable than what would be expected if there was no change in the current level of performance.
- This description is less likely to occur for this student than the "No Change" outcome but still represents reasonable outcome.

STEP 4. **Specify the "Much More" and "Much Less" Than Expected Levels of Outcome**
- Complete the extreme levels of the scale with descriptions of the indicators that are "much more" and "much less" favorable outcomes than can be realistically envisioned for the student.
- Each extreme level represents the outcome that might be expected to occur in 5% to 10% of similar at-risk students.

Box 6.2

SPOTLIGHT ON GOAL ATTAINMENT SCALING

As a method for setting, monitoring, and evaluating goals, goal attainment scaling has many appealing features. Goal attainment scaling involves systematic rigor in terms of assessment and yet is flexible enough to be applied to the scaling of a various content domains (Sladeczek et al., 2001). It has been found to be responsive to measuring diverse functional goals across services and sensitive to measuring intervention-inducted change, making it a strong outcome measure for groups of students where the rate of progress varies (MacKay, McCool, Cheseldine, & McCartney, 1993). Goal attainment scaling is also an easy to use for method for outcome determination that is both inexpensive and time efficient. A summary of the research regarding the utility and acceptability of goal attainment scaling for measuring students' progress can be found in Roach and Elliott (2005).

an academic intervention and a behavior intervention are presented in Table 6.2. The goal attainment scaling data can be displayed in the aggregate across a variety of interventions addressing a wide range of target behaviors (see Figure 6.4 for a graph of tier 2 behavior intervention outcomes).

Table 6.2 EXAMPLES OF GOAL ATTAINMENT SCALING APPLIED TO AN ACADEMIC
INTERVENTION GOAL AND A BEHAVIOR INTERVENTION GOAL

Level of Goal Attainment	Academic Intervention Example: Target Behavior: Oral Reading Fluency	Behavior Intervention Example Target Behavior: Aggression (hitting)
−2 Much less than expected	*Marquis will read fewer than 50 words correctly in 1 minute with Grade 2 reading passages.*	*Josh will demonstrate no aggressive bouts per week.*
−1 Somewhat less than expected	*Marquis will read 50 words correctly in 1 minute with Grade 2 reading passages.*	*Josh will demonstrate one to two aggressive bouts per week.*
0 No change	*Marquis will read 59 words correctly in 1 minute with Grade 2 reading passages.*	*Josh will demonstrate two to three aggressive bouts per week.*
+1 Somewhat more than expected	*Marquis will read 70 words correctly in 1 minute with Grade 2 reading passages.*	*Josh will demonstrate four aggressive bouts per week.*
+2 Much more than expected	*Marquis will read 87 or more words correctly in 1 minute with Grade 2 reading passages.*	*Josh will demonstrate five or more aggressive bouts per week.*

Percentage of Nonoverlapping Data

Calculating the PND involves counting the number of intervention data points
that exceed the highest baseline point (for studies seeking to increase a target
behavior) or counting the number of intervention data points lower than the

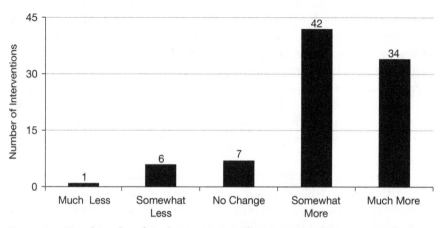

Figure 6.4. Visual Display of Goal Attainment Scaling Outcomes for 90 Tier 2 Behavior
Interventions

lowest baseline point (for studies seeking to decrease a target behavior). The number of nonoverlapping data points is then divided by the total number of intervention points to obtain the PND. Intervention effectiveness is interpreted using the following scale: a PND greater than or equal to 90% is considered "Highly Effective," a PND of 70% to less than 90% is judged as "Moderately Effective," a PND of 50% to less than 70% is considered "Mildly Effective," and a PND of less than 50% is rated as "Ineffective" (Scruggs, Mastropieri, Cook, & Escobar, 1986). PND should not be calculated when there are extreme scores in the baseline data (i.e., one or more extremely low baseline data points for a target behavior to be decreased or one or more extremely high baseline data points for a target behavior to be increased; Scruggs & Mastropieri, 1998; Scruggs, Mastropieri, & Casto, 1987). PND should also not be used when there is a clear trend in the data, as would be the case when there is a positive slope for skill fluency gains. In this evaluation of the Internship Program in School Psychology, PND was used as a supplemental summary statistic for behavioral interventions. PND was not recommended for use with academic interventions where the summary statistic would be confounded with expected academic skill fluency gains.

The use of PND as a summary statistic has wide support in the research literature because it is easy to calculate and interpret and it yields results that are consistent with the outcomes obtained through visual analysis of individual participant graphs and other summary statistics for single-case designs (Mathur, Kavale, Quinn, Forness, & Rutherford, 1998; Olive & Smith, 2005). The percentage of data points exceeding the median (PEM) is a variation of PND that accounts for data points in the baseline phase that have reached the ceiling or floor level, which would render the PND to be 0% (Ma, 2006). PEM also accounts for the fact that in the absence of an intervention effect, the intervention data points will fluctuate around the baseline median.

Effect Size

Effect size (ES) is a statistic that describes the magnitude of an effect on a standard scale. It is useful for comparing studies that use different outcome measures for similar interventions (National Center for Education Research, 2015). There are many ES estimation methods (Busk & Serlin, 1992; Thompson, 2007). In this evaluation, the standard mean difference was calculated by determining the difference between the mean baseline and mean intervention and then dividing by the standard deviation of the baseline (Busk & Serlin, 1992). ES is interpreted such that an intervention that yields an ES greater than or equal to 0.80 is considered to have a large effect; an ES between 0.50 and 0.79 represents a moderate effect, whereas an ES between 0.20 and 0.49 reflects a small effect. As a summary statistic, ES is well supported by the research literature because it is relatively easy to calculate and it yields results that are consistent with other summary statistics for single-case designs (Olive & Smith, 2005).

Table 6.3 SUPPORTING EVIDENCE FROM SUMMARY STATISTICS FOR ACADEMIC AND BEHAVIOR INTERVENTIONS SERVED IN THE OHIO INTERNSHIP IN SCHOOL PSYCHOLOGY

	Summary Statistic	Number of Interventions	Statistic Value	Interpretation
TIER 1: UNIVERSAL SUPPORTS				
Academic	ES	59	1.1	"Large Effect"
Behavior	ES	65	1.0	"Large Effect"
	PND	72	78.1%	"Moderately Effective"
TIER 2: TARGETED INTERVENTIONS				
Academic	ES	63	1.3	"Large Effect"
Behavior	ES	55	2.6	"Large Effect"
	PND	72	73.7%	"Moderately Effective"
TIER 3: INDIVIDUAL INTERVENTIONS				
Academic	ES	61	1.2	"Large Effect"
Behavior	ES	65	1.2	"Large Effect"
	PND	83	72.3%	"Mildly Effective"

NOTE: ES = effect size; PND = percentage of nonoverlapping data.

Case Study 2 Takeaway

Single-case designs are essential for determining the effects of an intervention in both research and practice. Single-case designs can also be used to evaluate the collective impact of a system of supports that provides academic and behavioral interventions to address a wide range of target behaviors at individual, small group, classwide, or buildingwide levels. Goal attainment scaling and summary statistics, such as the PND points and ES, provide the means for aggregating intervention outcomes over time and across settings to determine the merit and worth of a service delivery initiative and to inform its continuous improvement. These standard methods for summarizing intervention outcomes using single-case design data can be used to communicate results in a simple graph or chart that can be readily understood by teachers, staff, and school and district administrators (see Figure 6.4 and Table 6.3).

CASE STUDY 3: EVALUATING FIDELITY OF IMPLEMENTATION FOR TEACHER-BASED TEAMS' USE OF DATA-BASED DECISION MAKING AND INSTRUCTIONAL PLANNING

The implementation of an MTSS framework requires a degree of expertise and collaboration that necessitates the development of a variety of team structures at various levels—classroom, grade, school, and district (McIntosh & Goodman, 2016). Teacher teams are critical for expanding the knowledge, skills, and shared accountability needed to ensure that a system has the capacity of implement and sustain MTSS. Teacher-based teams, also known as grade-level teams, teacher learning teams, or teacher inquiry teams, are charged with evaluating the effects of instructional practices supporting all students within their specific grade and classrooms with a focus on continuous improvement and consistency across classrooms (McIntosh & Goodman, 2016). To this end, teacher-based teams use a structured, sequential, problem-solving process with an inquiry or continuous improvement focus in which teachers set and share an explicit goal for student learning, jointly plan instruction to address it, implement the plan, use common formative assessments to monitor progress, and either move on to a new shared goal or cycle back if the current goal had not been reached (Bird & Little, 1986; Gallimore, Ermeling, Saunders, & Goldenberg, 2009; Little, 1982). Previous research has shown that engaging teachers in collaborative teaming through the use of protocol-driven discussions of student work contributes to active teacher learning (Horn & Little, 2010), changes in instructional practices (Desimone, Porter, Garet, Yoon, & Birman, 2002), and increases in student achievement across subject areas (Jackson & Bruegmann, 2009; Koedel, 2009).

Evaluating the effectiveness of teacher-based teams could help identify targets for future professional learning that would advance teachers' use of data-driven problem solving and build the school's capacity for meeting the needs of all learners. Most of what is known about teachers' use of team-based problem-solving comes from the research on multidisciplinary problem-solving teams (Collier-Meek, Fallon, Sanetti, & Maggin, 2013) and schoolwide positive behavior support teams (Algozzine, Newton, Horner, Todd, & Algozzine, 2012; Sugai & Horner, 2009; Sugai et al., 2010; Todd et al., 2011). Aside from the Decision, Observation, Recording, and Analysis (DORA) for use with schoolwide behavior support teams (Algozzine et al., 2012) and implementation checklist for problem-solving teams developed by Burns, Wiley, and Viglietta (2008), however, instruments for measuring the data-based decision making and instructional planning practices of teachers in teams are scarce and sorely needed.

Early research on problem-solving team functioning reported inconsistent implementation fidelity (Bartels & Mortenson, 2005; Buck, Polloway, Smith-Thomas, & Cook, 2003; Burns & Symington, 2002), likely due to a lack of familiarity with the problem-solving procedures and a perception among the teachers that the process was complex and inefficient (Doll et al., 2005). In the interest of assessing and promoting implementation fidelity among problem-solving teams, Burns, Wiley, and Viglietta (2008) developed a 20-item implementation checklist detailing the core components of a team-based problem-solving process identified in the literature (Bahr & Kovaleski, 2006; Kovaleski, 2002; Minneapolis Public Schools, 2002; Rosenfield & Gravois, 1996). When used to examine implementation fidelity among problem-solving teams across three elementary schools, the results indicated that problem-solving teams did not consistently use data to monitor student progress, assess intervention effectiveness, or measure intervention adherence even after receiving performance feedback, although improvements were noted with the application of performance feedback (Burns, Peters, & Noell, 2008).

The Ohio Improvement Process and the Teacher-Based Team Five-Step Process

The Ohio Improvement Process is a statewide school improvement initiative that involves the use of structures and processes for data-based decision making to guide instructional planning and promote shared accountability among teams at the district, building, and teacher level. At the teacher level, teacher-based teams engaged in a cyclical, protocol-driven, problem-solving process that consists of five steps:

Step 1: Collect and chart data
Step 2: Analyze data
Step 3: Establish share expectations for implementing specific changes
Step 4: Implement changes consistently
Step 5: Collect, chart and analyze post data

A primary focus of the evaluation of the Ohio Improvement Process centers on the degree to which teacher-based teams implement the Five-Step Process with fidelity.

Method for Measuring Implementation Fidelity of Teacher-Based Teams

Methods most commonly used for assessing implementation fidelity include direct observation, self-reporting, and the use of permanent products (Sanetti & Collier-Meek, 2014; Sheridan, Swanger-Gagné, Welch, Kwon, & Garbacz, 2009). Although direct observation conducted by an independent observer is considered to be the "gold standard" for assessing the degree to which an academic or behavioral intervention is implemented as planned (Noell, 2008; Sanetti, Chafouleas, Christ, & Gritter, 2009), it may not be the method of choice for assessing implementation fidelity of teacher-based teams because one would not likely be able to observe all of the steps of a problem-solving protocol on one occasion. Direct observations are also resource intensive because they require independent observers to be available at designed times of the day and week to conduct multiple observations to ensure a representative sample of teacher practices. Direct observations may produce reactivity among teachers being observed participating in their teacher-based team and recent research has called into question how the scheduling of observations in schools (i.e., the day of the week, month of the year, and duration of the observation) can unduly influence the data gathered (Cash & Pianta, 2014). Furthermore, the vast majority of direct observations only gather evidence of adherence and neglect to measure quality or quantity dimensions of implementation (e.g., Gansle & McMahon, 1997; Noell, Duhon, Gatti, & Connell, 2002; Sanetti & Kratochwill, 2011).

As an alternative to direct observation, self-report measures assess implementation fidelity from the perspective of the individual responsible for implementing the intended practice. Self-report measures are typically structured as a written checklist of the steps of the intended practice as an estimate of the dimension of adherence. Although self-report requires fewer human and material resources than direct observation, several researchers have noted that self-reports tend to produce overestimates of intervention implementation by teachers (Lane, 2007; Noell, 2008; Sanetti et al., 2009; Wickstrom, Jones, LaFleur, & Witt, 1998). On the contrary, Sanetti and Kratochwill (2009) reported a high level of agreement between self-report and permanent product review. In light of these mixed findings, it is recommended that self-report not be used as the sole method for measuring fidelity (Noell, 2008; Sanetti et al., 2009; Sanetti & Collier-Meek, 2014).

A permanent product review is yet another method for assessing implementation fidelity. Permanent product reviews involve assessing implementation via written records/protocols or other products as indications of implementation (Sanetti & Collier-Meek, 2014; Sheridan et al., 2009). A permanent product review has several advantages over direct observation and self-report methods for assessing the implementation of a teacher-based team process in that it is a relatively simple measurement procedure that allows an independent evaluator to gather data on the implementation of a team process in its entirety. Given that fidelity estimates are based on tangible evidence, permanent product review functions best when there are permanent products generated for every step in the intervention protocol (Sanetti & Collier-Meek, 2014). A permanent product review does not produce reactivity among teachers or require additional work on the part of the teachers (i.e., teachers should be directed to *not* create new documents in anticipation of the review). Like direct observations, the majority of permanent product reviews only examine evidence of adherence (e.g., Gansle & McMahon, 1997; Noell et al., 2002; Sanetti & Kratochwill, 2011). In the evaluation featured in Case Study 3, a permanent product review was used for assessing the implementation fidelity of teacher-based teams' use of a structured protocol for data-driven problem solving across all three dimensions of fidelity: adherence, quality, and quantity.

The Teacher-Based Team Fidelity of Implementation Tool

The Teacher-Based Team Fidelity of Implementation Tool (FIT) was composed of 15 items designed to assess teacher-based teams' use of data-based decision making practices for instructional planning and intervention design (see Box 6.3). The

Box 6.3

TEACHER-BASED TEAM (TBT) FIDELITY OF IMPLEMENTATION (FIT) ITEMS

STEP 1: **Collect and Chart Data**

1.1. Common assessments of students are in place to monitor core instruction outcomes formatively.

1.2. Common formative assessments align to the instructional standards.

1.3. Common formative assessment data are collected for *all* students supported by this TBT.

1.4. Common formative assessment data are used to identify current level *and* expected level of student performance (e.g., benchmark, criterion for student mastery).

STEP 2: **Analyze Data**

2.1. Common formative assessment data are used to identify student or instructional need based on the gap between actual performance and expected level of performance.

2.2. TBT members identify obstacles, common errors and patterns in students' responding for this particular task/skill by grade level, subject area, and/or student subgroup.

2.3. Learner-centered problem(s) or problems of understanding common to many students is/are prioritized.

STEP 3: **Establish Shared Expectations for Implementing Specific Changes**

3.1. TBT members plan and implement their core instruction to address the student performance problem prioritized in Step 2.

3.2. TBT members identify strategies previously used and their outcomes.

3.3. A core instructional support, targeted intervention, or intensive, individual intervention is (a) developed collaboratively, (b) linked to specific standards and utilized with the intended rigor, and (c) uses research-based practices to accelerate learning and/or increase student engagement for the target student(s).

3.4. A written plan details intended implementation (i.e., who, what, when, how long/how frequent, where, how) of the core instruction, core instructional support, targeted intervention, or intensive, individual intervention.

STEP 4: **Implement Changes Consistently**

4.1. The TBT identifies what will be monitored in the classroom (i.e., teacher practices, student performances) to ensure implementation fidelity among the team members.

Box 6.3 (Continued)

STEP 5: **Collect, Chart and Analyze Postdata**

5.1. With the intervention/instructional support in place, common formative assessment data are used to identify changes in student performance relative to the expected level of performance.

5.2. With the intervention/instructional support in place, common formative assessment data are used to identify changes in student performance disaggregated by subgroup.

5.3. The direct relationship between adult implementation of the instructional support/intervention and its impact on student performance is determined using data.

---

items were culled from the state's structured protocol for the five-step teacher-based team process. Developed as a permanent product review, the Teacher-Based Team FIT is administered by an external consultant who meets with the team for approximately 45 to 50 minutes. For each of the items on the Teacher-Based Team FIT, the consultant asks the team members to describe how their team performs this specific practice and refer to team documents (e.g., student outcome data, team meeting notes on the five-step process form) to illustrate their efforts. After meeting with the team, the consultant reviews the documentation for each step and assigns a level of adherence rating for that step using the following scale: Implemented as intended ("2"), Implemented with deviation ("1"), and Not implemented ("0").

Two to four indicators of quality were developed for each step to feature desired data-based decision making practices that were not identified as an expected practice in the five-step structured protocol for teacher-based teams. Examples of the indicators of quality included common formative assessment data are displayed in a chart or graph (e.g., line graph or bar graph), a hypothesis is developed regarding how and why the concern is the student work exists, and interventions and supports are appropriately matched to level of intensity based on data. In addition to the level of adherence ratings and indicators of quality checklists, teacher team members were asked to report how often the team was scheduled to meet (i.e., how many times a week for how long?) to assess the quantity of the team's implementation.

The technical adequacy of the Teacher-Based Team FIT was established through its use with 43 teacher-based teams from 16 school districts representing urban, suburban, and rural regions. Teacher-based teams were selected by district leaders from among 29 school buildings. Eighteen teams were located in elementary schools, 7 teams were in middle schools, and 4 teams were selected at the high school level. Interrater agreement was measured by comparing the independent ratings of two consultants. The overall percentage of interrater agreement for the

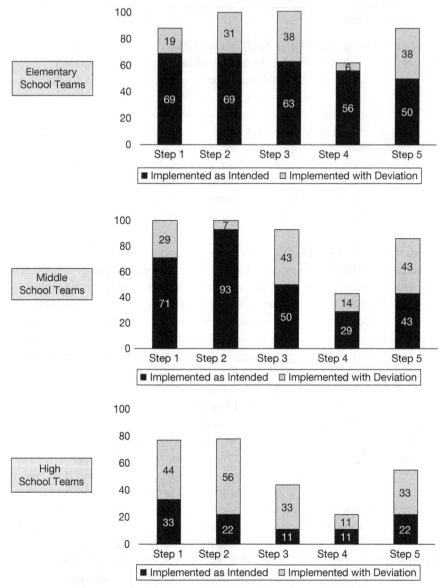

Figure 6.5. Percentage of Teacher-Based Team (TBTs) Implementing Each Step as Intended or with Deviation

level of adherence for each step was as follows: Step 1 (94.1%), Step 2 (90.2%), Step 3 (92.2%), Step 4 (90.2%), and Step 5 (88.2%). The percentage of interrater agreement for the level of quality was based on the independent ratings for the indicators of quality for each step: Step 1 (97.1% across four indicators), Step 2 (98.4% across three indicators), Step 3 (95.3% across two indicators), Step 4 (100% across two indicators), and Step 5 (96.6% across three indicators).

Teacher-Based Team FIT Outcomes

In year 4 of the Ohio Improvement Process initiative, the Teacher-Based Team FIT was completed with 39 teacher-based teams from 10 school districts serving students in urban, suburban, and rural regions of the state. Adherence to the Five-Step Process was highest among the 16 elementary school teams and lowest among the 9 high school teams (see Figure 6.5). At all of the grade levels, teams demonstrated higher levels of adherence for Step 1 (Collect and Chart Data), Step 2 (Analyze Data), and Step 5 (Collect, Chart, and Analyze Postdata). Levels of adherence were lower for Step 3 (Establish Shared Expectations for Implementing Specific Changes). Teacher-based teams demonstrated the lowest levels of adherence for Step 4 (Implement Changes Consistently).

Implementation fidelity quality was evaluated using the indicators of quality corresponding to each step in the five-step structured protocol for the 39 teacher-based teams. The results are presented in Table 6.4.

The quantity dimension of implementation fidelity was assessed by recording the amount of scheduled teacher-based team time reserved for each team (i.e., duration in minutes per week). Among the 39 teams, the scheduled meeting time ranged from 15 minutes (30 minutes every 2 weeks) to 80 minutes (40 minutes twice a week). Sixty-nine percent of the teams met weekly. The median scheduled meeting time was 45 minutes per week.

Case Study 3 Takeaway

Teacher team-based problem solving is a cornerstone of an MTSS and a variety of other school improvement initiatives. However, team-based problem solving requires a proficiency in data-based decision making that many teachers have not had the opportunity to develop. In fact, despite the prevalence of teaming in schools, very little is known about the extent to which teachers follow systematic steps during team meetings (Algozzine et al., 2012). Assessing the implementation fidelity of teacher teams could provide critical information for the evaluation and continuous improvement of a school's MTSS implementation efforts.

In this case study, we described the use of a permanent product review for assessing the implementation fidelity of teacher-based teams' use of a structured protocol for data-driven problem solving to address all three dimensions of fidelity: adherence, quality, and quantity. Although the items were culled directly from the structured protocol used by the Ohio Improvement Process, the tool could be adapted for use with a variety of team-based problem-solving protocols. Implementation adherence, quality, and quantity data were used to provide coaching feedback to teacher-based teams in the interest of increasing teams' fidelity of implementation and effectiveness in meeting students' needs. Implementation fidelity data were also used to inform the continuous improvement of the statewide initiative in terms of the professional learning supports (i.e., training and

Table 6.4. PERCENTAGE OF TEACHER-BASED TEAMS WITH EACH INDICATORS OF QUALITY EVIDENT

Indicators of Quality	Percentage of Teams
STEP 1: COLLECT AND CHART DATA	
1a. Common formative assessment data are summarized on a timely basis (within 1 week of assessment).	66.7%
1b. Step 1: Collect and Chart Data is completed at least once monthly.	74.4%
1c. Common formative assessment is research-based, technically adequate (i.e., reliable, valid), and sensitive to student growth.	23.1%
1d. Common formative assessment data are displayed in a chart or graph (e.g., line graph, bar graph).	53.8%
STEP 2: ANALYZE DATA	
2a. A specific, data-based problem is established reflecting the gap between actual and expected performance.	66.7%
2b. A hypothesis is developed regarding how and why the concern in the student work exists.	59.0%
2c. A hypothesis focuses on alterable variables, that is, factors within the teacher's control or problems of practice.	64.1%
STEP 3: ESTABLISH SHARED EXPECTATIONS FOR IMPLEMENTING SPECIFIC CHANGES	
3a. Interventions and supports are functionally matched to student need, based on data.	46.2%
3b. Interventions and supports are appropriately matched to level of intensity, based on data.	48.8%
STEP 4: IMPLEMENT CHANGES CONSISTENTLY	
4a. Feedback plan was provided to teachers regarding their implementation of this intervention/instructional support on a timely basis (within 1 week of observation).	41.0%
4b. Specific feedback plan based on data was provided to teachers regarding their implementation of this intervention/ instructional support.	23.1%
STEP 5: COLLECT, CHART AND ANALYZE POST-DATA	
5a. Student progress monitoring measures are directly linked to the problem being addressed.	59.0%
5b. Student formative assessments are sensitive to changes in student growth.	51.3%
5c. Adult implementation data are linked to student formative assessment data.	15.4%

coaching) teachers needed to advance their practices in data-based decision making and instructional planning.

IN CONCLUSION

Innovative applications of evaluation methods and techniques are often born of necessity. When school-based professionals come together in the pursuit of better outcomes for students, questions often arise that can be addressed through program evaluation:

- How do we know what we are doing is as effective as it needs to be?
- Are we really implementing the practices as we intended?

In this chapter and throughout this book, we hope you have come to see sticky, real-world challenges as opportunities to advance evidence-based practice through program evaluation.

Program Evaluation Standards

JOINT COMMITTEE ON STANDARDS
FOR EDUCATIONAL EVALUATION

The Joint Committee on Standards for Educational Evaluation is a coalition of professional organizations in education and psychology that have interests in evaluation. The Joint Committee published standards for evaluators and consumers of evaluation to use to judge the quality of evaluation. The *Program Evaluation Standards* were first developed in 1981 and revised in 1994 and 2010.

UTILITY STANDARDS

The utility standards are intended to increase the extent to which program stakeholders find evaluation processes and products valuable in meeting their needs.

U1	**Evaluator Credibility**

Evaluations should be conducted by qualified people who establish and maintain credibility in the evaluation context.

U2	**Attention to Stakeholders**

Evaluations should devote attention to the full range of individuals and groups invested in the program and affected by its evaluation.

U3	**Negotiated Purposes**

Evaluation purposes should be identified and continually negotiated based on the needs of stakeholders.

U4	**Explicit Values**

Evaluations should clarify and specify the individual and cultural values underpinning purposes, processes, and judgments.

U5	Relevant Information

Evaluation information should serve the identified and emergent needs of stakeholders.

U6	Meaningful Processes and Products

Evaluations should construct activities, descriptions, and judgments in ways that encourage participants to rediscover, reinterpret, or revise their understandings and behaviors.

U7	Timely and Appropriate Communicating and Reporting

Evaluations should attend to the continuing information needs of their multiple audiences.

U8	Concern for Consequences and Influence

Evaluations should promote responsible and adaptive use while guarding against unintended negative consequences and misuse.

FEASIBILITY STANDARDS

The feasibility standards are intended to increase evaluation effectiveness and efficiency.

F1	Project Management

Evaluations should use effective project management strategies.

F2	Practical Procedures

Evaluation procedures should be practical and responsive to the way the program operates.

F3	Contextual Viability

Evaluations should recognize, monitor, and balance the cultural and political interests and needs of individuals and groups.

F4	Resource Use

Evaluations should use resources effectively and efficiently.

PROPRIETY STANDARDS

The propriety standards support what is proper, fair, legal, right, and just in evaluations.

P1	Responsive and Inclusive Orientation

Evaluations should be responsive to stakeholders and their communities.

P2	Formal Agreements

Evaluation agreements should be negotiated to make obligations explicit and take into account the needs, expectations, and cultural contexts of clients and other stakeholders.

P3	Human Rights and Respect

Evaluations should be designed and conducted to protect human and legal rights and maintain the dignity of participants and other stakeholders.

P4	Clarity and Fairness

Evaluations should be understandable and fair in addressing stakeholder needs and purposes.

P5	Transparency and Disclosure

Evaluations should provide complete descriptions of findings, limitations, and conclusions to all stakeholders, unless doing so would violate legal and propriety obligations.

P6	Conflicts of Interests

Evaluations should openly and honestly identify and address real or perceived conflicts of interests that may compromise the evaluation.

P7	Fiscal Responsibility

Evaluations should account for all expended resources and comply with sound fiscal procedures and processes.

P8	Concern for Consequences and Influence

Evaluations should promote responsible and adaptive use while guarding against unintended negative consequences and misuse.

ACCURACY STANDARDS

The accuracy standards are intended to increase the dependability and truthfulness of evaluation representations, propositions, and findings, especially those that support interpretations and judgments about quality.

A1	Justified Conclusions and Decisions

Evaluation conclusions and decisions should be explicitly justified in the cultures and contexts where they have consequences.

A2	Valid Information

Evaluation information should serve the intended purposes and support valid interpretations.

A3	**Reliable Information**

Evaluation procedures should yield sufficiently dependable and consistent information for the intended uses.

A4	**Explicit Program and Context Descriptions**

Evaluations should document programs and their contexts with appropriate detail and scope for the evaluation purposes.

A5	**Information Management**

Evaluations should employ systematic information collection, review, verification, and storage methods.

A6	**Sound Designs and Analyses**

Evaluations should employ technically adequate designs and analyses that are appropriate for the evaluation purposes.

A7	**Explicit Evaluation Reasoning**

Evaluation reasoning leading from information and analyses to findings, interpretations, conclusions, and judgments should be clearly and completely documented.

A8	**Communication and Reporting**

Evaluation communications should have adequate scope and guard against misconceptions, biases, distortions, and errors.

EVALUATION ACCOUNTABILITY STANDARDS

The evaluation accountability standards encourage adequate documentation of evaluations and a metaevaluative perspective focused on improvement and accountability for evaluation processes and products.

E1	**Evaluation Documentation**

Evaluations should fully document their negotiated purposes and implemented designs, procedures, data, and outcomes.

E2	**Internal Metaevaluation**

Evaluators should use these and other applicable standards to examine the accountability of the evaluation design, procedures employed, information collected, and outcomes.

E3	**External Metaevaluation**

Program evaluation sponsors, clients, evaluators, and other stakeholders should encourage the conduct of external metaevaluations using these and other applicable standards.

The Standards statements were reprinted with permission from the Joint Committee on Standards for Educational Evaluation. A full description of these statements can be found at Yarbrough, D. B., Shulha, L. M., Hopson, R. K., & Caruthers, F. A. (2011). *The program evaluation standards: A guide for evaluators and evaluation users* (3rd ed.). Thousand Oaks, CA: Sage.

Observation Checklist for High-Quality
Professional Development Training

The *Observation Checklist for High-Quality Professional Development* was designed to be completed by an observer to determine the level of quality of professional development training. It can also be used to provide ongoing feedback and coaching to individuals who provide professional development training. Furthermore, it can be used as a guidance document when designing or revising professional development. The tool represents a compilation of research-identified indicators that should be present in high-quality professional development. Professional development training with a maximum of one item missed per domain on the checklist can be considered high quality.

Context Information	
Date: _____	Location: _____
Topic: _____	Presenter: _____
Observer: _____	Role: _____

The professional development provider:	
Preparation	**Observed?** (Check if Yes)
1. Provides a description of the training with learning objectives prior to training • *EXAMPLE 1: Training description and objectives e-mailed to participants in advance* • *EXAMPLE 2: Training description and goals provided on registration website* • *EXAMPLE 3: Agenda including learning targets provided with materials via online file sharing before training*	☐

Preparation (*continued*)	Observed? (Check if Yes)
Evidence or example:	
2. Provides readings, activities, and/or questions in accessible formats to think about prior to the training • *EXAMPLE 1: Articles for prereading e-mailed to participants in advance* • *EXAMPLE 2: Book for prereading distributed to schools before training* • *EXAMPLE 3: Materials made available via online file sharing*	☐
Evidence or example:	
3. Provides an agenda (i.e., schedule of topics to be presented and times) before or at the beginning of the training • *EXAMPLE 1: Paper copy of agenda included in training packet for participants* • *EXAMPLE 2: Agenda included in pretraining e-mail*	☐
Evidence or example:	
4. Quickly establishes or builds on previously established rapport with participants • *EXAMPLE 1: Trainer gives own background, using humor to create warm atmosphere* • *EXAMPLE 2: Trainer praises group's existing skills and expertise to create trust* • *EXAMPLE 3: Trainer uses topical videos to break the ice with the audience*	☐
Evidence or example:	
Introduction	**Observed? (Check if Yes)**
5. Connects the topic to participants' context • *EXAMPLE 1: The state leader introducing the presenter explains that the topic is related to the initiative being implemented across the state* • *EXAMPLE 2: Trainer shows examples from classrooms, then asks participants to compare the examples to what happens in their school* • *EXAMPLE 3: Trainer shares participating district data profiles and asks participants to consider how the intervention might affect students*	☐
Evidence or example:	

Introduction (*continued*)	Observed? (Check if Yes)
6. Includes the empirical research foundation of the content • *EXAMPLE 1: Trainer provides a list of references supporting evidence-based practices* • *EXAMPLE 2: Citations to research are given during PowerPoint presentation* • *EXAMPLE 3: Trainer references key researchers and details their contributions to the training content during presentation*	☐
Evidence or example:	
7. Content builds on or relates to participants' previous professional development • *EXAMPLE 1: Trainer explains how intervention relates to other existing interventions within the state* • *EXAMPLE 2: Trainer refers to content provided in previous trainings within the sequence* • *EXAMPLE 3: Trainer uses participants' knowledge of other interventions to inform training*	☐
Evidence or example:	
8. Aligns with organizational standards or goals • *EXAMPLE 1: Trainer shows how the intervention fits in with the Elementary and Secondary Education Act and Individuals with Disabilities Education Act* • *EXAMPLE 2: Trainer discusses how the district selected this intervention for implementation as part of an improvement plan* • *EXAMPLE 3: Trainer refers to the program as part of a federally funded State Personnel Development Grant*	☐
Evidence or example:	
9. Emphasizes impact of content (e.g., student achievement, family engagement, client outcomes) • *EXAMPLE 1: Participants brainstorm the ways the intervention will impact students, especially students with disabilities* • *EXAMPLE 2: Trainer uses data to show that the intervention is shown to positively impact postschool outcomes and inclusion in the general education classroom for students with disabilities* • *EXAMPLE 3: Trainer shares research that shows that the use of the instructional strategies improved academic achievement for students*	☐
Evidence or example:	

Demonstration	Observed? (Check if Yes)
10. Builds shared vocabulary required to implement and sustain the practice • *EXAMPLE 1: Trainer has participants work together to formulate definitions of the intervention components and then goes over the definitions as a group* • *EXAMPLE 2: Trainer defines instructional practices according to established literature* • *EXAMPLE 3: Trainer introduces acronyms and mnemonics to help participants remember training content*	☐
Evidence or example:	
11. Provides examples of the content/practice in use (e.g., case study, vignette) • *EXAMPLE 1: Trainer provides video examples of the intervention in place within classrooms at different grade levels* • *EXAMPLE 2: Trainer provides hands-on demonstrations of how to use new technology tools* • *EXAMPLE 3: Trainer uses a case study to demonstrate how to implement the intervention*	☐
Evidence or example:	
12. Illustrates the applicability of the material, knowledge, or practice to the • *EXAMPLE 1: Trainer describes how the intervention will benefit schools/classrooms* • *EXAMPLE 2: Trainer shows trend data before and after the practice was implemented in a school* • *EXAMPLE 3: Trainer presents a case study of a teacher who has successfully implemented the intervention*	☐
Evidence or example:	
Engagement	**Observed? (Check if Yes)**
13. Includes opportunities for participants to apply content and/or practice skills during training • *EXAMPLE 1: Trainer has participants perform a mock lesson using the new instructional strategy* • *EXAMPLE 2: After receiving training on how to complete a form, participants practice completing the form with a sample case* • *EXAMPLE 3: Participants practice identifying various instructional strategies from sample videos*	☐

Engagement (*continued*)	Observed? (Check if Yes)
Evidence or example:	
14. Includes opportunities for participants to express personal perspectives (e.g., experiences, thoughts on concept) • *EXAMPLE 1: Participants use their experiences and prior knowledge to fill in a worksheet on the advantages and disadvantages of various instructional approaches* • *EXAMPLE 2: Participants work together to strategize ways to overcome barriers to implementation in their school* • *EXAMPLE 3: In groups, participants share personal and professional experiences related to the topic*	☐
Evidence or example:	
15. Facilitates opportunities for participants to interact with each other related to training content • *EXAMPLE 1: Participants independently answer questions, then discuss those answers as a large group* • *EXAMPLE 2: Participants work in groups to assess implementation progress in their building* • *EXAMPLE 3: Participants think/pair/share about questions within the training*	☐
Evidence or example:	
16. Adheres to agenda and time constraints • *EXAMPLE 1: Breaks, lunch, and dismissal occur on schedule according to written or verbal agenda* • *EXAMPLE 2: Trainer adjusts training content to accommodate adjustments to agenda (e.g., participants arriving late due to inclement weather)*	☐
Evidence or example:	
Evaluation/Reflection	Observed? (Check if Yes)
17. Includes opportunities for participants to reflect on learning • *EXAMPLE 1: Participants strategize how to apply the knowledge from the training in their own schools* • *EXAMPLE 2: Participants record three main points, two lingering questions, and one action they will take* • *EXAMPLE 3: Green, yellow, and red solo cups at tables used to visually check for understanding at key points throughout training*	☐
Evidence or example:	

Evaluation/Reflection (*continued*)	Observed? (Check if Yes)
18. Includes specific indicators—related to the knowledge, material, or skills provided by the training—that would indicate a successful transfer to practice • EXAMPLE 1: *Participants work in district-level teams to use a graphic organizer to create an action plan* • EXAMPLE 2: *Expectations for completing classroom observations outlined for coaches* • EXAMPLE 3: *Materials provided for educators to do midsemester self-assessment to see if intervention is being implemented*	☐
Evidence or example:	
19. Engages participants in assessment of their acquisition of knowledge and skills • EXAMPLE 1: *Posttest to assess trainees' grasp of learning objectives* • EXAMPLE 2: *After guided practice on how to complete an observation form, participants use the form to individually rate a video example and compare their responses to the trainer* • EXAMPLE 3: *Participants complete performance based assessment, illustrating that they have mastered the learning targets*	☐
Evidence or example:	
Mastery	Observed? (Check if Yes)
20. Details follow-up activities that *require* participants to apply their learning • EXAMPLE 1: *Participants complete an action plan with clear activities, a timeline, and individuals responsible* • EXAMPLE 2: *Due dates for steps of student behavioral assessment process reviewed at end of training* • EXAMPLE 3: *Implementation timeline with due dates provided and discussed*	☐
Evidence or example:	
21. Offers opportunities for continued learning through technical assistance and/or resources • EXAMPLE 1: *Trainer describes future trainings and explains how training fits into the series* • EXAMPLE 2: *Trainer provides contact information for technical assistance including e-mail address and phone number* • EXAMPLE 3: *Trainer shows participants where to find additional materials and readings on the project website*	☐
Evidence or example:	

Mastery (*continued*)	Observed? (Check if Yes)
22. Describes opportunities for coaching to improve fidelity of implementation • *EXAMPLE 1: Trainer describes follow-up in-building support to be provided by state-level coaches* • *EXAMPLE 2: Trainer provides monthly two-hour phone calls to discuss barriers and strategize solutions* • *EXAMPLE 3: Series of coaching webinars scheduled to provide follow-up support and additional information on how to implement the intervention*	☐
Evidence or example:	

AUTHORS' NOTE

This checklist is not designed to evaluate all components of professional development, because as Guskey (2000) points out, professional development is an intentional, ongoing, and systemic process. However, training (e.g., workshops, seminars, conferences, webinars) is the most common form of professional development because it is "the most efficient and cost-effective professional development model for sharing ideas and information with large groups" (p. 23). Therefore, this checklist is designed to improve and evaluate the quality of training.

SOURCE: Noonan, P., Gaumer Erickson, A., Brussow, J., & Langham, A. (2015). *Observation checklist for high-quality professional development in education* [Updated version]. Lawrence, KS: University of Kansas, Center for Research on Learning, www.researchcollaboration.org. Reprinted with permission from the authors.

Associated Publication

Gaumer Erickson, A. S., Noonan, P. M., Brussow, J., & Carter, K. S. (2016). Measuring the quality of professional development training. *Professional Development in Education*. doi: 10.1080/19415257.2016. 1179665

REFERENCES

Archibald, S., Coggshall, J. G., Croft, A., & Goe, L. (2011). High-quality professional development for all teachers: Effectively allocating resources (Research and Policy Brief). Retrieved from National Comprehensive Center for Teacher Quality website: http://www.tqsource.org/publications/HighQualityProfessionalDevelopment.pdf

Cooper, J. D. (n.d.). *Professional development: An effective research-based model.* Houghton Mifflin Harcourt. Available at http://www.washingtonstem.org/STEM/

media/Media/Resources/Professional-DeveloPment-An-Effective-Research-Based-Model-COOPER.pdf.

Duda, M. A., Van Dyke, M., Borgmeier, C., Davis, S., & McGlinchey, M. (2011, February). *Evidence-based professional development.* Presented at the 2011 State Personnel Development Grants Regional Meeting, Washington, DC.

Dunst, C. J., & Trivette, C. M. (2009). Let's be PALS: An evidence-based approach to professional development. *Infants & Young Children, 22*(3), 164–176.

Guskey, T.R. (2000). *Evaluating professional development.* Thousand Oaks, CA: Corwin.

Hunzicker, J. (2010). *Characteristics of effective professional development: A checklist.* Unpublished manuscript, Department of Teacher Education, Bradley University, Peoria, Illinois.

Joyce, B., & Showers, B. (2002). *Student achievement through staff development* (3rd ed.). Alexandria, VA: Association for Supervision and Curriculum Development.

Knowles, M. S. (1980). *The modern practice of adult education: From pedagogy to andragogy.* New York: Cambridge.

Knoff, H. M. (2011). Arkansas SPDG research-based professional development: Evaluation form. Unpublished instrument.

Learning Forward. (2012). Standards for Professional Learning. Retrieved from, http://learningforward.org/standards-for-professional-learning#.U-EvhPldXFo.

National Research Council. (1999). *How People Learn: Bridging Research and Practice.* Washington, DC: The National Academies Press.

Trivette, C. M., Dunst, C. J., Hamby, D.W., & O'Herin, C. E. (2009). Characteristics and consequences of adult learning methods and strategies (Winterberry Research Synthesis, Vol. 2, No. 2). Asheville, NC: Winterberry Press.

Wei, R. C., Darling-Hammond, L., & Adamson, F. (2010). *Professional learning in the United States: Trends and challenges.* Dallas, TX: National Staff Development Council.

This evaluation instrument was developed under a grant from the U.S. Department of Education, #H323A120018. However, content does not necessarily represent the policy of the U.S. Department of Education, and endorsement by the Office of Special Education Programs should not be assumed.

APPENDIX C

Norwegian Teacher Self-Efficacy Scale

How certain are you that you can:	Not at all certain		Quite uncertain		Quite certain		Absolutely certain
1. Explain central themes in your subjects so that even the low-achieving students understand.	①	②	③	④	⑤	⑥	⑦
2. Get all students in class to work hard with the schoolwork.	①	②	③	④	⑤	⑥	⑦
3. Cooperate well with most parents.	①	②	③	④	⑤	⑥	⑦
4. Successfully use any instructional method that the school decides to use.	①	②	③	④	⑤	⑥	⑦
5. Organize schoolwork to adapt instruction and assignments to individual needs.	①	②	③	④	⑤	⑥	⑦
6. Maintain discipline in any school class or group of students.	①	②	③	④	⑤	⑥	⑦
7. Find adequate solutions to conflicts of interest with other teachers.	①	②	③	④	⑤	⑥	⑦
8. Provide good guidance and instruction to all students regardless of their level of ability.	①	②	③	④	⑤	⑥	⑦
9. Control even the most aggressive students.	①	②	③	④	⑤	⑥	⑦
10. Awake the desire to learn even among the lowest achieving students.	①	②	③	④	⑤	⑥	⑦
11. Provide realistic challenge for all students even in mixed ability classes.	①	②	③	④	⑤	⑥	⑦
12. Answer students' questions so that they understand difficult problems.	①	②	③	④	⑤	⑥	⑦
13. Collaborate constructively with parents of students with behavioral problems.	①	②	③	④	⑤	⑥	⑦

	1	2	3	4	5	6	7
14. Get students with behavioral problems to follow the classroom rules.	①	②	③	④	⑤	⑥	⑦
15. Get students to do their best even when working with difficult problems.	①	②	③	④	⑤	⑥	⑦
16. Explain subject matter so that most students understand the basic principles.	①	②	③	④	⑤	⑥	⑦
17. Manage instruction regardless of how it is organized (group composition, mixed age groups, etc.).	①	②	③	④	⑤	⑥	⑦
18. Adapt instruction to the needs of low-ability students while you also attend to the needs of other students in class.	①	②	③	④	⑤	⑥	⑦
19. Get all students to behave politely and respect the teachers.	①	②	③	④	⑤	⑥	⑦
20. Manage instruction even if the curriculum has changed.	①	②	③	④	⑤	⑥	⑦
21. Motivate students who show low interest in schoolwork.	①	②	③	④	⑤	⑥	⑦
22. Cooperate effectively and constructively with other teachers, for example, teaching teams.	①	②	③	④	⑤	⑥	⑦
23. Organize classroom work so that both low- and high-ability students work with tasks that are adapted to their abilities.	①	②	③	④	⑤	⑥	⑦
24. Teach well even if you are told to use instructional methods that would not be your choice.	①	②	③	④	⑤	⑥	⑦

SOURCE: Skaalvik, E. M., & Svaalvik, S. (2007). Dimensions of teacher self-efficacy and relations with strain factors, perceived collective teacher efficacy, and teacher burnout. *Journal of Educational Psychology*, 99(3), 611–625. doi: 10.1037/0022-0663.99.3.611. Reprinted with permission from the authors. This full reference must be included in written reports that result from the use of the Norwegian Teacher Self-Efficacy Scale.

Example of a Logic Model

Academic goal: By [year], the percentage of students at grade 5 at or above the proficient level on the state-mandated assessment in reading will increase from ____% to at least ____%.

INPUTS	OUTPUTS		OUTCOMES		
	Activities	Participants	Short-Term	Medium-Term	Long-Term
Curriculum materials	Professional development for teachers on new curriculum (fidelity of use)	All teachers receive professional development on new curriculum	Teachers demonstrate knowledge and skills in new curriculum (fidelity of use)	Increase in student performance based on the formative assessments	Increase in the percentage of student at or above the proficient level in Reading
Materials for universal screening/ progress monitoring	Professional development for teachers/staff on how to administer universal screening/progress monitoring formative assessment	All teachers and selected staff receive professional development on formative assessment	Teachers/staff demonstrate knowledge and skills in formative assessment	Decrease in the number of students who need more intensive Tier 2 and Tier 3 interventions	
tier 2 intervention materials	Professional development for teachers/staff on how to implement tier 2 interventions	Selected teachers/staff receive professional development on tier 2 interventions.	Selected teachers/ staff demonstrate knowledge and skills in tier 2 interventions (adherence)		
Funds for materials		Universal screening and progress monitoring for all students			
Time for professional development and adherence checks		Selected students identified and received tier 2			

APPENDIX E

Evaluation Planning Template

Evaluation Questions or Objectives	Source	Data Collection Method	Data Collection		Criteria	Reporting		
			By Whom	When		To Whom	How	When
Sample Objective 1	Building Leadership Team	TFI	PBIS Coach to Facilitate	May	Tier 1 = 70%	District PBIS Team	District Database	Annual (June)

NOTE: PBIS = Positive Behavioral Intervention and Supports; TFI = Tiered Fidelity Inventory.

APPENDIX F

Assessment Schedule

Activity	Jul	Aug	Sep	Oct	Nov	Dec	Jan	Feb	Mar	Apr	May	Jun
Adult Implementation/Fidelity Measures												
Example: Tiered Fidelity Inventory			X						X			
Student Outcome Data												
Example: Universal Screening: DIBELS Next			X				X				X	
Feedback for Continuous Improvement												
Example: Professional Development Evaluations					X			X				

NOTE: Examples have been provided. Adult Implementation/Fidelity Measures could include schoolwide measures, such as the SWPBIS Tiered Fidelity Inventory or the Reading-Tiered Fidelity Inventory as well as individual and small group intervention fidelity measures or intervention logs. Student Outcome Data could include universal screening in reading, math, writing, and office discipline referrals, as well as progress monitoring data for students receiving academic or behavior interventions. Student Outcome Data could also include a student survey of school climate. Feedback for Continuous Improvement could include professional development evaluations completed following each training session and coaching feedback surveys.

Responsibility Matrix

KEY	
E	Execution responsibility
C	Must be consulted
I	Must be informed
A	Approval authority

Tasks	Date to Accomplish	Implementation Team	Trainers/Presenters	Evaluator/Data Coach	Instructional Coach
1.					
2.					
3.					
4.					
5.					
6.					
7.					
8.					
9.					
10.					
11.					
12.					

APPENDIX H

District Implementation Team (DIT) Communication Plan

NOTE: Includes linking communication protocols.

Groups/Teams: Internal and external to intentionally communicate	Designees	Linking Communication Protocol? (Y/N)	Date to survey groups/teams about effectiveness of communication
MIBLSI	DIT: MIBLSI		
Central office	DIT: Liaison:		
Administrative team	DIT: Administrative team:		
School coaches	DIT: School names and coach names—or coach coordinator:		
School leadership teams	DIT School names and designees:		
ISD	DIT ISD		
Add others as needed	DIT (other group designee)		

Communication Protocol: DIT and MIBLSI

Purpose	Communicate information that is critical to staff's ability successfully use the components of an integrated behavior and reading MTSS model	

Information necessary to be gathered and communicated	**From:** MIBLSI
	Professional learning information/ updates:
	• Upcoming training dates/details for your district team and school cohorts including reminders to register
	• Other statewide and regional professional learning opportunities for the year (e.g., Implementer's Conference, Anita Archer trainings)
	
	Data (measures, data system, data coordination capacity):
	• MIDATA start-up activities and support navigating data system at the district and school levels
	• Data coordination training events: (SWIS Facilitator training, PBIS Assessment Coordinator, DIBELS Mentor training, R-TFI Facilitator, Early Warning Systems Coordination, District Capacity Assessment Facilitator)
	• Timelines for installation of measures
	• Changes to the required measures or training expectations
	• Data collection windows (measures, timeline for administering, and data entry)
	
	District Implementation Infrastructure Development/Refinement:
	• Monthly prompting and planning for DIT meeting agenda items/areas of work for the team to focus efforts
	
	State suggestions for removing implementation barriers:
	Statewide policy and funding opportunities to strengthen the MTSS implementation effort
		To: MIBLSI
		Implementation challenges:
		• Barriers encountering that are difficult to remove
		
		Team logistics:
		• Staffing changes:
		  o DIT membership
		  o Leadership
		  o District MTSS Coordinator
		  o Individuals providing data coordination
		• Meeting schedule
		• Dates for district events/ presentations to build knowledge and/ or communicate implementation efforts
		
		Existing and new initiatives/ programs:
		• Impact on district resource allocation (time, personnel, etc.) the integrated behavior and reading MTSS work

(*Continued*)

Communication Protocol: DIT and MIBLSI (*Continued*)

Team Designees	Name of MIBLSI designee(s): 1. Implementation specialist 2. Data coordination support designees:	**MTSS coordinator**
Format for gathering necessary information	Possible options: Implementation specialist at DIT meeting, e-mail, phone call	Possible options: implementation specialist at DIT meeting, e-mail, phone call
Timelines for responding to and addressing challenges	Possible options: • Timelines for responding to challenges and acting on challenges are determined as they are identified	Insert agreed-upon timelines for responding to challenges and acting on challenges (e.g., 5–10 days)
Format for responding to challenges	E-mail communication regarding how challenges are being responded to and the status of the action	E-mail communication regarding how challenges are being responded to and the status of the action

Communication Protocol: DIT and Central Office

Purpose	Communicate information that is critical to staff's ability successfully use effective innovations (e.g., components of an integrated behavior and reading MTSS model)	
Information necessary to be gathered and communicated	**From: Central Office** (Add suggestions from District Implementation Presession)	**To: Central Office** (Add suggestions from District Implementation Presession)
Team designees		
Format for gathering necessary information		
Timelines for responding to and addressing challenges		
Format for responding to challenges		

Communication Protocol: DIT and Administrative Team

Purpose	Communicate information that is critical to staff's ability successfully use effective innovations (e.g., components of an integrated behavior and reading MTSS model)	
Information necessary to be gathered and communicated	**From: Administrative Team** (Add suggestions from District Implementation Presession)	**To: Administrative Team** (Add suggestions from District Implementation Presession)
Team designees		
Format for gathering necessary information		
Timelines for responding to and addressing challenges		
Format for responding to challenges		

Communication Protocol: DIT and School Leadership Teams

Purpose	Communicate information that is critical to staff's ability successfully use effective innovations (e.g., components of an integrated behavior and reading MTSS model)	
Information necessary to be gathered and communicated	**From: School Leadership Teams**	**To: School Leadership Teams**
Team designees		
Format for gathering necessary information		
Timelines for responding to and addressing challenges		
Format for responding to challenges		

Communication Protocol: DIT and School Coaches

Purpose	Communicate information that is critical to staff's ability successfully use effective innovations (e.g., components of an integrated behavior and reading MTSS model)	
Information necessary to be gathered and communicated	**From: School Coaches**	**To: School Coaches**
Team designees		
Format for gathering necessary information		
Timelines for responding to and addressing challenges		
Format for responding to challenges		

Communication Protocol: DIT and Regional Independent School District

Purpose	Communicate information that is critical to staff's ability successfully use effective innovations (e.g., components of an integrated behavior and reading MTSS model)	
Information necessary to be gathered and communicated	**From: ISD**	**To: ISD**
Team designees		
Format for gathering necessary information		
Timelines for responding to and addressing challenges		
Format for responding to challenges		

Generic Communication Effectiveness Survey (sent out to the group/team during the designated timelines listed on page 1 of the Communication Plan):

Introduction statement: The District Implementation Team continues to be focused on effective communication in order to help support your school's use of integrated behavior and reading MTSS components. We would like to hear from you about how effective communication has been to and from our team.

Directions: Please complete this brief survey. The data will be used by the District Implementation Team to refine and improve how effectively we communicate to you!

Select your primary role:
- Central office administrator
- Administrator
- School leadership team member
- Coach
- MIBLSI
- ISD
- (Add any other group/team roles that are included in your communication plan)

1. I am kept informed about critical aspects of the MTSS work (MIBLSI collaboration with our district and schools).
   o Agree
   o Disagree
   o Strongly Disagree

2. I feel the level of communication with my District Implementation Team designee is adequate.
   o Agree
   o Disagree
   o Strongly Disagree

3. What other feedback about communication with the District Implementation Team would you like to share?

NOTE: ISD = Independent School District; MIBLSI = Michigan's Integrated Behavior and Learning Support Initiative; MSST = multi-tier system of supports.

SOURCE: Michigan's Integrated Behavior and Learning Support Initiative. (2016). District Implementation Team Communication Plan. Holland, MI: Author. Reprinted with permission from the author.

Attribution (vs. contribution) claims the program being evaluated caused the observed changes in outcomes. Contribution claims acknowledge the influence of the program that acknowledging other factors might also have influenced observed changes in outcomes.

Compatibility refers to the degree to which the innovation is seen to be a good fit within the local context in terms of its consistency with past practices, prevailing values, and current needs, according to diffusion theory.

Complexity in diffusion theory is the degree to which an innovation is perceived as difficult to understand and use. Innovations that are perceived as being simple to use will be more easily adopted.

Context, Input, Process, and Product (CIPP) is a decision-oriented evaluation approach involving a process of delineating, obtaining, reporting and applying descriptive and judgmental information about a program's merit, worth, and significance to guide decisions, support accountability, disseminate effective practices, and increase understanding of the program.

Curriculum-based measurement (CBM) involves the use of short-cycle, formative assessment measures of academic skill fluency that have empirically derived cut points that represent categories of relative risk.

Data-based decision making (also known as data literacy) is defined as the ability to understand and use data effectively to inform decisions.

Diffusion theory accounts for the process by which an innovation is communicated through certain channels over time among the members of a social system.

Dissemination (vs. diffusion) are distinct terms. Dissemination describes the spread of an innovation that maintains its fidelity, whereas diffusion describes a process by which an innovation is adopted and likely adapted to fit the local context.

District Capacity Assessment is a tool developed to measure the capacity of a school district to support implementation of a given innovation.

Effect size is a statistic that describes the magnitude of an effect on a standard scale.

Evaluation capacity building is the ability to conduct an effective evaluation that meets acceptable standards of the discipline.

Evidence-based practices are practices and programs shown by high-quality research to have meaningful effects on student outcomes.

Experimental designs tests the effect of an intervention on an outcome, controlling for all other actors that might influence the outcome.

External evaluator is an individual who is not a member of or affiliated with the organization implementing the program who functions as an evaluator.

Formative evaluation has as its primary purpose the role of providing information for program improvement.

Goal attainment scaling process involves (a) the selection of the target behavior; (b) a specific, observable, measurable description of the desired intervention outcome; and (c) the development of five descriptions of that target behavior scaled to approximate varied levels of attainment of the desired outcome.

Internal evaluator is an individual who is a member of the organization implementing the program who functions as an evaluator.

Impact evaluation (See Outcome evaluation).

Implementation includes all of the activities focused on the actual operation of a program.

Implementation fidelity is the degree to which the core components of the initiative are implemented as planned.

Instructional Hierarchy model describes a learning progression across four stages: skill acquisition stage, fluency stage, generalization stage, and the adaptation stage.

Internal validity is the extent to which changes in one variable (an intervention) brings about changes in another variable(s); an outcome) in the context of an experimental research study. Interval validity determines the confidence one has in establishing a cause-effect relationship.

Logic models provide a graphic display of the theory of change and further help articulate the program's goals, activities, and intended outcomes.

Mixed-methods approach involves the use of both qualitative and quantitative data and includes philosophical assumptions that guide every aspect of the evaluation regarding the nature of ethics, the nature of reality, the nature of knowledge, and the nature of systematic inquiry.

Multiple-baseline design is a single-case design in which one participant, behavior, or setting is measured over time under baseline and intervention conditions, with the introduction of the intervention staggered in time for each participant, behavior, or setting. For example, if three students were identified to participate in an individual, intensive reading intervention, following three weeks of baseline data collection, student A might begin intervention in week 4, student B might begin the intervention in week 7, and student C might begin the intervention in week 10 in a study designed to determine the effects of the reading intervention.

Multi-tier system of supports (MTSS) is a framework designed to meet the academic and behavioral needs of all students through the use of high-quality instruction and a continuum of instructional and behavioral supports and targeted, evidence-based interventions of increasing intensity matched to student need.

Needs assessment involves identifying and prioritizing needs for the purpose of determining the causes of the needs and developing solutions.

Observability is the degree to which the use and benefits of an innovation made visible to others, according to diffusion theory.

Office discipline referrals (ODRs) are events in which (a) a student engages in a behavior that violates a rule/social norm in the school, (b) a problem behavior is observed by a member of the school staff, and (c) the event results in a consequence delivered by administrative staff who produces a permanent product defining the whole event.

Opinion leaders are influential individuals within an organization that can help facilitate the adoption of a new practice among the other members of their peer group.

Organizational learning refers to building an organization's capacity to learn and manage in difficult times.

Outcome evaluation focuses on the changes that occur as a result of a program's implementation.

Percentage of nonoverlapping data (PND) points is a summary statistics used with single-case design data, which involves counting the number of intervention data points that exceed the highest baseline point (for studies seeking to increase a target behavior) or counting the number of intervention data points lower than the lowest baseline point (for studies seeking to decrease a target behavior). The number of PND points are then divided by the total number of intervention points to obtain the percentage of nonoverlapping data.

Permanent products are school organizational records (e.g., an activity or participation log) or intervention products (e.g., charts, tokens, home/school notes) that are generated on site at frequent intervals by teachers or other program practitioners.

Positive Behavioral Interventions and Supports (PBIS) is a framework for implementing evidence-based practices, providing a three-tiered continuum of support to students, using systems to support staff in implementation, and using data for decision making.

Practice profiles are tools for operationally defining the critical components of a program in order to promote fidelity and consistency across practitioners.

Process evaluation examines the delivery of a program.

Professional learning refers to a process that leads to increases in knowledge and skills among professionals, which occurs as a result of experience and increases the potential for improved performance and future learning.

Program evaluation involves the identification, clarification, and application of defensible criteria to document a program's worth and merit in relation to those criteria.

Quasi-experimental designs are a variation of experimental designs in which individuals are not randomly assigned to a group (i.e., intervention group vs. comparison group).

Reading-Tiered Fidelity Inventory (R-TFI) a tool developed to measure the implementation of schoolwide research-based reading systems within a school: tier I (whole school universal prevention/core instruction), tier II (targeted intervention), and tier III (intensive, individualized intervention).

Regional Capacity Assessment is a tool developed to measure the capacity of a regional education agencies to support implementation of a given innovation.

Relative advantage is the extent to which the innovation is perceived to have significant advantages over the status quo or current alternatives, according to diffusion theory.

Response-shift bias is evident when individual self-rate their knowledge as higher prior to a professional learning experience only to self-rate their knowledge lower on a post-test measure, thus generating a negative gain score.

Response to Intervention (RTI) is a preventive systems approach to improving schoolwide and individual achievement through high-quality universal instruction and additional tiered supports provided in response to student need.

Rubrics are tools for assessing performance. They are structured as a grid with gradations of quality operationalized for each criterion on the grid (i.e., highly proficient, proficient, developing proficiency, not proficient).

Single-case designs are research designs used to examine the effects of an intervention on a particular case (i.e., individual or group of individual) and to provide evidence of the effectiveness of the intervention using a relatively small sample size.

S.M.A.R.T. goals are Specific, Measurable, Attainable (or Achievable), Relevant, and Time-bound.

Spillover effects are defined as the effects of professional learning that extend above and beyond the direct effects on the teachers who participated in the experience.

SUCCESs Model outlines six communication strategies for dissemination information so that it is understood and memorable: Simple, Unexpected, Concrete, Credible, Emotional, and Stories.

Summative evaluation focus on providing information to inform decisions, including judgments regarding the overall worth or merit of the program in relation to important criteria.

Teacher self-efficacy refers to a teacher's belief in their capabilities to perform a particular skill, task, or domain to attain a valued outcome.

Theory of change is defined as the process through which program components are presumed to affect outcomes and the conditions under which these processes are believed to operate.

Tiered Fidelity Inventory (TFI) is a tool designed to measure the extent to which Positive Behavioral Interventions and Supports (PBIS) core features are in place within a school.

Trialability refers to the extent to which components of an innovation can be tried out before a potential user decides to adopt it, according to diffusion theory.

Universal screening is the systematic assessment of all children within a given classroom, grade level, school building, or school district using brief assessments academic and/ or social-behavioral skills that are highly predictive of future outcomes.

REFERENCES

Aaronson, D., Barrow, L., & Sander, W. (2007). Teachers and student achievement in the Chicago public high schools. *Journal of Labor Economics, 25,* 95–135.

Al Otaiba, S., & Torgensen, J. (2007). Effects from intensive standardized kindergarten and first-grade interventions for the prevention of reading difficulties. In S. E. Jimerson, M. K. Burns, & A. M. VanDerHeyden (Eds.), *Handbook of response to intervention: The science and practice of assessment and intervention* (pp. 212–222). New York: Springer.

Algozzine, B., Barrett, S., Eber, L., George, H., Horner, R., Lewis, T., . . . Sugai, G. (2014). *School-wide PBIS Tiered Fidelity Inventory.* OSEP Technical Assistance Center on Positive Behavioral Interventions and Supports. Retrieved from www.pbis.org

Algozzine, B., Horner, R. H., Sugai, G., Barrett, S., Dickey, C. R., Eber, L., . . . Tobin, T. (2010). *Evaluation blueprint for school-wide positive behavior support.* Eugene, OR: National Technical Assistance Center on Positive Behavior Interventions and Support. Retrieved from www.pbis.org

Algozzine, B., Newton, J. S., Horner, R. H., Todd, A. W., & Algozzine, K. (2012). Development and technical characteristics of a team decision-making assessment tool: Decision, Observation, Recording, and Analysis (DORA). *Journal of Psychoeducational Assessment, 30,* 237–249.

Alibali, M. W. (1999). How children change their minds: Strategy change can be gradual or abrupt. *Developmental Psychology, 35,* 127–145.

Allinder, R. M. (1994). The relationship between efficacy and the instructional practices of special education teachers and consultants. *Teacher Education and Special Education, 17,* 86–95.

Altschuld, J. W., Hung, H.-L., & Lee, Y.-F. (2014). Needs assessment and asset/capacity building: A promising development in practice. *New Directions for Evaluation, 144,* 89–103.

Altschuld, J. W., & Watkins, R. (2014). A primer on needs assessment: More than 40 years of research and practice. *New Directions for Evaluation, 144,* 5–18.

Ambrose, S. A., Bridges, M. W., DiPietro, M., Lovette, M. C., & Norman, M. K. (2010). *How learning works: Seven research-based principles for smart teaching.* San Francisco: Jossey-Bass.

American Evaluation Association. (2004). *Guiding principles for evaluators.* Available from http://www.eval.org/p/cm/ld/fid=51

Anderson, C. M., Childs, K., Kincaid, D., Horner, R. H., George, H., Todd, A. W., . . . Spaulding, S. A. (2012). *Benchmarks for advanced tiers*. Unpublished instrument, Educational and Community Supports, University of Oregon & University of South Florida.

Anderson, C. M., Lewis-Palmer, T., Todd, A. W., Horner, R. H., Sugai, G., & Sampson, N. K. (2011). *Individual-Student Systems Evaluation Tool, Version 2.8*. Eugene: University of Oregon, Educational and Community Supports.

Anderson, L. W., & Krathwohl, D. R. (Eds.) (2001). *A taxonomy for learning, teaching, and assessing: A revision of Bloom's taxonomy of educational objectives*. New York: Longman.

Andrade, H. (2000). Using rubrics to promote thinking and learning. *Educational Leadership, 57*(5), 13–18.

Angelucci, M., & Di Maro, V. (2010). *Program evaluation and spillover effects: Impact-evaluation guidelines*. Washington, DC: Inter-American Development Bank.

Archer, A., & Hughes, C. A. (2011). *Explicit instruction: Effective and efficient teaching (What works for special needs learners)*. New York: The Guilford Press.

Ardoin, S. P., & Daly E. J., III, (2007). Introduction to the special series: Close encounters of the instructional kind—How the instructional hierarchy is shaping instructional research 30 years later. *Journal of Behavioral Education, 16*, 1–6.

Ashley, S. R. (2009). Innovation diffusion: Implications for evaluation. In J. M. Ottoson & P. Hawe (Eds.), Knowledge utilization, diffusion, implementation, transfer, and translation: Implications for evaluation. *New Directions for Evaluation, 124*, 35–45.

Ashton, P. T., & Webb, R. B. (1986). *Making a difference: Teachers' sense of efficacy and student achievement*. New York: Longman.

Atkins, M. S., Frazier, S. L., Leathers, S., Graczyk, P., Talbott, E., Jakobsons, L., . . . Bell, C. C. (2008). Teacher key opinion leaders and mental health consultation in urban low-income schools. *Journal of Consulting and Clinical Psychology, 76*, 905–908. doi:10.1037/a0013036

Bachrach, L. L. (1988). The chronic patient: On exporting and importing model programs. *Hospital and Community Psychiatry, 39*, 1257–1258.

Bahr, M. W., & Kovaleski, J. F. (2006). The need for problem-solving teams: Introduction to the special series. *Remedial and Special Education, 27*, 2–6.

Balu, R., Zhu, P., Doolittle, F., Schiller, E., Jenkins, J., & Gersten, R. (2015). *Evaluation of Response to Intervention Practices for Elementary School Reading (NCEE 2016-4000)*. Washington, DC: National Center for Education Evaluation and Regional Assistance, Institute of Education Sciences, U.S. Department of Education.

Bandura, A. (1997). *Self-efficacy: The exercise of control*. New York: Freeman.

Barnett, D. W., VanDerHeyden, A. M., & Witt, J. C. (2007). Achieving science-based practice through response to intervention: What it might look like in preschools. *Journal of Educational and Psychological Consultation, 17*, 31–54.

Barrett, S., & Scott, T. M. (2006). Evaluating time saved as an index of cost effectiveness in PBIS schools. *Technical Assistance Center on Positive Behavior Support Newsletter, 3*(4). Available at: https://www.pbis.org/common/cms/files/Newsletter/Volume3Issue4.pdf

Barron, K., & Harackiewicz, J. (2001). Achievement goals and optimal motivation: Testing multiple goal models. *Journal of Personality and Social Psychology, 80*, 706–722.

Bartels, S. M., & Mortenson, B. P. (2005). Enhancing adherence to a problem-solving model for middle school pre-referral teams: A performance feedback and checklist approach. *Journal of Applied School Psychology, 22*, 109–123. doi:10.1300/J008v22n01_06

Bartunek, J. M. (2007). Academic-practitioner collaboration need not require joint or relevant Research: Toward a relational scholarship of integration. *Academy of Management Journal, 50*, 1323–1333.

Batsche, G., Elliot, J., Graden, J. L., Grimes, J., Kovaleski, J. F., & Prasse, D. (2005). Response to intervention: Policy considerations and implementation. Alexandria, VA: National Association of State Directors of Special Education.

Bird, T., & Little, J. W. (1986). How schools organize the teaching profession. *Elementary School Journal, 86*, 493–512.

Blakely, C. H., Mayer, J. P., Gottschalk, R. G., et al. (1987). The fidelity-adaptation debate: Implications for the implementation of public sector social programs. *American Journal of Community Psychology, 15*, 253–268.

Blase, K. A., Fixsen, D. L., Van Dyke, M., & Duda, M. A. (2013). *Implementation Drivers—Best Practices for Coaching.* Chapel Hill, NC: National Implementation Research Network. Available at: http://nirn.fpg.unc.edu

Blase, K., Kiser, L., & Van Dyke, M. (2013). *The Hexagon Tool: Exploring Context.* Chapel Hill, NC: National Implementation Research Network, FPG Child Development Institute, University of North Carolina at Chapel Hill.

Bloom, B. S. (Ed.) (1956). *A taxonomy of educational objectives: Handbook I: Cognitive domain.* New York: David McKay.

Bloom, M., Fischer, J., & Orme, J. G. (2005). *Evaluating practice: Guidelines for the accountable professional* (5th ed.). Boston: Allyn & Bacon.

Bond, G. R., Evans, L., Salyers, M. P., Williams, J., & Kim, H. W. (2000). Measurement of fidelity in psychiatric rehabilitation. *Mental Health Services Research, 2*(2), 75–87.

Bong, M. (2006). Asking the right question. How confident are you that you could successfully perform these tasks? In F. Pajares & T. Urdan (Eds.), *Self-efficacy beliefs of adolescents* (pp. 287–305). Greenwich, CT: Information Age.

Bong, M., & Skaalvik, E. M. (2003). Academic self-concept and self-efficacy: How different are they really? *Educational Psychology Review, 15*, 1–40.

Borko, H., Jacobs, J., Eiteljorg, E., & Pittman, M. E. (2008). Video as a tool for fostering productive discourse in mathematics professional development. *Teaching and Teacher Education, 24*, 417–436.

Brandt, R. (1978). On evaluation: An interview with Daniel Stufflebeam. *Educational Leadership, 35*, 249–254.

Bresciani, M. J., Oakleaf, M., Kolkhorst, F., Nebeker, C., Barlow, J., Duncan, K., & Hickmott, J. (2009). Examining design and inter-rater reliability of a rubric measuring research quality across multiple disciplines. *Practical Assessment, Research, and Evaluation, 14*(12). Available at http://pareonline.net/

Brown-Chidsey, R., Steege, M. W., & Mace, F. C. (2008). Best practices in evaluating the effectiveness of interventions using case study data. In A. Thomas & J. Grimes (Eds.), *Best Practices in School Psychology V.* (pp. 2177–2191). Bethesda, MD: National Association of School Psychologists.

Brunvand, S. (2010). Best practices for producing video content for teacher education. *Contemporary Issues in Technology and Teacher Education, 10*, 247–256.

Bryk, A., & Schneider, A. (2002). *Trust in schools: A core resource for improvement.* New York, NY: Russell Sage Foundation.

Bryk, A., Sebring, P. B., Allensworth, E., Luppescu, S., & Easton, J. (2010). *Organizing schools for improvement: Lessons from Chicago.* Chicago, IL: University of Chicago Press.

Buck, G. H., Polloway, E. A., Smith-Thomas, A., & Cook, K. W. (2003). Pre-referral intervention processes: A survey of state practices. *Exceptional Children, 69,* 349–360.

Burns, C. E. (2015). Does my program really make a difference? Program evaluation utilizing aggregate single-subject data. *American Journal of Evaluation, 36,* 191–203.

Burns, M. K., Peters, R., & Noell, G. H. (2008). Using performance feedback to enhance implementation fidelity of the problem-solving team process. *Journal of School Psychology, 46,* 537–555. doi: 10.1016/j.jsp/2008.04.0001

Burns, M. K., & Symington, T. (2002). A meta-analysis of pre-referral intervention teams: Student and systemic outcomes. *Journal of School Psychology, 40,* 437–447.

Burns, M. K., VanDerHeyden, A. M., Jiban, C. L. (2006). Assessing the instructional level for mathematics: A comparison of methods. *School Psychology Review, 35,* 401–418.

Burns, M. K., Wiley, H. I., & Viglietta, E. (2008). Best practices in facilitating problem-solving teams. In A. Thomas, & J. Grimes (Eds.), *Best practices in school psychology V* (pp. 163–1644). Bethesda, MD: National Association of School Psychologists.

Busk, P. L., & Serlin, R. C. (1992). Meta-analysis for single-case research. In T. R. Kratochwill & J. R. Levin (Eds.), *Single-case research designs and analysis: New directions for psychology and education* (pp. 187–212). Hillsdale, NJ: Lawrence Erlbaum Associates.

Campbell, D. T., & Stanley, J. C. (1963). *Experimental and quasi-experimental designs for research.* Chicago: Rand-McNally College Publishing Company.

Carroll, C., Patterson, M., Wood, S., Booth, A., Rick, J., & Balain, S. (2007). A conceptual framework for implementation fidelity. *Implementation Science, 2,* 40. doi: 10.1186/1748-5908-2-40

Carver, C. S., & Scheier, M. F. (1998). *On the self-regulation of behavior.* Cambridge: Cambridge University Press.

Casabianca, J. M., McCaffrey, D. F., Gitomer, D. H., Bell, C. A., Hamre, B. K., & Pianta, R. C. (2013). Effect of observation mode on measures of secondary mathematics teaching. *Educational and Psychological Measurement, 73,* 757–783. doi: 10.1177/0013164413486987

Cash, A. H., & Pianta, R. C. (2014). The role of scheduling in observing teacher-child interactions. *School Psychology Review, 43,* 428–449.

Castro, E. G., Barrera, M., & Martinez, C. R. (2004). The cultural adaptation of prevention interventions: Resolving tensions between fidelity and fit. *Prevention Science, 5,* 41–45. doi: 10.1023/B:PREV.0000013980.124l2.cd

Chi, M. T. H., & Roscoe, R. D. (2002). The process and challenges of conceptual change. In M. Limon & L. Mason (Eds.), *Reconsidering conceptual change: Issues in theory and practice* (pp. 3–27). The Netherlands: Kluwer.

Chen, H. T. (2015). Practical program evaluation: Theory-driven evaluation and the integrated evaluation perspective, Second Edition. Thousand Oaks: Sage Publications, Inc.

Christie, C. A., Ross, R. M., & Klein, B. M. (2004). Moving toward collaboration by creating a participatory internal-external evaluation team: A case study. *Studies in Educational Evaluation, 30,* 125–134.

Coburn, C. E. (2004). Beyond decoupling: Rethinking the relationship between the institutional environment and the classroom. *Sociology of Education*, *77*, 211–244.

Coburn, C. E., Russell, J. L., Kaufman, J. H., & Stein, M. K. (2012). Supporting sustainability: Teachers' advice networks and ambitious instructional reform. *American Journal of Education*, *119*, 137–182.

Cohen, D. K. (1990). A revolution in one classroom: The case of Mrs. Oublier. *Educational Evaluation and Policy Analysis*, *12*, 311–329.

Cohen, R., Kincaid, D., & Childs, K. E. (2007). Measuring school-wide positive behavior support implementation: Development and validation of the Benchmarks of Quality. *Journal of Positive Behavior Support*, *9*, 203–213.

Collier-Meek, M. A., Fallon, L. M., Sanetti, L. M. H., & Maggin, D. M. (2013). Focus on implementation: Strategies for problem-solving teams to assess and promote treatment fidelity. *Teaching Exceptional Children*, *45*, 52–59.

Connell, J. P., & Klem, A. M. (2000). You can get there from here: Using a theory of change approach to plan urban education reform. *Journal of Educational and Psychological Consultation*, *11*, 93–120.

Cook, B. G., Cook, L., & Landrum, T. J. (2013). Moving research into practice: Can we make dissemination stick? *Exceptional Children*, *79*, 163–180.

Cook, B. G., & Cook, S. C. (2011). Unraveling evidence-based practices in special education. *Journal of Special Education*, *47*, 71–82. doi: 10.1177/0022466911420877

Cook, B. G., & Odom, S. L. (2013). Evidence-based practices and implementation science in special education. *Exceptional Children*, *79*(2), 135–144.

Cook, B. G., & Smith, G. J. (2012). Leadership and instruction: Evidence-based practices in special education. In J. B. Crockett, B. S. Billingsley, & M. L. Boscardin (Eds.), *Handbook of leadership in special education* (pp. 281–296). London, England: Routledge.

Cook, C. R., Rasetshwane, K. B., Truelson, E., Grant, S., Dart, E. g., Collins, T. A., & Sprague, J. (2011). Development and validation of the Student Internalizing Behavior Screener: Examination of reliability, validity, and classification accuracy. *Assessment for Effective Intervention*, *36*, 71–79.

Cooper, J. O., Heron, T. E., & Heward, W. L. (2007). *Applied behavior analysis* (2nd ed.) Upper Saddle River, NJ: Pearson.

Cordray, D. S., & Pion, G. M. (2006). Treatment strength and integrity: Models and methods. In R. R. Bootzin & P. E. McKnight (Eds.), *Strengthening research methodology: Psychological measurement and evaluation* (pp. 103–124). Washington, DC: American Psychological Association.

Cousins, J. B., & Earl, L. (1995). *Participatory evaluation in education: Studies in evaluation use and organizational learning*. London: Falmer.

Cousins, J. B., Goh, S., & Clark, S. (2005). Data use leads to data valuing: Evaluative inquiry for school decision making. *Leadership and Policy in Schools*, *4*, 155–176.

Cousins, J. B., Goh, S. C., Elliott, C. J., & Bourgeois, I. (2014). Framing the capacity to do and use evaluation. In J. B. Cousins & I. Bourgeois (Eds.), Organizational capacity to do and use evaluation. *New Directions for Evaluation*, *141*, 7–23.

Creswell, J. & Plano Clark, V. (2007). *Designing and conducting mixed methods research*. Thousand Oaks, CA: Sage.

Dahler-Larsen, P. (2009). Learning oriented educational evaluation in contemporary society. In K. E. Ryan & J. B. Cousins (Eds.), *The Sage International Handbook of Educational Evaluation*. Thousand Oaks, CA: Sage.

Daly, E. J. III, Martens, B. K., Barnett, D., Witt, J. C., & Olson, S. C. (2007). Varying inter-vention delivery in response-to-intervention: Confronting and resolving challenges with measurement, instruction, and intensity. *School Psychology Review, 36,* 562–581.

Dane, A. V., & Schneider, B. H. (1998). Program integrity in primary and early second-ary prevention: Are implementation effects out of control? *Clinical Psychology Review, 18,* 23–45.

Darling-Hammond, L., Wei, R. C., Andree, A., Richardson, N., & Orphanos, S. (2009). *Professional learning in the learning profession: A status report on teacher development in the United States and abroad.* Washington, DC: National Staff Development Council.

Datnow, A., Hubbard, L., & Mehan, H. (2002). *Extending educational reform: From one school to many.* London: Routledge/Falmer.

Dearing, J. W. (2008). Evolution of diffusion and dissemination theory. *Journal of Public Health Management and Practice, 14,* 99–108.

Dearing, J. W., & Kreuter, M. W. (2010). Designing for diffusion: How can we increase the uptake of cancer communication innovations? *Patient Education and Counseling, 81S,* S100–S110.

D'Eon, M., Sadownik, L., Harrison, A., & Nation, J. (2008). Using self-assessments to detect workshop Success: do they work? *American Journal of Evaluation, 29,* 92–98.

Deno, S. L. (1985). Curriculum-based measurement: The emerging alternative. *Exceptional Children, 52,* 219–232.

Deno, S. L., Mirkin, P. K., & Chang, B. (1982). Identifying valid measures of reading, *Exceptional Children, 49,* 36–45.

Desimone, L. M. (2009). Improving impact studies of teachers' professional develop-ment: Toward better conceptualizations and measures. *Educational Researcher, 38*(3), 181–199. doi: 10.3102/0013189X08331140

Desimone, L. M., Porter, A. C., Garet, M. S., Yoon, K. S., & Birman, B. F. (2002). Effects of professional development on teachers' instruction: Results from a three-year longi-tudinal study. *Educational Evaluation and Policy Analysis, 24,* 81–112.

Doll, B., Haack, K., Kosse, S., Osterloh, M., Siemers, E., & Pray, B. (2005). The dilemma of pragmatics: Why schools don't use quality team consultation practices. *Journal of Educational and Psychological Consultation, 16,* 127–155.

Donaldson, S. I. (2007). *Program theory-driven evaluation science: Strategies and applica-tions.* New York: Lawrence Erlbaum Associates.

Donovan, M. S., Bransford, J. D., & Pellegrino, J. W. (Eds.). (1999). *How people learn: Bridge research and practice.* Washington, DC: National Academy Press.

Doran, G. T. (1981). There's a S.M.A.R.T. way to write management's goals and objectives. *Management Review, 70*(11), 35–36.

Drake, R., Goldman, H., Leff, H., Lehman, A., Dixon, L., Mueser, K., & Torrey, W. (2001). Implementing evidence-based practices in routine mental health service set-tings. *Psychiatric Services, 52,* 179–182.

Drummond, T. (1994). *The Student Risk Screening Scale (SRSS).* Grants Pass, OR: Josephine County Mental Health Program.

Durlak, J. A. (1998). Why program implementation is important. *Journal of Prevention & Intervention in the Community, 17,* 5–18.

Durlak, J. A. (2010). The importance of doing well in whatever you do: A commentary on the special section, "Implementation research in early childhood education." *Early Childhood Research Quarterly, 25,* 348–357. doi: 10.1016/j.ecresq.2010.03.003

Durlak, J. A., & DuPre, E. P. (2008). Implementation matters: A review of research on the influence of implementation on program outcomes and the factors affecting implementation. *American Journal of Community Psychology, 41*, 327–350. doi: 10.1007/s10464-008-9165-0

Dusenbury, L., Brannigan, R., Falco, M., & Hansen, W. B. (2003). A review of research on fidelity of implementation: Implications for drug abuse prevention in school settings. *Health Education Research, 18*, 237–256.

Engeström, Y. (2011). From design experiments to formative interventions. *Theory and Psychology, 21*, 598–628.

Erickson, F. (1986). Qualitative methods in research on teaching. In M. Wittrock (Ed.), *Handbook of research on teaching* (3rd ed., pp. 119–161). New York: Macmillan.

Ervin, R. A., Schaughency, E., Goodman, S. D., McGlinchey, M. T., & Matthews, A. (2006). Merging research and practice agendas to address reading and behavior school-wide. *School Psychology Review, 35*, 198–223.

Eva, K. W., Cunnington, J. P. W., Reiter, H. I., Keane, D. R., & Norman, G. R. (2004). How can I know what I don't know? Poor self-assessment in a well-defined domain. *Advances in Health Sciences Education: Theory to Practice, 9*, 211–224.

Evergreen, S. (2017). *Effective data visualization: The right chart for the right data.* Thousand Oaks, CA: Sage.

Fagerlin, A., Wang, C., & Udel, P. A. (2005). Reducing the influence of anecdotal reasoning on people's health care decisions: is a picture worth a thousand statistics? *Medical Decision Making, 25*(4), 398–405.

Fairweather, G. W., & Tornatzsky, L. G. (1971). *Experimental methods for social policy research.* New York, NY: Pergamon Press.

Few, S. (2013). *Information dashboard design: Displaying data for at-a-glance monitoring.* Burlingame, CA: Analytics Press.

Fisher, W. W., Piazza, C. C., & Roane, H. S. (Eds.). (2011). *Handbook of applied behavior nalysis.* New York, NY: Guilford Press.

Fitzpatrick, J. L., Sanders, J. R., & Worthen, B. R. (Eds.). (2011). *Program evaluation: Alternative approaches and practical guidelines* (4th ed.). Boston: Pearson Education, Inc.

Fixsen, D., Blase, K., Metz, A., & Van Dyke, M. (2013). Statewide implementation of evidence-based programs. *Exceptional Children, 79*, 213–230.

Fixsen, D., Blase, K., Naoom, S., & Duda, M. (2013). *Implementation Drivers: Assessing Best Practices.* University of North Carolina at Chapel Hill.

Fixsen, D. L., Naoom, S. F., Blase, K. A., Friedman, R. M., & Wallace, F. (2005). *Implementation research: A synthesis of the literature.* Tampa, FL: University of South Florida, Louis de la Parte Florida Mental Health Institute, The National Implementation Research Network (FMHI Publication #231).

Fletcher, J. M., Coulter, W. A., Reschly, D. J., & Vaughn, S. (2004). Alternative approaches to the definition and identification of learning disabilities: Some questions and answers. *Annuals of Dyslexia, 54*, 304–331.

Frykholm, J. A. (1996). Pre-service teachers in mathematics: Struggling with the standards. *Teaching and Teacher Education, 12*(6), 665–681.

Fuchs, L. S., Fuchs, D., & Bishop, N. (1992). Instructional adaptation for students at risk. *Journal of Educational Research, 86*, 70–84.

Fuchs, L. S., Fuchs, D., Hosp, M., & Jenkins, J. R. (2001). Oral reading fluency as an indicator of reading competence: A theoretical, empirical, and historical analysis. *Scientific Studies of Reading, 5*, 239–256.

Fuchs, L. S., Fuchs, D., & Maxwell, L. (1988). The validity of informal measures of reading comprehension. *Remedial and Special Education, 9*(2), 20–28.

Gallimore, R., Ermeling, B. A., Saunders, W. M., & Goldenberg, C. (2009). Moving the learning of teaming closer to practice: Teacher education implications of school-based inquiry teams. *The Elementary School Journal, 109*(5), 537–553.

Gansle, K. A., & McMahon, C. M. (1997). Component integrity of teacher intervention management behavior using a student self-monitoring treatment: An experimental analysis. *Journal of Behavioral Education, 7*, 405–419.

Gansle, K. A., Noell, G. H., VanDerHeyden, A. M., Slider, N., Hoffpauir, L. D., Whitmarsh, E. L., & Naquin, G. M. (2004). An examination of the criterion validity and sensitivity to brief intervention of alternate curriculum-based measures of writing skill. *Psychology in the Schools, 41*, 291–300.

Gansle, K. A., VanDerHeyden, A. M., Noell, G. H., Reseter, J. L., Williams, K. L. (2006). The technical adequacy of curriculum-based and rating-based measures of written expression for elementary school students. *School Psychology Review, 35*, 435–450.

Gersten, R. (2001). Sorting out the roles of research in the improvement of practice. *Learning Disabilities: Research & Practice, 16*(1), 45–50.

Gersten, R., Fuchs, L. S., Compton, D., Coyne, M., Greenwood, C, & Innocenti, M. S. (2005). Quality indicators for group experimental and quasi-experimental research in special education. *Exceptional Children, 71*, 149–164.

Goldhaber, D. D. (2002). The mystery of good teaching. *Education Next, 2*, 50–55.

Good, R. H., & Kaminski, R. A. (2002). *Dynamic Indicators of Basic Early Literacy Skills: Administration and Scoring Guide.* Eugene, OR: University of Oregon.

Good, R. H., Simmons, D. C., & Kame'enui, E. J. (2001). The importance and decision-making utility of a continuum of fluency-based indicators of foundational reading skills for third-grade high-stakes outcomes. *Scientific Studies of Reading, 5*, 257–288.

Graden, J. L., Stollar, S. A., & Poth, R. L. (2007). The Ohio Integrated Systems Model: Overview and lessons learned. In S. E. Jimerson, M. K. Burns, & A. M. VanDerHeyden (Eds.), *Handbook of response to intervention: The science and practice of assessment and intervention* (pp. 288–299). New York: Springer.

Gresham, F. M., Dart, E. H., & Collins, T. A. (2017). Generalizability of multiple measures of treatment integrity: Comparisons among direct observation, permanent products, and self-report. *School Psychology Review, 46*, 108–121.

Gresham, F. M., Gansle, K., & Noell, G. H. (1993). Treatment integrity in applied behavior analysis with children. *Journal of Applied Behavior Analysis, 26*, 257–263. doi: 10.1901/jaba.1993.26-257

Gresham, F. M., MacMillan, D. L., Beebe-Frankenberger, M. E., & Bocian, K. M. (2000). Treatment integrity in learning disabilities intervention research: Do we really know how treatments are implemented? *Learning Disabilities Research & Practice, 15*, 198–205. doi: 10.1207/SLDRP1504_4

Griffiths, A., VanDerHeyden, A. M., Skokut, M., & Lilles, E. (2009). Progress monitoring in oral reading fluency within the context of RTI. *School Psychology Quarterly, 24*, 13–23.

Guskey, T. R. (1982). The effects of change in instructional effectiveness upon the relationship of teacher expectations and student achievement. *Journal of Educational Research, 75*(6), 345–349.

Guskey, T. R. (1988). Teacher efficacy, self-concept, and attitudes toward the implementation of instructional innovation. *Teaching and Teacher Education, 4*, 63–69.

Guskey, T. R. (2000). *Evaluating Professional Development.* Thousand Oaks, CA: Corwin Press, Inc.

Guskey, T. R., & Huberman, M. (1995). *Professional development in education: New paradigms and practices.* New York: Teachers College Press.

Gutierrez, K. D., & Penuel, W. R. (2014). Relevance to practice as a criterion for rigor. *Educational Researcher, 43*, 19–23. doi: 10.3102/0013189X13510189

Hall, G. E., & Hord, S. M. (2011). *Implementing change: Patterns, principles, and potholes* (3rd ed.). Boston, MA: Allyn & Bacon.

Hall, G. E., & Loucks, S. F. (1978). *Innovation configurations: Analyzing the adaptation of innovations.* Austin, TX: Research and Development Center for Teacher Education.

Hamre, B. K., Pianta, R. C., Downer, J. T., DeCoster, J., Mashburn, A. J., Jones, S. M., . . . Hamagami, A. (2013). Teaching through interactions: Testing a developmental framework of teacher effectiveness in over 4,000 classrooms. *The Elementary School Journal, 113*, 461–487. doi: 10.1086/669616

Harackiewicz, J., Barron, K., Taucer, J., Carter, S., & Elliot, A. (2000). Short-term and long-term consequences of achievement goals: Predicting interest and performance over time. *Journal of Educational Psychology, 92*, 316–330.

Haring, N. G. & Eaton, M. D. (1978). Systematic procedures: An instructional hierarchy. In N. G. Haring, T. C. Lovitt, M. D., Eaton, & C. L. Hansen (Eds.), *The fourth R: Research in the classroom.* Columbus, OH: Charles E. Merrill Publishing Company.

Harms, A., & Oskam, R. (2014). *MIBLSI Database.* Michigan Department of Education, Michigan's Integrated Behavior and Learning Support Initiative.

Harn, B., Parisi, D., & Stoolmiller, M. (2013). Balancing fidelity with flexibility and fit: What do we really know about fidelity of implementation in schools? *Exceptional Children, 79*, 181–193.

Hasbrouck, J. E., & Tindal, G. (1992). Curriculum-based oral reading fluency norms for students in Grades 2 through 5. *Teaching Exceptional Children, 24*, 41–44.

Hasbrouck, J. E., & Tindal, G. (2005). *Oral reading fluency: 90 years of measurement* (Technical Report No. 33). Eugene, OR: Behavioral Research and Training.

Hattie, J. (2009). *Visible learning: A synthesis of over 800 meta-analyses relating to achievement.* New York: Routledge.

Hawkins, R. O., Morrison, J. Q., Musti-Rao, S., & Hawkins, J. A. (2008). Treatment integrity for academic interventions in real world settings. *School Psychology Forum: Research in Practice, 2*(3), 1–15.

Heath, C., & Heath, D. (2008). *Made to stick: Why some ideas survive and others die.* New York, NY: Random House.

Heibert, J., Gallimore, R., & Stigler, W. (2002). A knowledge base for the teaching profession: What would it look like and how can we get one? *Educational Researcher, 31*(5), 3–15.

Henry, G. T., McTaggert, M. J., & McMillan, J. H. (1992). Establishing benchmarks for outcome indicators: A statistical approach to developing performance standards. *Evaluation Review, 16*, 131–150.

Hintze, J. M. (2005). Psychometrics of direct observation. *School Psychology Review, 34*, 507–519.

Hintze, J., & Matthews, W. (2004). The generalizability of systematic direct observations across time and setting: A preliminary investigation of the psychometrics of behavioral observation. *School Psychology Review, 33*, 258–270.

Hintze, J. M., & Silberglitt, B. (2005). A longitudinal examination of the diagnostic accuracy and predictive validity of R-CBM and high-stakes testing. *School Psychology Review, 34*, 372–386.

Hinyard, L. J., & Kreuter, M. W. (2007). Using narrative communication as a tool for health behavior change: A conceptual, theoretical, and empirical overview. *Health Education & Behavior, 34*, 777–792.

Hohmann, A. A., & Shear, M. K. (2002). Community-based intervention research: Coping with the "noise" of real life in study design. *American Journal of Psychiatry, 159*, 201–207.

Hood, P. (2002). Perspectives on knowledge utilization in education. San Francisco, CA: WestEd. Retrieved from http://www.wested.org/online_pubs/perspectives.pdf.

Horn, I. S., & Little, J. W. (2010). Attending to problems of practice: Routines and resources for professional learning in teachers' workplace interactions. *American Educational Research Journal, 47*, 181–217.

Horner, R. H., Carr, E.G., Halle, J., McGee, G., Odom, S., & Wolery, M. (2005). The use of single-subject research to identify evidence-based practice in special education. *Exceptional Children, 71*, 165–179.

Horner, R. H., Todd, A. W., Lewis-Palmer, T., Irvin, L. K., Sugai, G., & Boland, J. B. (2004). The School-wide Evaluation Tool (SET): A research instrument for assessing school-wide positive behavior support. *Journal of Positive Behavior Interventions, 6*, 3–12.

Hosp, M. K. & Fuchs, L. S. (2005). Using CBM as an indicator of decoding, word reading, and comprehension: Do the relations change with grade? *School Psychology Review, 34*, 9–26.

Hosp, J. L., Hosp, M. K., Howell, K. W., & Allison, R. (2014). The ABCs of curriculum-based evaluation: A practical guide to effective decision making. New York: The Guilford Press.

Howard, G. S. (1980). Response-shift bias: A problem in evaluating interventions with pre/post self-reports. *Evaluation Review, 4*, 93–106.

Hubbard, L., & Mehan, H. (1999). Scaling up an untracking program: A co-constructed process. *Journal of Education for Students Placed at Risk, 4*(10), 83–100.

Huberman, M., & Miles, M. B. (1984). Innovation up close: How school improvement works. New York: Plenum.

Humphry, S. M., & Heldsinger, S. A. (2014). Common structural design features of rubrics may represent a threat to validity. *Educational Researcher, 43*, 253–263.

Hyman, R. B. (1993). Evaluation of an intervention for staff in long-term care facility using a retrospective pretest design. *Evaluation in the Health Professions, 16*, 212–224.

Irvin, L. K., Tobin, T. J., Sprague, J. R., Sugai, G., & Vincent, C. G. (2004). Validity of office discipline referral measures as indices of school-wide behavioral status and effects of school-wide behavioral interventions. *Journal of Positive Behavior Interventions, 6*, 131–147.

Jackson, C. K., & Bruegmann, E. (2009). Teaching students and teaching each other: The importance of peer learning for teachers. *American Economic Journal: Applied Economics, 1*, 85–108.

Johnson, R. B., & Stefurak, T. (2013). Considering the evidence-and-credibility discussion in evaluation through the lens of dialectical pluralism. In D. M. Mertens & S. Hesse-Biber (Eds.), *Mixed methods and credibility of evidence in evaluation. New Directions for Evaluation, 138,* 37–48.

Jonsson, A., & Svingby, G. (2007). The use of scoring rubrics: Reliability, validity and educational consequences. *Educational Research Review, 2,* 130–144.

Joyce, B., & Showers, B. (1995). *Student achievement through staff development: Fundamentals of school renewal* (2nd ed.). New York: Longman.

Justice, L. M., Mashburn, A. J., Hamre, B. K., & Pianta, R. C. (2008). Quality of language and literacy instruction in preschool classrooms serving at-risk pupils. *Early Childhood Research Quarterly, 23,* 51–68. doi: 10.1016/j.ecresq.2007.09.004

Kaderavek, J. N., & Justice, L. M. (2010). Fidelity: An essential component of evidence-based practice in speech-language pathology. *American Journal of Speech-Language Pathology, 19,* 369–379. doi: 10.1044/1058-0360(2010/09-0097)

Kamphaus, R. W., & Reynolds, C. R. (2007). *BASC-2 Behavioral and Emotional Screening System.* Minneapolis, MN: Pearson.

Kazdin, A. E. (1981). Drawing valid inferences from case studies. *Journal of Consulting and Clinical Psychology, 49,* 183–192.

Kazdin, A. (2011). *Single-case research designs* (2nd ed.). New York, NY: Oxford University Press.

Kilgus, S. P., Chafouleas, S. M., & Riley-Tillman, T. C. (2013). Development and initial validation of the Social and Academic Behavior Risk Screener for elementary grades. *School Psychology Quarterly, 28,* 210–226. doi:10.1037/spq0000024

Killion, J. (2008). *Assessing impact: Evaluating staff development* (2nd ed.). Thousand Oaks, CA: Corwin Press, Inc.

Killion, J., Harrison, C., Bryan, C., & Clifton, H. (2012). *Coaching matters.* Thousand Oaks, CA: Learning Forward.

Kiresuk, T. J., Smith, A., & Cardillo, J. E. (Eds.) (1994). *Goal attainment scaling: Applications, theory, and measurement.* Hillsdale, NJ: Lawrence Erlbaum Associates.

Kirkpatrick, D. L., & Kirkpatrick, J. D. (2006). *Evaluating training programs.* San Francisco, CA: Berrett-Koehler Publishers, Inc.

Kirkpatrick, D. L., & Kirkpatrick, J. D. (2007). *Implementing the four levels: A practical guide for effective evaluation of training programs.* San Francisco, CA: Berrett-Koehler Publishers, Inc.

Knaflic, C. N. (2015). *Storytelling with data: A data visualization guide for business professionals.* Hoboken, NY: John Wiley & Sons.

Knight, J. (2007). *Instructional coaching: A partnership approach to improving instruction.* Thousand Oaks, CA: Corwin Press and Learning Forward.

Koedel, C. (2009). An empirical analysis of teacher spillover effects in secondary school. *Economics of Education Review, 28,* 682–692.

Kovaleski, J. F. (2002). Best practices in operating pre-referral intervention teams. In A. Thomas, & J. Grimes (Eds.), *Best practices in school psychology IV* (pp. 645–656). Bethesda, MD: National Association of School Psychologists.

Kraft, M. A., & Papay, J. P. (2014). Can professional environments in schools promote teacher development? Explaining heterogeneity in returns to teaching experience, *Educational Evaluation and Policy Analysis, 36,* 476–500. doi: 10.3102/0162373713519496

Kratochwill, T. R., Volpiansky, P., Clements, M., & Ball, C. (2007). Professional development in implementing and sustaining multitier prevention models: Implications for response to intervention. *School Psychology Review, 36*, 618–631.

Lamb, T. A., & Tschillard, R. (2005). Evaluating learning in professional development workshops: Using the retrospective pretest. *The Journal of Research in Professional Learning.* Retrieved from http://nsdc.org/library/publications/research/lowden.pdf

Lane, K. L. (2007). Identifying and supporting students at risk for emotional and behavioral disorders within multi-level models: Data driven approaches to conducting secondary interventions with an academic emphasis. *Education and Treatment of Children, 30*, 135–164.

Lane, K. L., Kalberg, J. R., Parks, R. J., & Carter, E. W. (2008). Student Risk Screening Scale: Initial evidence for score reliability and validity at the high school level. *Journal of Emotional and Behavioral Disorders, 16*, 178–190.

Lane, K. L., Oakes, W. P., Menzies, H. M., Major, R., Allegra, L., Powers, L., & Schatschneider, C. (2015). The Student Risk Screening Scale for Early Childhood: An initial validation study. *Topics in Early Childhood Special Education, 34*, 234–249.

Lane, K. L., Parks, R. J., Kalberg, J. R., & Carter, E. W. (2007). Systematic screening at the middle school level: Score reliability and validity of the Student Risk Screening Scale. *Journal of Emotional and Behavioral Disorders, 15*, 209–222.

Lane, K. L., Richards, C., Oakes, W. P., & Connor, K. (2014). Initial evidence for the reliability and validity of the Student Risk Screening Scale with elementary age English learners. *Assessment for Effective Intervention, 39*, 219–232.

Langberg, J., & Smith, B. (2006). Developing evidence-based interventions for deployment into school settings: A case example highlighting key issues of efficacy and effectiveness. *Evaluation and Program Planning, 29*, 323–334.

Learning Forward. (2012). Standards for Professional Learning. Retrieved from, http://learningforward.org/standards-for-professional-learning#.U-EvhPldXFo.

Leviton, L. C. (2001). Presidential address: Building evaluation's collective capacity. *American Journal of Evaluation, 22*, 1.

Lewis-Palmer, T., Todd, A. W., Horner, R. H., Sugai, G., & Sampson, N. K. (2006). *Individual-Student Systems Evaluation Tool.* Eugene: University of Oregon, Educational and Community Supports.

Lieberman, A., & Wood, D. R. (2003). *Inside the National Writing Project: Connecting network learning and classroom teaching.* New York, NY: Teachers College Press.

Lipkus, I. M., & Hollands, J. G. (1999). The visual communication of risk. *Journal of the National Cancer Institutes Monograph, 25*, 149–163.

Lipsey, M. W. (2009). The primary factors that characterize effective interventions with juvenile offenders: A meta-analytic overview. *Victims and Offenders, 4*, 124–147.

Little, J. (1982). Norms for collegiality and experimentation: Workplace conditions of school success. *American Educational Research Journal, 19*, 325–340.

Loewenberg, A. (2015, December 1). New raises questions about RTI Implementation. *EdCentral.* Available at: http://www.edcentral.org/rtistudy/

Loucks-Horsley, S., Hewson, P. W., Love, N., & Stiles, K. (1998). *Designing professional development for teachers of science and mathematics.* Thousand Oaks, CA: Corwin Press.

Love, A. J. (2003). *Beyond the black box: Strengthening performance measurement through implementation evaluation.* Presentation to the Canadian Evaluation Society National

Capital Chapter. Available: http://www.evaluationcanada.ca/distribution/20031126_love_arnold.pdf

Luborsky, L., McLellan, A. T., Diguer, L., Woody, G., & Seligman, D. A. (1997). The psychotherapist matters: Comparison of outcomes across twenty-two therapists and seven patient samples. *Clinical Psychology: Science & Practice, 4*, 53–65.

Ma, H.-H. (2006). An alternative method for quantitative synthesis of single-subject researches: Percentage of data points exceeding the median. *Behavior Modification, 30*, 598–617. doi: 10.1177/0145445504272974

MacKay, G., McCool, S., Cheseldine, S., & McCartney, E. (1993). Goal attainment scaling: A technique for evaluating conductive education. *British Journal of Special Education, 20*, 143–147.

Mahajan, V., & Peterson, R. A. (1985). *Models for innovation diffusion.* Thousand Oaks, CA:Sage.

Mandinach, E. B., & Gummer, E. S. (2013). A systemic view of implementing data literacy in educator preparation. *Educational Researcher, 42*(1), 30–37. doi: 10.3102/0013189X12459803

Mathur, S. R., Kavale, K. A., Quinn, M. M., Forness, S. R., & Rutherford, R. B. (1998). Social skills interventions for students with emotional and behavioral problems: A quantitative synthesis of single-subject research. *Behavioral Disorders, 23*, 193–201.

Mayer, D. P. (1999). Measuring instructional practice: Can policymakers trust survey data? *Educational Evaluation and Policy Analysis, 21*(1), 29–45.

McDonald, P. W., & Viehbeck, S. (2007). From evidence-based practice making to practice-based evidence making: Creating communities of (research) and practice. *Health Promotion Practice, 8*(2), 140–144.

McGregor, H., & Elliot, A. (2002). Achievement goals as predicators of achievement-relevant processes prior to task engagement. *Journal of Educational Psychology, 94*, 381–395.

McGrew, J. H., Bond, G. R., Dietzen, L., & Salyers, M. (1994). Measuring the fidelity of implementation of a mental health program model. *Journal of Consulting and Clinical Psychology, 62*, 670–678.

McIntosh, K., Chard, D. J., Boland, J. B., & Horner, R. H. (2006). Demonstrations of combined efforts in school-wide academic and behavioral systems and incidence of reading and behavior challenges in early elementary grades. *Journal of Positive Behavior Interventions, 8*, 146–154.

McIntosh, K., & Goodman, S. (2016). *Integrated multi-tiered systems of support: Blending RTI and PBIS.* New York, NY: The Guilford Press.

McIntosh, K., Frank, J. L., & Spaulding, S. A. (2010). Establishing research-based trajectories of office discipline referrals for individual students. *School Psychology Review, 39*, 380–394.

McIntosh, K., Massar, M. M., Algozzine, R. F., George, H. P. Horner, R. H., Lewis, T. J., & Swain-Bradway, J. (2016). Technical adequacy of the SWPBIS Tiered Fidelity Inventory. *Journal of Positive Behavior Interventions.* Available at http://pbi.sagepub.com/content/early/2016/03/17/1098300716637193

McLaughlin, M., & Talbert, J. (2003). *Reforming districts: How districts support school reform. A research report.* Seattle, WA: Center for the Study of Teaching and Policy, University of Washington. Retrieved November 9, 2006, from http://depts.washington.edu/ctpmail/PDFs/ReformingDistricts-09-2003.pdf

Meijer, C. J. W., & Foster, S. F. (1988). The effect of teacher self-efficacy on referral change. *Journal of Special Education, 22*, 378–385.

Menzies, H. M. & Lane, K. L. (2012). Validity of the Student Risk Screening Scale: Evidence of predictive validity in a diverse, suburban elementary setting. *Journal of Emotional and Behavioral Disorders, 20*, 82–91.

Metz, A. (2012). Developing, measuring, and improving program fidelity: Achieving positive outcomes through high-fidelity implementation. Invited presentation at the State Personnel Development Grant (SPDG) National Conference, Washington, DC.

Meyer, P. J. (2003). *What would you do if you knew you couldn't fail? Creating S.M.A.R.T. Goals. Attitude is Everything: If You Want to Succeed Above and Beyond.* Scotts Valley, CA: Meyer Resource Group, Inc.

Midgley, C., Feldlaufer, H., & Eccles, J. (1989). Change in teacher efficacy and student self- and task-related beliefs in mathematics during the transition to junior high school. *Journal of Educational Psychology, 81*, 247–258.

Millar, A., R.S., Simeone, & J.T. Carnevale. (2001). Logic models: a systems tool for performance management. *Evaluation and Program Planning, 24*, 73–81.

Miller, A. H. (1987). Course design for university lecturers. New York: Nichols Publishing.

Miller, R., Greene, B., Montalvo, G., Ravindran, B., & Nichols, J. (1996). Engagement in academic work: The role of learning goals, future consequences, pleasing others and perceived ability. *Contemporary Educational Psychology, 21*, 388–422.

Mills, S. C., & Ragan, T. J. (2000). A tool for analyzing implementation fidelity of an integrated learning system (ILS). *Educational Technology Research and Development, 48*, 21–41.

Minneapolis Public Schools. (2002). Problem solving model. Minneapolis, MN: author. Available online at http://pic.mpls.k12.mn.us/Problem_Solving_Model_Worksheets_1__2_and_3.html

Moncher, F. J., & Prinz, R. J. (1991). Treatment fidelity in outcome studies. *Clinical Psychology Review, 11*, 247–266. doi: 10.1016/0272-7358(91)90103-2

Morrison, J. Q. (2013). Performance evaluation and accountability for school psychologists: Challenges and opportunities. *Psychology in the Schools, 50*, 314–324. doi: 10.1002/ pits.21670

Morrison, J. Q. (2015). Technical adequacy of the Student Protective Factors Screening Scale (SPF-7) as a universal screening tool. *Psychology, 6*, 817–832. Available from http://dx.doi.org/10.4236/psych.2015.67081

Morrison, J. Q., Ellenwood, A., Sansosti, F., Cochrane, W., Jenkins, J., Evans, J., . . . Miranda, A. H. (2011). Evaluation of the Ohio Internship Program in School Psychology: Five-Year Summary, 2004-05 to 2008-09. *Trainers of School Psychologists: Trainers' Forum, 29*(4), 36–56.

Morrison, J. Q., Graden, J. L., & Barnett, D. W. (2009). Steps to evaluating a state-wide internship program: Model, trainee, and student outcomes. *Psychology in the Schools, 46*, 989–1005.

Moskal, B. M., & Leydens, J. A. (2000). Scoring rubric development: Validity and reliability. *Practical Assessment, Research and Evaluation, 7*(10) Available: http://pareonline.net/getvn.asp?v=7&n=10.

Mowbray, C. T., Holter, M. C., Teague, G. B., & Bybee, D. (2003). Fidelity criteria: Development, measurement, and validation. *American Journal of Evaluation, 24*, 315–340.

Muijs, D., & Reynolds, D. (2002). Teacher beliefs and behaviors: What matters. *Journal of Classroom Interaction, 37,* 3–15.

National Center for Education Research. (2015). The role of between-case effect size in conducting, interpreting, and summarizing single-case research (NCER 2015-002). Institute of Education Sciences, U. S. Department of Education, Washington D. C.

Nelson, S. R., Leffler, J. C., & Hansen, B. A. (2009). *Toward a research agenda for understanding and improving the use of research evidence.* Portland, OR: Northwest Regional Educational Laboratory. Retrieved from http://educationnorthwest.org/webfm_send/311

Nevo, D. (2001). School evaluation: Internal or external? *Studies in Educational Evaluation, 27,* 95–106.

Noell, G. H. (2008). Studying relationships among consultation process, treatment integrity, and outcomes. In W. P. Erchul & S. M. Sheridan (Eds.), *Handbook of research in school consultation: Empirical foundations for the field* (pp. 323–342). Mahwah, NJ: Erlbaum.

Noell, G. H., Duhon, G. J., Gatti, S. L., & Connell, J. E. (2002). Consultation, follow-up, and implementation of behavior management interventions in general education. *School Psychology Review, 31,* 217–234.

Noell, G. H., & Gresham, F. M. (1993). Functional outcome analysis: Do the benefits of consultation and prereferral intervention justify the costs? *School Psychology Quarterly, 8*(3), 200–226.

Noonan, P., Gaumer Erickson, A. S., Brussow, J. A., & Langham, A. (2015). *Observation checklist for high-quality professional development in education* [Updated version]. Lawrence, KS: University of Kansas, Center for Research on Learning. Available at http://www.researchcollaboration.org/page/high-quality-professional-development-checklist.

Oakes, W. P., Wilder, K. S., Lane, K. L., Powers, L., Yokoyama, L. T. K., O'Hare, M. E., & Jenkins, A. B. (2010). Psychometric properties of the Student Risk Screening Scale: An effective tool for use in diverse urban elementary schools. *Assessment for Effective Intervention, 35*(4), 231–239.

Odom, S. L., Fleming, K., Diamond, K., Lieber, J., Hanson, M., Butera, G., Marquis, J. (2010). Examining different forms of implementation and in early childhood curriculum research. *Early Childhood Research Quarterly, 25,* 314–328. doi: 10.10l6/j.ecresq.2010.03.001

O'Donnell, C. L. (2008). Defining, conceptualizing, and measuring fidelity of implementation and its relationship to outcomes in K–12 curriculum intervention research. *Review of Educational Research, 78,* 33–84. doi: 10.3102/0034654307313793

Olive, M. L., & Smith, B. W. (2005). Effect size calculations and single subject designs. *Educational Psychology, 25,* 313–324.

Oliver, R. B., Wehby, J. H., & Nelson, J. R. (2015). Helping teachers maintain classroom management practices using a self-monitoring checklist. *Teaching and Teacher Education, 51,* 113–120.

OSEP Center on Positive Behavioral Interventions and Supports. (2009). *What is School-wide Positive Behavioral Interventions and Supports?* Eugene, OR: Author. Available: www.PBIS.org.

Otis-Wilborn, A. K., Winn, J. A., & Ford, A. (2000). Standards, benchmarks, and indictors. *Teaching Exceptional Children, 32*(5), 20–28.

Ottoson, J. M. (2009). Knowledge-for-action theories in evaluation: Knowledge utilization, diffusion, implementation, transfer, and translation. In J. M. Ottoson & P. Hawe (Eds.), Knowledge utilization, diffusion, implementation, transfer, and translation: Implications for evaluation. *New Directions for Evaluation, 124,* 7–20.

Ottoson, J. M., & Hawe, P. (2009). Knowledge utilization, diffusion, implementation, transfer, and translation: Implications for evaluation. *New Directions for Evaluation, no. 124*. Hoboken, NJ: Wiley Periodicals, Inc.

Owen, N., Glanz, K., Sallis, J. F., & Kelder, S. H. (2006). Evidence-based approaches to dissemination and diffusion of physical activity interventions. *American Journal of Preventive Medicine, 31*(4S), S35–S44.

Owen, J. & Lambert, K. (1995). Roles for evaluators in learning organizations. *Evaluation, 1*, 237–250.

Patton, M. Q. (2008). *Utilization-focused evaluation* (4th ed.). Thousand Oaks, CA: Sage.

Paulson, R. I., Post, R. L., Herincks, H. A., & Risser, P. (2002). Beyond components: Using fidelity scales to measure and assure choice in program implementation and quality assurance. *Community Mental Health Journal, 38*, 119–128.

Penuel, W. R., & Spillane, J. P. (2014). Learning sciences and policy design and implementation: Key concepts and tools for collaborative engagement. In R. K. Sawyer (Ed.), *The Cambridge Handbook of the Learning Sciences* (2nd ed.) (pp. 649–667). New York, NY: Cambridge University Press.

Perepletchikova, F., & Kazdin, A. E. (2005). Treatment integrity and therapeutic change: Issues and research recommendations. *Clinical Psychology: Science and Practice, 12*, 365–383.

Peterson, L., Homer, A. L., & Wonderlich, S. A. (1982). The integrity of independent variables in behavior analysis. *Journal of Applied Behavior Analysis, 15*, 477–492.

Phillips, J. J., & Stone, R. D. (2002). *How to measure training results*. New York, NY: McGraw Hill.

Pianta, R. C., La Paro, K. M., & Hamre, B. K. (2008). *Classroom assessment scoring system*. Baltimore, MD: Brookes.

Porter, A. C., Kirst, M. W., Osthoff, E. J., Smithson, J. L., & Schneider, S. A. (1993). *Reform up close: An analysis of high school mathematics and science classrooms*. New Brunswick, NJ: Consortium for Policy Research in Education.

Power, T. J., Blom-Hoffman, J., Clarke, A. T., Riley-Tillman, T. C., Kelleher, C., & Manz, P. H. (2005). Reconceptualizing intervention integrity: A partnership-based framework for linking research with practice. *Psychology in the Schools, 42*, 495–507. doi: 10.1002/pits.20087

Pratt, C. C., McGuigan, W. M., & Katzev, A. R. (2000). Measuring program outcomes: Using retrospective pretest methodology. *American Journal of Evaluation, 21*, 341–349.

Predy, L., McIntosh, K., & Frank, J. L. (2014). Utility of number and type of office discipline referrals in predicting chronic problem behavior in middle school. *School Psychology Review, 43*(4), 472–489.

Preskill, H., & Boyle, S. (2008). A multidisciplinary model of evaluation capacity building. *American Journal of Evaluation, 29*, 443–459.

Preskill, H., & Jones, N. (2009). A practical guide for engaging stakeholders in developing evaluation questions. Robert Wood Johnson Foundation. Available from http://bit.ly/eq-rwjf

Preskill, H., & Torres, R. T. (1999). *Evaluative inquiry for learning in organizations*. Thousand Oaks, CA: Sage.

Ravallion, M. (2009). Evaluating three stylised interventions. *Journal of Development Effectiveness, 1*(3), 227–236.

Reddy, Y. M., & Andrade, H. (2010). A review of rubric use in higher education. *Assessment and Evaluation in Higher Education, 35*(4), 435–448.

Rezaei, A. R., & Lovorn, M. (2010). Reliability and validity of rubrics for assessment through writing. *Assessing Writing, 15*(1), 18–39.

Rivkin, S. G., Hanushek, E. A., & Kain, J. F. (2005). Teachers, schools, and academic achievement. *Econometrica, 73*, 417–458.

Roach, A. T., & Elliott, S. N. (2005). Goal attainment scaling: An efficient and effective approach to monitoring student progress. *Teaching Exceptional Children, 37*(4), 8–17.

Rockoff, J. E. (2004). The impact of individual teachers on student achievement: Evidence from panel data. *American Economic Review, 94*, 247–252.

Rogers, E. (2003). *Diffusion of innovations* (5th ed.). New York, NY: Free Press.

Rogers, P. (2009). Matching impact evaluation design to the nature of the intervention and the purpose of the evaluation. *Journal of Development Effectiveness, 1*(3), 217–229.

Rosenfield, S. A., & Gravois, T. A. (1996). Instructional consultation teams: Collaborating for change. New York, NY: Guilford.

Ross, J. A. (1992). Teacher efficacy and the effect of coaching on student achievement. *Canadian Journal of Education, 17*, 51–65.

Ross, J. A., McDougall, D., Hogaboam-Gray, A., & LeSage, A. (2003). A survey measuring elementary teachers' implementation of standards-based mathematics teaching. *Journal for Research in Mathematics Education, 34*(1), 344–363.

Rossi, P., & Freeman, H. (1982). *Evaluation: A systematic approach* (2nd ed.). Beverly Hills, CA: SAGE.

Rouse, H. L., & Fantuzzo, J. W. (2006). Validity of the dynamic indicators for basic early literacy skills as an indicator of early literacy for urban kindergarten children. *School Psychology Review, 35*(3), 341–355.

Russell, C., & Harms, A. (2016). Michigan's integrated behavior and learning support initiative a statewide system of support for MTSS. In K. McIntosh & S. Goodman (Eds.) *Multi-tiered Systems of Support: Integrating Academic RTI and School-wide PBIS.* (pp. 305–324). New York, NY: Guilford Press.

Sanetti, L. M. H., Chafouleas, S. M., Christ, T. J., & Gritter, K. L. (2009). Extending use of Direct Behavior Rating beyond student assessment: Applications to treatment integrity assessment within a multi-tier model of school-based intervention delivery. *Assessment for Effective Intervention, 34*, 251–258.

Sanetti, L. M. H., & Collier-Meek, M. A. (2014). Increasing the rigor of procedural fidelity assessment: An empirical comparison of direct observation and permanent product review methods. *Journal of Behavioral Education, 23*, 60–88. doi: 10.1007/s10864-013-9179-z

Sanetti, L. M. H., & Kratochwill, T. R. (2009). Treatment integrity assessment in the schools: An evaluation of the treatment integrity planning protocol. *School Psychology Quarterly, 24*, 24–35.

Sanetti, L. M. H., & Kratochwill, T. R. (2011). An evaluation of the treatment integrity planning protocol and two schedules of treatment integrity self-report: Impact on implementation and report accuracy. *Journal of Educational and Psychological Consultation, 21*, 284–308.

Sanetti, L. M. H., & Kratochwill, T. R. (2014). *Treatment integrity: A foundation for evidence-based practice in applied psychology.* Washington, DC: American Psychological Association.

Scheirer, M. A. (1994). Designing and using process evaluation. In J. S. Wholey, H. P. Hatry, & K. E. Newcomer (Eds.), *Handbook of Practical Program Evaluation* (pp. 40–68). San Francisco: Jossey-Bass, Inc.

Scott, T. M., & Barrett, S. B. (2004). Using staff and student time engaged in disciplinary procedures to evaluate the impact of school-wide PBS. *Journal of Positive Behavior Interventions, 6*(1), 21–27.

Scribner, J. P., Sawyer, R. K., Watson, S., & Myers, V. L. (2007). Teacher teams and distributed leadership: A study of group discourse and collaboration. *Educational Administration Quarterly, 43,* 67–100.

Scriven, M. (1967). The methodology of evaluation. In R. E. Stake (Ed.), *Curriculum evaluation* (American Educational Research Association Monograph Series on Evaluation, No. 1, pp. 39–83). Chicago: Rand McNally.

Scriven, M. (1991). Beyond formative and summative evaluation. In M. W. McLaughlin & D. C. Phillips (Eds.), *Evaluation and education: At quarter century.* Ninetieth Yearbook of the National Society for the Study of Education (pp. 19–64). Chicago: University of Chicago Press.

Scruggs, T. E., & Mastropieri, M. A. (1998). Summarizing single-subject research: Issues and applications. *Behavior Modification, 22,* 221–242.

Scruggs, T. E., Mastropieri, M. A., & Casto, G. (1987). The quantitative synthesis of single-subject research: Methodology and validation. *Remedial and Special Education, 8,* 24–33.

Scruggs, T. E., Mastropieri, M. A., Cook, S. B., & Escobar, C. (1986). Early intervention for children with conduct disorders: A quantitative synthesis of single-subject research. *Behavioral Disorders, 11,* 260–271.

Severson, H. H., Walker, H. M., Hope-Doolittle, J., Kratochwill, T. R., & Gresham, F. M. (2007). Proactive, early screening to detect behaviorally at-risk students: Issues, approaches, emerging innovations, and professional practices. *Journal of School Psychology, 45,* 193–223.

Shapiro, E. S. (2011). *Academic skills problems: Direct assessment and intervention* (4th Ed.). New York, NY : The Guilford Press.

Shapiro, E. S., & Clemens, N. H. (2009). A conceptual model for evaluating systems effects of response to intervention. *Assessment for Effective Intervention, 35,* 3–16. doi: 10.1177/1534508408330080

Shapiro, E. S., & Heick, P. F. (2004). School psychologist assessment practices in the evaluation of students referred for social/behavioral/emotional problems. *Psychology in the Schools, 41,* 551–561. doi: 10.1002/pits.10176

Shapiro, E. S., Solari, E., & Petscher, J. (2008). Use of a measure of reading comprehension to enhance prediction on the state high stakes assessment. *Learning and Individual Differences, 18,* 316–328.

Sheridan, S. M., Swanger-Gagné, M., Welch, G. W., Kwon, K., & Garbacz, S. A. (2009). Fidelity measurement in consultation: Psychometric issues and preliminary examination. *School Psychology Review, 38,* 476–495.

Shinn, M.R. (Ed.). (1989). *Curriculum-Based Measurement: Assessing Special Children.* New York, NY: Guilford.

Shinn, M.R. (Ed.). (1998). *Advanced Applications of Curriculum-Based Measurement.* New York, NY: Guilford.

Shinn, M. R., Good, R. H., Knutson, N., Tilly, W. D., & Collins, V. L. (1992). Curriculum-based measurement of oral reading fluency: A confirmatory analysis of its relation to reading. *School Psychology Review, 21*, 459–479.

Siegel, W., & Yates, C. (2007). *Improving the evaluation of professional development presentations using retrospective pre-testing of existing knowledge and self-efficacy.* National Council of Professors of Educational Administration. Retrieved January 21, 2008 from https://cnx.org/content/m14362/latest

Silversti, L., & Oescher, J. (2006). Using rubrics to increase the reliability of assessment in health classes. *International Electronic Journal of Health Education, 9*, 25–30.

Skaalvik, E. M., & Skaalvik, S. (2007). Dimensions of teacher self-efficacy and relations with strain factors, collective teacher efficacy, and teacher burnout. *Journal of Educational Psychology, 99*, 611–625. doi: 10.1037/0022-0663.99.3.611

Sladeczek, I. E., Elliott, S. N., Kratochwill, T. R., Robertson-Mjaanes, S., & Stoiber, K. (2001). Application of goal attainment scaling to a conjoint behavioral consultation case. *Journal of Education and Psychological Consultation, 12*, 45–58.

Somuncuoglu, Y., & Yildirim, A. (1999). Relationship between achievement goal orientations and use of learning strategies. *Journal of Educational Research, 92*, 267–277.

Sonnichsen, R. C. (2000). *High impact internal evaluation: A practitioner's guide to evaluating and consulting inside organizations.* Thousand Oaks, CS: Sage.

Soodak, L. C., & Podell, D. M. (1993). Teacher efficacy and student problem as factors in special education referral. *Journal of Special Education, 27*, 66–81.

Soodak, L. C., & Podell, D. M. (1996). Teacher efficacy: Toward the understanding of a multi-faceted construct. *Teaching and Teacher Education, 12*, 401–411.

Sparks, S. D. (2015, November 6). Study: RTI practice falls short of promise. *Education Week, 35*(12), 1, 12. Available online at http://www.edweek.org/ew/articles/2015/11/11/study-rti-practice-falls-short-of-promise.html

Speece, D. L., & Case, L. (2001). Classification in context: An alternative to identifying early reading disability. *Journal of Educational Psychology, 93*, 735–749.

Spillane, J. P., & Zeuli, J. (1999). Reform and teaching: Exploring patterns of practice in the context of national and state mathematics reforms. *Educational Evaluation and Policy Analysis, 21*, 1–27.

State Implementation and Scaling-Up of Evidence-Based Practices (2016). *Communications Protocol.* University of North Carolina at Chapel Hill.

Steege, M. W., Brown-Chidsey, R., & Mace, F. C. (2002). Best practices in evaluating interventions. In A. Thomas & J. Grimes (Eds.). *Best Practices in School Psychology IV.* (pp. 517–534). Bethesda, MD: National Association of School Psychologists.

Stein, M., Berends, M., Fuchs, D., McMaster, K., Saenz, Yen, L., . . . Compton, D. L. (2008). Scaling up an early reading program: Relationships among teacher support, fidelity of implementation, and student performance across different sites and years. *Education Evaluation and Policy Analysis, 30*, 368–388. doi: 10.3102/0162373708322738

Stigler, J. W., Gallimore, R., & Hiebert, J. (2000). Using video surveys to compare classrooms and teaching across cultures: Examples and lessons from the TIMSS video studies. *Educational Psychologist, 35*(2), 87–100.

St. Martin, K. (2016). *District Communication Plan.* Michigan Department of Education, Michigan's Integrated Behavior and Learning Support Initiative.

St. Martin, K., Nantais, M., & Harms, A. (2015). *Reading Tiered Fidelity Inventory Secondary-Level Edition*. Michigan Department of Education, Michigan's Integrated Behavior and Learning Support Initiative.

St. Martin, K., Nantais, M., & Harms, A., Huth, E. (2015). *Reading Tiered Fidelity Inventory Elementary-Level Edition*. Michigan Department of Education, Michigan's Integrated Behavior and Learning Support Initiative.

St. Martin, K., Ward, C., Fixsen, D. L., Harms, A., & Russell, C. (2015). *Regional Capacity Assessment*. National Implementation Research Network, University of North Carolina at Chapel Hill.

Stoolmiller, M., Eddy, J. M., & Reid, J. B. (2000). Detecting and describing preventive intervention effects in a universal school-based randomized trial targeting delinquent and violent behavior. *Journal of Consulting and Clinical Psychology, 68*, 296–306. doi.10.1037/0022-006X.68.2.296

Stringfield, S., & Datnow, A. (1998). Scaling up school restructuring designs in urban schools. *Education and Urban Society, 30*(3), 269–276.

Stufflebeam, D. L. (2004). The 21st-Century CIPP model: Origins, development, and use. In M. Alkin (Ed.), *Evaluation roots: Tracing theorists' views and influences* (pp. 245–266). Thousand Oaks, CA: Sage.

Stufflebeam, D. L. (2005). CIPP model (contest, input, process, product). In S. Mathison (Ed.), *Encyclopedia of evaluation* (pp. 60–65). Thousand Oaks, CA: Sage.

Stufflebeam, D. L., & Coryn, C. L. S. (2014). *Evaluation theory, models, and applications.* (2nd ed.). San Franscisco: Jossey-Bass, Inc.

Sugai, G., & Horner, R. H. (2009). Responsiveness-to-intervention and school-wide positive behavior supports: Integration of multi-tiered system approaches. *Exceptionality, 17*, 223–237.

Sugai, G., Horner, R., Algozzine, B., Barrett, S., Lewis, T., Anderson, C., . . . Simonsen, B. (2010). *Implementation blueprint and self-assessment: Positive behavior interventions and supports*. Eugene, OR: OSEP Center on Positive Behavioral Interventions and Supports. Retrieved from http://www.pbis.org/

Sugai, G., Horner, R. H., Lewis-Palmer, T., & Rossetto Dickey, C. (2011). *Team Implementation Checklist, Version 3.1*. Eugene, OR: Educational and Community Supports, University of Oregon.

Sugai, G., Horner, R. H., & Todd, A. W. (2003). The PBIS Self-Assessment Survey (SAS): Version 2.0. Eugene, OR: University of Oregon, Educational and Community Supports. Retrieved from https://www.pbisassessment.org/Evaluation/Surveys

Sugai, G., Sprague, J. R., Horner, R. H., & Walker, H. M. (2000). Preventing school violence. The use of office discipline referrals to assess and monitor school-wide discipline interventions. *Journal of Emotional and Behavioral Disorders, 8*, 94–101. doi: 10.1177/106342660000800205

Sun, M., Loeb, S., & Grissom, J. A. (2017). Building teacher teams: Evidence of positive spillovers from more effective colleagues. *Educational Evaluation and Policy Analysis, 39*, 104–125. doi: 10.3102/0162373716665698

Sun, M., Penuel, W. R., Frank, K. A., Gallagher, H. A., & Youngs, P. (2013). Shaping professional development to promote the diffusion of instructional expertise among teachers. *Educational Evaluation and Policy Analysis, 35*(3), 344–369. doi: 10.3102/0162373713482763

Szulanski, G., & Winter, S. (2002). Getting it right the second time. *Harvard Business Review, 80*, 62–69.

Teague, G. B., Bond, G. R., & Drake, R. E. (1998). Program fidelity and assertive community treatment: Development and use of a measure. *American Journal of Orthopsychiatry, 68*, 216–232.

Thompson, B. (2007). Effect sizes, confidence intervals, and confidence intervals for effect sizes. *Psychology in the Schools, 44*, 423–432.

Todd, A., Horner, R., Newton, J. S., Algozzine, R., Algozzine, K. M., & Frank, J. L (2011). Effects of team initiated problem solving on decision making by school-wide behavior support teams. *Journal of Applied School Psychology, 27*, 42–59.

Todd, A. W., Lewis-Palmer, T., Horner, R. H., Sugai, G., Sampson, N. K., & Phillips, D. (2012). *School-wide evaluation tool (SET) implementation manual: Version 2.0.* Eugene, OR: University of Oregon.

Trivette, C. M., Dunst, C. J., Hamby, D. W., & O'Herin, C. E. (2009). Characteristics and consequences of adult learning methods and strategies. *Winterberry Research Synthesis, 2*(2), 1–33.

Tschannen-Moran, M., Hoy, A. W., & Hoy, W. K. (1998). Teacher efficacy: Its meaning and measure. *Review of Educational Research, 68*, 202–248.

Tschannen-Moran, M., & Woolfolk Hoy, A. (2001). Teacher efficacy: Capturing an elusive construct. *Teaching and Teacher Education, 17*, 783–805. doi:10.1016/S0742-051X(01)00036-1

Tseng, V. (2012). The uses of research in policy and practice. *Social Policy Report, 26*(2). Retrieved from http://www.srcd.org/index.php?option=com_content&task=view&id=232&itemid=658

Van Norman, E. R., Nelson, P. M., Shin, J., & Christ, T. J. (2013). An evaluation of the effects of graphic aids in improving decision accuracy in a continuous treatment design. *Journal of Behavioral Education, 22*, 283–301.

VanDerHeyden, A. M. (2010). Determining early mathematical risk: Ideas for extending the research. *School Psychology Review, 39*, 196–202.

VanDerHeyden, A. M. (2013). Universal screening may not be for everyone: Using a threshold model as a smarter way to determine risk. *School Psychology Review, 42*, 402–414.

VanDerHeyden, A. M., Broussard, C., & Cooley, A. (2006). Further development of measures of early math performance for preschoolers. *Journal of School Psychology, 44*, 533–553.

VanDerHeyden, A. M., Broussard, C., Snyder, P., George, J., Lafleur, S. M., & Williams, C. (2011). Measurement of kindergartners' understanding of early mathematical concepts. *School Psychology Review, 40*, 296–306.

VanDerHeyden, A. M., & Burns, M. K. (2005a). Effective instruction for at-risk minority populations. In C. L. Frisby & C. R. Reynolds (Eds.), *Comprehensive handbook of multicultural school psychology* (pp. 483–515). Hoboken, NJ: John Wiley & Sons, Inc.

VanDerHeyden, A. M., & Burns, M. K. (2005b). Using curriculum-based assessment and curriculum-based measurement to guide elementary mathematics instruction: Effect on individual and group accountability scores. *Assessment for Effective Interventions, 30*, 15–31.

VanDerHeyden, A., Burns, M., Brown, R., Shinn, M. R., Kukic, S., Gibbons, K., Batsche, G., & Tilly, W. D. (2016, January 5). Four steps to implement RTI correctly. *Education*

Week, 35, 25. Available at: http://www.edweek.org/ew/articles/2016/01/06/four-steps-to-implement-rti-correctly.html

VanDerHeyden, A. M., & Witt, J. C. (2005). Quantifying context in assessment: Capturing the effect of base rates on teacher referral and a problem-solving model of identification. *School Psychology Review, 34,* 161–183.

VanDerHeyden, A. M., Witt, J. C., & Barnett, D. W. (2005). The emergence and possible futures of response to intervention. *Journal of Psychoeducational Assessment, 23,* 339–361.

VanDerHeyden, A. M., Witt, J. C., & Gilbertson, D. (2007). A multi-year evaluation of the effects on a Response to Intervention (RTI) model on identification of children for special education. *Journal of School Psychology, 45,* 225–256.

VanDerHeyden, A. M., Witt, J. C., & Naquin, G. (2003). Development and validation of a process for screening referrals to special education. *School Psychology Review, 32,* 204–227.

VanHoof, J., & Van Petegem, P. (2007). Matching internal and external evaluation in an era of accountability and school development: Lessons from a Flemish perspective. *Studies in Educational Evaluation, 33,* 101–119.

Vaughn, S., Wanzek, J., Woodruff, A. L., & Linan-Thompson, S. (2007). Prevention and early identification of students with reading disabilities. In D. Haager, J. Klingner, & S. Vaughn (Eds.), *Evidence-based reading practices for response to intervention* (pp. 11–27). Baltimore: Paul H. Brookes Publishing.

Vincent, C., Spaulding, S., & Tobin, T. J. (2010). A reexamination of the psychometric properties of the school-wide evaluation tool (SET). *Journal of Positive Behavior Interventions, 12,* 161–179. doi: 10.1177/1098300709332345

Volkov, B. B. (2011a). Internal evaluation a quarter-century later: A conversation with Arnold J. Love. In B. B. Volkov & M. E. Baron (Eds.), *Internal evaluation in the 21st century. New Directions for Evaluation, 132,* 5–12.

Volkov, B. B. (2011b). Beyond being an evaluator: The multiplicity of roles of the internal evaluator. In B. B. Volkov & M. E. Baron (Eds.), *Internal evaluation in the 21st century. New Directions for Evaluation, 132,* 25–42.

Volpe, R. J., DiPerna, J. C., Hintze, J. M., & Shapiro, E. S. (2005). Observing students in classroom settings: A review of seven coding schemes. *School Psychology Review, 34,* 454–474.

Wald, H. S., Borkan, J. M., Scott Taylor, J., Anthony, D., & Schmuel, P. R. (2012). Fostering and evaluating reflective capacity in medical education: Developing the REFLECT rubric for assessing reflective writing. *Academic Medicine, 87*(1), 41–50.

Wallace, E, Blase, K., Fixsen, D., & Naoom, S. (2008). *Implementing the findings of research: Bridging the gap between knowledge and practice.* Washington, DC: Education Research Service.

Ward, C., St. Martin, K., Horner, R., Duda, M., Ingram-West, K., Tedesco, M., Putnam, D., Buenrostro, M., & Chaparro, E. (2015). *District Capacity Assessment.* University of North Carolina at Chapel Hill.

Watling, R., & Arlow, M. (2002). Wishful thinking: Lessons from the internal and external evaluations of an innovatory education project in Northern Ireland. *Evaluation and Research in Education, 16,* 166–181.

Wayne, A. J., Yoon, K. S., Zhu, P., Cronen, S., & Garet, M. S. (2008). Experimenting with teacher professional development: Motives and methods. *Educational Researcher, 37,* 469–479.

Webster-Stratton, C., Reinke, W. W., Herman, K. C., & Newcomer, L. L. (2011). The incredible years teacher classroom management training: The methods and principles that support fidelity of training and delivery. *School Psychology Review, 40*, 509–529.

Wedman, J. (2014). Needs assessments in the private sector. In J. W. Altschuld & R. Watkins (Eds.), *Needs assessment: Trends and a view toward the future. New Directions for Evaluation, 144,* 47–60.

Weiss, C. H. (1998). *Evaluation: Methods for studying programs and policies* (2nd ed.). Upper Saddle River, NJ: Prentice-Hall.

What Works Clearinghouse. (2011). *Procedures and standards handbook* (Version 2.1). Retrieved from http://ies.ed.gov/ncee/wwc/pdf/reference_resources/wwc_procedures_v 2_1_standards_handbook.pdf

Wheatley, K. F. (2005). The case for reconceptualizing teacher efficacy research. *Teaching and Teacher Education, 21,* 747–766.

Wheldall, K., & Madelaine, A. (1997). Should we measure reading progress and if so how? Extrapolating the curriculum based measurement model for monitoring low-progress readers. *Special Education Perspectives, 6,* 29–35.

White, H. (2013). The use of mixed methods in randomized control trials. In D. M. Mertens & S. Hesse-Biber (Eds.), *Mixed methods and credibility of evidence in evaluation. New Directions for Evaluation, 138,* 61–73.

Wickstrom, K. F., Jones, K. M., LaFleur, L. H., & Witt, J. C. (1998). An analysis of treatment integrity in school-based behavioral consultation. *School Psychology Quarterly, 13,* 141–154.

Williams, J. (2013). *The Remarkable Half-Naked Rubric: Creating Collaboratively Developed Tools to Measure Results of Education as Intervention.* Workshop presented at Evaluation 2013, the annual meeting of the American Evaluation Association, Washington, DC.

Wingate, L., & Schroeter, D. (2015). *Evaluation Question Checklist for Program Evaluation.* Western Michigan University. Available from https://www.wmich.edu/sites/default/files/attachments/u58/2016/eval-questions-checklist.pdf

Winton, P. (2006). The evidence-based practice movement and its effect on knowledge utilization. In V. Buysse & P. Wesley (Eds.), Evidence-based practice in the early childhood field (pp. 71–115). Washington, DC: Zero to Three.

Winton, P. J., & Turnbull, A. (1982). Dissemination of research to parents. *The Exceptional Parent, 12*(4), 32–36.

Witt, J. C., & VanDerHeyden, A. M. (2007). The System to Enhance Educational Performance (STEEP): Using science to improve achievement. In S. E. Jimerson, M. K. Burns, & A. M. VanDerHeyden (Eds.), *Handbook of response to intervention: The science and practice of assessment and intervention* (pp. 343–353). New York, NY: Springer.

Wong, D. M. (2013). *The Wall Street Journal guide to information graphics: the dos and don'ts of presenting data, facts, and figures.* New York, NY: W. W. Norton.

Woolfolk, A. E., Rosoff, B., & Hoy, W. K. (1990). Teachers' sense of efficacy and their beliefs about managing students. *Teacher and Teacher Education, 6,* 137–148.

Yarbrough, D. B., Shulha, L. M., Hopson, R. K., & Caruthers, F. A. (2011). *The program evaluation standards: A guide for evaluators and evaluation users* (3rd ed.). Thousand Oaks, CA: Sage.

Yeaton, W. M., & Sechrest, L. (1981). Critical dimensions in the choice and maintenance of successful treatments: Strength, integrity, and effectiveness. *Journal of Consulting and Clinical Psychology, 49*, 156–167. doi: 10.1037/0022-006X.49.2.156

Yoon, K. S., Duncan, T., Lee, S. W.-Y., Scarloss, B., & Shapley, K. L. (2007). *Reviewing the evidence on how teacher professional development affects student achievement.* Washington, DC: U.S. Department of Education, Institute of Education Sciences, National Center for Education Evaluation and Regional Assistance, Regional Educational Laboratory Southwest.

Zikmund-Fisher, B. J., Fagerlin, A., & Ubel, P. A. (2008). Improving understanding of adjuvant therapy options by using simpler risk graphics. *Cancer, 113*, 3382–3390.

Zimmerman, B. J., & Cleary, T. J. (2006). Adolescents' development of personal agency. The role of self-efficacy beliefs and self-regulatory skills. In F. Pajares & T. Urdan (Eds.), *Self-efficacy beliefs of adolescents* (pp. 45–69). Greenwich, CT: Information Age.

Zvoch, K., Letourneau, L. E., & Parker, R. P. (2007). A multilevel multisite outcomes-by-implementation evaluation of an early childhood literacy model. *American Journal of Evaluation, 28*, 132–150.

Julie Q. Morrison, PhD, is an Associate Professor in the School Psychology Program at the University of Cincinnati, Cincinnati, Ohio. Her research interests include evaluating the effectiveness of universal and targeted interventions to address the academic and behavioral needs of school-age children and youth within a multi-tier system of supports framework. She has more than 20 years of experience as an evaluator of educational initiatives implemented at a state, regional, and district level. Currently, she serves on the Joint Committee on Standards in Educational Evaluation as a liaison member representing the National Association of School Psychologists.

Anna L. Harms, PhD, is the Evaluation and Research Coordinator for Michigan's Integrated Behavior and Learning Support Initiative (MIBLSI). MIBLSI is a statewide initiative designed to support regional educational service agencies, districts, and schools in the development and implementation of evidence-based practices within a multi-tiered delivery system. In her current role, she leads the design and implementation of internal evaluation for MIBLSI. This includes work on three federally funded grants. She coordinates a team that provides support to local districts and schools around multi-tiered system of supports measurement and evaluation, including research projects on universal screening, data-based decision making, and assessment construction and validation.

CPSIA information can be obtained
at www.ICGtesting.com
Printed in the USA
BVHW031706170520
579674BV00007B/11

9 780190 609108